The Story of Architecture

The Story of Architecture

Patrick Nuttgens

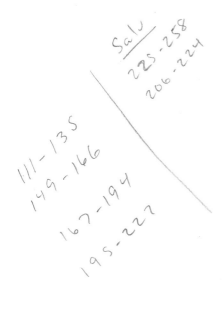

PRENTICE-HALL, INC.
Englewood Cliffs
New Jersey 07632

© Phaidon Press Limited 1983
Text © Patrick Nuttgens 1983

First published in the United States of America 1984 by Prentice-Hall, Inc.,
Englewood Cliffs, New Jersey 07632

Printed in Great Britain by
Butler & Tanner Ltd, Frome and London

Library of Congress Cataloging in Publication Data

Nuttgens, Patrick
    The story of architecture
    1. Architecture—History.   I. Title.
NA200.N8   1984   720′.9   83-3430
ISBN 0-13-850149-1
ISBN 0-13-850131-9 (pbk.)

Marginal drawings by James Nuttgens except for those on pp. 54, 92, 100, 102, 105
(bottom), 130, 203, 260 (bottom)

frontispiece, *Trulli,*
Alberobello

Contents

9 - 40
85 - 110

Preface

This book is the fruit of a collaboration. It is a story which unfolds as it goes along. For that reason it does not have footnotes, and there is no glossary at the end; the words used about buildings are explained as they come into the story.

My collaborator is my wife Bridget. At first my research assistant, in the event she has been more than that; she has drafted much of the book and has been wholly responsible for some chapters, though I take responsibility for all of them and for all the judgements contained in them.

We have been visiting buildings for some thirty years together in many parts of the world and talking about architecture incessantly. But this is our first attempt at collaboration in research and writing and is thus our first literary offspring.

1
Origins

Whether we are aware of it or not, architecture is part of everbody's personal history. The chances are that it is in a building that we are born, make love, and die; that we work and play and learn and teach and worship; that we think and make things; that we sell and buy, organize, negotiate affairs of state, try criminals, invent things, care for others. Most of us wake up in a building in the morning, go to another building or series of buildings to pass our day, and return to a building to sleep at night.

Simply from living in buildings, we all possess sufficient expertise to embark on the study of the story of architecture. But before we can do so there is one fundamental point we have to note, which makes architecture both different from the many other arts and more difficult to judge. It has to be practical as well as attractive, useful on the one hand and beautiful on the other.

In the early seventeenth century Sir Henry Wotton, adapting the maxim of an earlier theorist, the first-century Roman architect Vitruvius, wrote that 'Well-building has three conditions: firmness, commodity and delight'. His first two conditions are concerned with the down-to-earth side of architecture; his third, with its aesthetic aspect. *Commodity* covers what the building is for: are the spaces formed by the building suitable for the purpose for which it is being built? *Firmness* concerns whether it is structurally sound: are the materials and the construction right for that particular building in that particular place, in that climate? *Delight* includes the aesthetic pleasure and satisfaction that both viewer and user derive from a building: and that involves a multiplicity of personal judgements.

The story I am telling in this book is a story told by an architect, and it is a story that covers the whole of the world. The knowledge we now have, increasing with every year, of the architecture of Eastern and Middle-Eastern countries and of prehistory, affects the way we look at our own immediate environment, changing its shape, its position in history and its relative importance. The view I take of architecture is that of a person trained to design buildings. It may be a different view from that taken by an art historian, because I have to try to understand the problem in my own way, which means to imagine what the designer was thinking as he approached the problem.

So the main question I am going to ask about a building is: why is it like that? There are many and various reasons. If we can discover some of them, such as the influence of history and politics and religion and social aspirations, we may be able to see more clearly why a certain designer thought the way he did and why he chose a particular way to build it. For not only is there no single reason for a building,

Inca fortress, Sacsahuaman, Peru

Taos Pueblo, New Mexico

Reed hut on the Tigris, Iraq

there is also no single solution to its needs. Ultimately the designer has a choice. What we have to ask is why he made that particular one.

Before we can start on the story it is necessary to establish some basic facts about building of any kind.

Throughout the whole of history until our own century (which has revolutionized technological developments, as we shall see in a later chapter) there have been only two basic ways of building: you could either put one block upon another or you could make a frame or skeleton and cover it with a skin.

Almost everywhere in the world people have built by assembling blocks—of dried mud or clay bricks or stones. They piled one upon another, inventing ways of turning corners, leaving holes so as to get in and out, to let light in and smoke out. Finally they covered the whole structure for shelter. In some parts of the world people have built by making a skeleton of wood or rushes in bundles (or later iron and steel) and covering it with skins of many kinds—animal hides, cloth and canvas, mud and straw (and later many kinds of slab).

Blocks can be made from almost anything: from alluvial mud, sometimes bound with straw to make it more cohesive and lasting, as in ancient Mesopotamia or Egypt; from kiln-dried bricks, as in most of Europe and the Middle East; from stone, dressed or undressed; even ice as in the Esquimo igloos of Arctic regions. Of all the materials used, the most adaptable, permanent and expressive is stone. Of the skeleton and skin type of structure, the North American Indian tepee is the classic example, with poles leaning against one another, bound at the top with their ends overlapping, and wrapped round with an animal skin. And there are many variations—the skin tents of Lapland, structures made of brushwood, of clay and reed, and the wood and paper houses of the Japanese. They are the precursors of the nineteenth-century frame structures of iron and glass and the steel and glass of our own time.

Let us first look at the practical problems. To the person originally thinking it out and facing the architectural challenge, the great problem from the start was not so much how to leave holes in the sides (central as those are to the character of a style of architecture, as we shall see later) as how to finish the building at the top. Again, there are two ways of doing that. The commonest is one of those described above—making a frame of wood, either flat or sloping, and covering it with some material which will keep out the sun and rain and wind, and maybe fastening it down so that it does not blow away. But the most primitive (and in the end the architecturally most exciting) is to lay the stones of the walls on one another so that the upper ones project enough gradually to curve the walls inwards and ultimately meet at the top. Such *corbelling*, as it is called, can lead to a tunnel, or, if it runs all round a building, to a dome.

The most attractive examples that still remain are in Apulia—the *trulli* at Alberobello. Although most of the stone-domed houses are probably no older than the sixteenth century, it is known that they are replacements in a tradition that goes back to primitive times, merely becoming more decorative with the centuries.

Now let us take the problem a stage further. When the earliest house-makers were devising ways of building their homes, it must sooner or later have occurred to them that materials could be used in only a few ways. They could be pressed together, stretched or bent. In modern structural engineering terms, strength depended upon compression or tension or bending. The block structures depend on pressing one stone or brick down on another—on compression. Skeleton structures depend on the great quality timber has—of bending. More sophisticated structures, as well as some primitive ones, using man-made ropes, depend upon their resistance to stretching—on tension.

Because some materials are better at compression and others at tension or at bending, it follows that the kind of structure adopted in any part of the world depended upon what materials were available. Almost anything can be used for building and in practice almost everything has been used. Naturally it was the readily available materials that had the most profound effect upon architecture all over the world: stone, clay, wood, skins, grass, leaves, sand and water. But much depends on the distribution of such materials, where they are found in nature or what man has done to make them more accessible.

Of all the structural means that have been used to put those materials together, two are so fundamental and so lasting in their influence that it is worth at this point showing how they arose from the solution of basic building problems.

As any child playing with building blocks discovers sooner or later the next stage once he has made a wall is to balance a block horizontally so as to span two upright blocks and make a lintel. Primitive man discovered the same trick, sometimes investing it with magical and ceremonial significance, and siting it so that it formed a gateway for the beams of the rising or setting sun, like the stone circle at Stonehenge. Whatever its elaboration, the post and lintel is the funda-

Stonehenge, Wiltshire

mental form used in buildings all over the world. The Egyptians translated it into columns supporting entablatures, leading to its metamorphosis into the classical colonnade of Greek architecture, which was used to confer power and dignity upon important buildings such as the Parthenon in Athens. The Chinese, with ready supplies of light wood, adapted it to that material, evolving a roof-structure composed of a pyramid of decreasing post-and-lintel gateways, piled one on top of the other to carry the wide eaves of the roofs. The Japanese used the form in the gateways to temples.

The second fundamental structural form is the arch. We have already seen a primitive form of it in the arrangement of stones in a wall, where each course of stones on either side of an opening juts out beyond the course below until, without the need of a capstone or

Great Baths, Mohenjo-Daro

Corbelled arch

True arch

lintel, they meet to form a bridge. That corbelled arch was developed in many parts of the world—in the brick-work cisterns of Mohenjo-Daro in India's earliest civilization, in the Chinese vaulted tombs of the third century BC, in the arches supporting the waterways that fed the hanging gardens of Babylon. The true arch, built of radiating wedge-shaped stones or *voussoirs*, arranged to form a semi-circle, was an act of the imagination that released all sorts of architectural possibilities.

Having looked at the basic materials and the basic structural forms, we shall now look at the basic kind of building—that is, the house.

Man's earliest dwellings were single rooms, sometimes caves or semi-caves hollowed out of the ground and covered with a tent structure or with mud-bricks and entered from the roof. Such early dwellings are found all over the world. There are very early examples in Jordan and Anatolia (now Turkey), some of which date back to 8000 BC. Another example (200 BC–AD 200) is the Yayoi tent-house of the Japanese, which is sunk into the ground and has a roof of sticks

Red Lion Hotel, Weobley, Hereford

and turf. However many variations his successors later made, the early house-maker seems to have used only two basic shapes for a house and two basic ways of grouping its components.

In shape it could be either round or rectangular. The round buildings probably came first, if only because they did not pose the problems of making a corner, which requires the cutting of stone or the making of bricks. Even when the shape was rectangular, as in the early *bothans* of Scotland and the *clachans* of Ireland, the corners were rounded. Rectangular houses are usually found in regions where there was timber available for spanning roofs or making frames. For example, the long houses of the Scandinavian countries and the cruck-framed houses of England—made with timber-framed arches with their feet stuck in the ground and the walls and roof built around them.

As soon as man began to go beyond the single unit for dwelling, he had two ways of grouping the component rooms. He could make a multiple dwelling—that is, one made up of a number of separate units, each with its own roof system, grouped together closely or more freely. The *trullo* at Alberobello, referred to earlier, is the best surviving example of that type; the vaulted stone rooms could be grouped together in twos, threes or fours, and ultimately made into an elaborate and fascinating complex. Tents, as in Arab desert settlements, could be similarly grouped together. Especially fascinating is Skara Brae, Orkney. In 1850 a great storm undid the work of another storm possibly 3000 years earlier and uncovered a Stone Age village of stone houses connected by passageways, their walls corbelled inwards to form smoke-holes, which were probably originally covered by turfs. The houses had stone hearths, stone beds, even a stone dresser.

Alternatively, man could make a single compact dwelling with all the rooms under the one roof. Originally that entailed the housing of animals and humans under the same roof. The earliest houses of the Scottish Highlanders were like that. They housed people on one side of the fireplace, which later became a wall, and cattle on the other. Once the animals had been put out and given a separate shelter, that type developed into the cottage of two rooms (the but-and-ben), one for living and one for sleeping.

This pattern became more sophisticated when one room was assigned more importance than the other. The classic pattern was the Greek *megaron*, which started on the Mycenaean mainland—a hall with an entrance room off it. That simple pattern was in due course to become the basic component of any great house or castle. Then houses moved upwards. The addition of an upper floor or a balcony required the construction of a stair, either internal or external.

Further refinements came with the development of ways of regulating the temperature. For the sake of coolness it became common in the East to group houses or rooms around a courtyard; it was a pattern adopted by the earliest monks, the desert hermits, and was found so convenient that it spread by way of European monastic establishments to academic institutions like the universities. In harsher climates like that of most of Europe, especially the northern parts, the most important development was the making of a fireplace. In the earliest houses the fire was in the centre of the floor, the smoke escaping through a hole in the roof, with or without a lid to keep the rain out at other times. It was the moving of the fireplace to the wall, usually the outer wall in a rectangular house, and the gradual development of a chimney, at first of timber and then of stone, which created the house-form. The increase in convenience and fresh air more than compensated for the heat that may have been lost by having the fireplace on the outside wall. It was, I suspect, the first architectural exercise in putting comfort before technical efficiency—a process which has continued ever since.

The story of *great* architecture is the astonishing story of how individuals and groups have taken the structures, groupings, plans, access and service arrangements originally evolved to satisfy basic human needs and transformed them into one of the greatest manifestations of the human spirit. It is that story that we shall now tell.

2

Barbaric Splendour

The story of architecture begins with the story of civilization, at the stage when primitive man found himself able to improve upon hunting and gathering by establishing a settlement. Not just a single building—if that was all he needed he could have stayed in a cave. Instead, with others, he established the beginning of a town or city.

So intimate is the connection between man's building of the first cities and his development of a civilized way of life that the very word *civilization* comes from the Latin word *civis*, which means citizen, or dweller in a city. Sir Kenneth Clark points out that a sense of permanence is the prerequisite of civilization, and what could more explicitly indicate that man meant to give up his wandering ways and settle down permanently than his building of a city? Men, said Aristotle, come together in cities in order to live; they remain there to live the good life.

The earliest indications we have of this settling-down process, between 8000 and 6000 BC, have been found in agricultural villages on the hill fringes of Anatolia and the Zagros Mountains, and to the west in the Levant. Jericho, today a palm-tufted oasis town dotted with lemon trees in the Judean desert, is the oldest recorded city in the world, and it is in such remains and those of cities further east that we shall find the earliest known architecture.

Until the birth of archaeology, however, there was little to draw historians' attention to the land, now generally accepted as the cradle of civilization. The Greeks called it Mesopotamia; in the Bible it is the Land of Shinar. This land occupied an area between modern Iran and Iraq along the 700 mile course of the rivers Tigris and Euphrates from their sources in the mountains of Anatolia southwards down to the Persian Gulf, and is said by tradition to have been the site of the Garden of Eden, the place where Genesis says human life began.

Today it looks unprepossessing. But archaeologists have established that, during the 5000-year gestation period of civilization, this desolate area was a rich alluvial delta, teeming with fish and wildfowl. It was, as Leonard Cottrel described it in *Lost Cities* (1957), 'the most fertile land on earth, mile after mile of flat green fields, palm-groves and vineyards, criss-crossed by a network of irrigation canals ... which at dawn and sunset still show as dark lines across the alluvial plain.' The area has come to be known as the 'fertile crescent', but as each generation discovers more remains of early man, its shape resembles less a crescent than an ink blot bounded by a scattered circle of seas—the Black and Caspian Seas, the Persian Gulf, the Red Sea and the Mediterranean.

From the fifth to the first millennium BC, the fertile crescent was the hub of the world and a melting pot of vast tribal movements. Three great early civilizations, of Sumer-Akkad, Babylon and Assyria, flourished here. Here rose the great cities of Ur of the Chaldees in Sumeria, the first and second cities of Babylon, and the Assyrian capitals of Ashur (before 2000 BC) and later, Nimrud, Khorsabad and Nineveh. Here too was the awesome capital of the fierce Hittites in Anatolia, which dates from about 1400 BC, Hattushash, unusually large for a Bronze-age city, perched on a ridge above the modern Turkish city of Boghazkoy and surrounded by sheer cliffs, down which cataracts plunge.

Sumer was not so much a country as a collection of city states, each with its own organization and proprietary rights to one particular god. It had a continuing Mesopotamian culture in the thousand years of its greatness before one state, Akkad, under Sargon the Great, conquered all the others and, in a brief but brilliant two hundred years, welded them together into the world's first empire. When archaeologists began to explore the strange mounds that travellers had described as standing up above the Mesopotamian desert, they did not at first appreciate that, in a treeless and stoneless country where the common building material was sun-baked mud, the mounds were in fact buildings which had crumbled back into the landscape from which they had come.

It is now clear that the planning and architecture of the cities were closely related to their civic and religious organization. A raised area in each city was allocated to that city's special god; here the god lived,

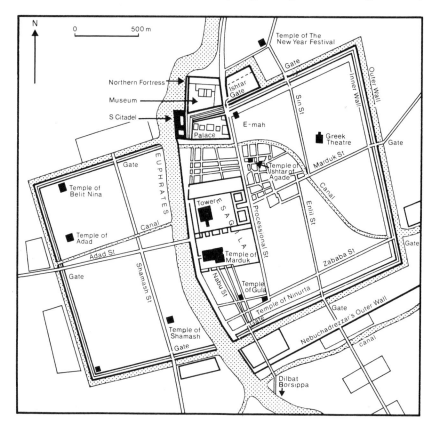

Map of Babylon

and the priests and princes, as the god's agents, ruled. In the northwest corner of Ur, for instance, Nanna the Moon God had his own enclosure, raised above the rest of the city, which included his house, the ziggurat, temples dedicated to himself and his wife, Nin-gal, and administrative buildings from which officials dispensed justice and collected taxes on his behalf. Ur had 350,000 people packed into five square miles of alleys and bazaars; houses were single, semicircular or built round courtyards. Citizens rich enough to afford wood, a scarce material in that area, had outside stairs leading to a simple wooden balcony, which connected the upstairs rooms along the outside of the house.

Babylon was even more impressive. The river Euphrates ran through the city. Here the first Babylonian Empire was set up by Semitic Amorites, and their first great building period was under

Hammurabi (1762–1750 BC). The magnificence of the city was even greater during the second (Chaldean) Empire, a city provided by Nebuchadnezzar II (605–562 BC) with stone defences, navigable moats, palaces—one of which contained the banqueting hall where King Belshazzar is said, in the Book of Daniel, to have seen the writing on the wall.

It was a planned city: its great processional way swept from the north through the town parallel to the river and through the Ishtar Gate to the palace/temple complex. Six bridges crossed the moats to six gates. The ordinary houses were congested and perhaps four or five storeys high—a vernacular pattern which can be seen today in Iraq, Syria and Egypt—grouped round courtyards, and made from mud packed on timber frames or brick vaults.

One of the glories of the city was the use of glazed bricks, predominantly blue, tinted with lapis lazuli, with gold for contrast—the very colours we will find later in the sumptuous decorations of the palaces and mosques of Islamic architecture, in much the same area of the world. Nebuchadnezzar's Ishtar Gate is resplendent with blue tiles patterned with 152 golden beasts, almost lifesize. These have been identified as bulls alternating with the mythological 'sirrush', which had the front legs of a lynx, the back legs of an eagle, and the head and tail of a snake. Recent studies have suggested that Babylon was so attractive a place that the leaders of the Israelites had considerable difficulty in persuading their countrymen to go back to Israel when Nebuchadnezzar ended their captivity and set them free.

Not all the states of Mesopotamia appear to have been so contented. Although the standard of sophistication in Nineveh was so high that King Sennacherib brought drinking water into the city by canals and stone aqueducts, the Assyrian cities and those of Anatolia generally present a harsher aspect.

Massive fortifications were essential for states that were constantly threatened by rival states and tribal war. Materials for fortification varied with local supply—mud-brick in south Mesopotamia, stone for the Hittite cities of Anatolia, usually with a superstructure of mud-brick. They were often built in concentric rings, a practical defensive pattern which persisted into the Middle Ages, indeed until the invention of gunpowder made the fortified castle obsolete. The outer wall was studded with look-out turrets and punctured with gateways, some built with lintels, some—those at Hattushash, the Hittite capital, and at Tiryns in Mycenaean Greece—with elliptical arches. The main gateway was guarded by sentinel towers.

Cities were usually on raised ground and important areas—the citadel of the palace/temple complex—were frequently raised on another podium, usually heavily buttressed. Buttresses served a double purpose. Reinforced with reed-matting they gave strength; and they varied the monotony of the mud-brick walls by presenting a series of alternating projecting and recessed panels. Different methods of decorating these potentially grim surfaces developed. The Sumerians used clay cones, sometimes coloured cream, black and red and arranged in patterns, as can be seen in the Temple of Warka (Iraq), of

Hittite warrior from the King's Gate, Hattushash

*c.*2000 BC. Both the Assyrians and later the Persians decorated exterior and interior walls and bronze doors with reliefs depicting their history, sometimes with cuneiform inscriptions to explain the scenes. The writing on the walls of the palaces of Ashurbanipal and Ezarhaddon in Nimrud bears out the reputation for blood-thirst ascribed to the Assyrians in the Bible: 'I built a wall before the great gate of the city; I flayed the chief men of the rebels, and I covered the wall with their skins. Some of them I enclosed alive within the bricks of the wall, some of them were crucified with stakes along the wall; I caused a great multitude of them to be flayed in my presence and I covered the wall with their skins.'

Palace of Ctesiphon

The architectural achievement of these early nations remained simple in both structure and plan. Many buildings were impressive in their monumental power or soaring simplicity, like the superb masonry of the ziggurat of Choga Zambil in the little kingdom of Elam. There was nothing very sophisticated about the structure of even the important buildings: stone was piled on stone or brick on brick, and the roof finished off with a corbelled arch. True structural sophistication did not appear in this area until the sixth century AD, over 2500 years later, when the builders of the second wave of Persian supremacy, the Sassanians, set their kiln-baked bricks obliquely to raise parabolic vaults over the great hall or *iwan* of the palace of Ctesiphon on the Tigris. One end-arch remains for us to see today. But in Babylon of the eighteenth century BC, architectural progress was

Ziggurat of Ur-Nammu at Ur

limited to mortar. They sandwiched their mud-bricks together with a thin skimming of hot asphalt (a natural substance often found alongside oil deposits and plentiful in this area), reinforced every so often with a layer of reed-matting, thus creating a bond so strong that, three thousand years later, a pickaxe had to be used to break them apart. Plans for the ceremonial buildings were likewise little more complex than the houses of the ordinary citizens.

In only one building-type did Mesopotamia achieve distinctive form: the ziggurat. This is a stepped pyramid made in mud and brick, with great ceremonial staircases leading to a temple-room at the top. In the plain of Sumer these temple-mounts were landmarks, and men working in the fields far from the city could assure themselves that their god was keeping a protective eye on them. Their origin was probably accidental: the short life of mud-brick meant that constant rebuilding was required. But since the god owned the temple-area in perpetuity, each successive rebuilding took place on an accumulative platform made from the debris of previous temples; possibly, too, the high-priest's grave was embedded in the platform and built over. This may indeed have led to the procedure used in building the Egyptian pyramids, of working on each successive level from a ramp of packed earth which spiralled around the building.

Inevitably the ziggurat form became imbued with a religious symbolism common in the East: the god on his temple-mountain brought the life-giving rains to Sumer. The most complete remains are those

Ziggurat at Choga Zambil,
near Susa, Iran

at Choga Zambil, capital of the Elamite kingdom, twenty-five miles south-east of Susa, now in Iran. Five out of a possible six stages survive, approached by stairways from three sides, and these flights of steps (unlike those of the Mesopotamian ziggurat, which rise sheerly up the face of the ramped building) here pass through vaulted passages into the structure of the building before emerging to move up to the next level.

The Tower of Babel was probably a ziggurat. It has now been almost certainly identified with the temple-tower of Etemenanki, which stands in its own precinct off the processional way, between the remains of Nebuchadnezzar's palace and the temple of Marduk, Babylon's own god. And so were the 'Hanging Gardens', once considered one of the wonders of the world. The gardens were in fact stepped terraces, built over a vaulted building which contained not only the wells whose pumped waters made the trees and flowers flourish at the different levels, but also an ice-house or refrigerator, to store, it has been suggested, sherbet for the delectation of the Medean princess for whose relaxation the gardens had been created.

Some of the myths and history of Mesopotamia figure in the Bible and so have become part of Western cultural tradition. In contrast, the building tradition of Mesopotamia appears barbaric and alien. It is only towards the end of the early civilizations that we begin to glimpse the kind of architecture with which we are more familiar, when for example outside influences from Egypt creep into the fringe

Apadana with the Palace of Darius in the background, Persepolis

(opposite) *Lion Gateway, Mycenae, mainland Greece*

civilizations of Persia and the cultures of Crete and Mycenae. We find ourselves on more familiar ground in the ruins at Persepolis, the remains of the Persian empire in Iran, which, through the Achaemenid Dynasty, founded by Cyrus II (*c.*600–529 BC), created the largest empire the world had known up to that time, absorbing all the civilizations we have talked of so far, as well as Egypt and the people of the Indus Valley.

No early example is more drastic and memorable than the architecture of Persepolis built in sixty years during the sixth and fifth centuries BC by Darius I, Xerxes I and Artaxerxes. Great flights of steps lead to the platform on which the palaces were built, with a carved frieze of 23 vassal states bringing tribute to the Persian Emperor. A gateway and passage along the north side of the platform gave access to the Apadana on the western side and the throne room on the eastern side. Behind these ceremonial rooms to the south lay the living quarters. Only the stumps of the 100 columns of Xerxes' throne room survive; the pillars of the Apadana, Darius' audience hall, were each

Throne Room in the Palace of Knossos, Crete

topped with unique capitals shaped like the forefront of an animal. Looking at those awe-inspiring ruins we can appreciate why Christopher Marlowe, somewhat anachronistically, makes Tamburlaine, the Mongol conqueror of Persia, thus give utterance to his dreams of greatness:

> Is it not passing brave to be a king
> and ride in triumph through Persepolis?

Similarly grand and evocative is the architecture of the forerunners of classical Greek splendour: the Minoan people in Crete from about 3000 BC, so christened after their legendary king, Minos, who kept the dreaded Minotaur in his labyrinth. The Minoans on the islands of the Aegean give an impression of complacence among the butterflies and flowers and bare-breasted goddesses; and it is possible that this carefree attitude spelt the downfall of their civilization—that they were overrun by more war-like Greeks from the Mycenaean mainland, their palaces at Knossos and Phaestus burnt and obliterated.

The impression of ease and comfort is vividly suggested by the ruins of the palace at Knossos, Crete, where the archaeologist Sir Arthur Evans re-created the slim wooden pillars, seeming upside-down because they taper towards the bottom, and retouched the frescoes of young princes and maidens idling in meadows.

Very different from the palace are the fortress-walls of ancient Sumer and Babylon, or the northern kingdoms of the Assyrians and the Hittites, even of mainland Greece at Mycenae: by comparison gross, uncouth and hostile. The masonry is sometimes referred to as 'cyclopean' because the scale of the stonework makes it look as if it has been built by a race of giants. What leaves us open-mouthed with wonder is the megalomania of these expressions of power, fierce and elaborate, rich with carvings and figures—aspiring gloriously to the mountain tops in an architecture of ramps and stairs which arrogantly disregards the ordinary man in his reed hut below. It is an architecture of barbaric splendour.

The civilizations which generated it were eventually destroyed and dispersed by Alexander the Great. Their architectural influences were spread to India and thence to China and Japan, and ultimately around the world.

But long before that, in these countries far from the fertile crescent, metamorphosis into civilization had taken place, commencing, characteristically (as in the Middle East), along fertile river valleys. In India a string of settlements of about 2500 BC have been excavated along the Indus Valley (now Pakistan)—a precursor of the Aryan civilization of 1500 BC. About 1600 BC, when Hammurabi was in power in Babylon and Crete was already in decline, China's cultural chrysalis broke into her first civilization along the Yellow River (the Hwang Ho). Across the barriers of the great seas, the New World cultures developed independently in Central America and in Peru.

We shall follow the story to those countries in due course. But first we shall stay in the Middle East and explore the remains of the most inscrutable of all the early civilizations—that of ancient Egypt.

3

The Geometry of Immortality

The key to Egypt's story is the Nile, that river with the singular characteristic that it never dries up: although virtually no rain falls along its course, it is constantly filled by the White Nile from the great lakes of central Africa. The two distinct topographical areas into which the river divides provided the basis for the division of Ancient Egypt into a Lower and Upper Kingdom.

Dotted along the west bank of the Nile for about fifty miles southwest of Cairo, some eighty pyramids raise their inscrutable and monumental bulk to the sun's disc. Our immediate reaction might be that here was a civilization very similar to those of Mesopotamia. After all, they all started along river valleys and in the Middle East, and at roughly the same era in evolutionary terms, and they are all characterized by mammoth buildings, whether ziggurat or pyramids. But in fact their architecture is very different. Where Mesopotamia exhibits the aggrandizement of defence and aggression, Egypt reflects 3000 years of splendour, serenity and mystery.

The plains of Mesopotamia were so located as to make them a seething cauldron of races seeking lands through settlement or war. In contrast, Egypt, isolated in the fastness of the Nile Valley, had, one might say, peace thrust upon her. Her people had no need to pack together into fortified cities for defence. In fact, she was slow to develop cities at all; the earliest approximation to cities were her cities of the dead, with streets of tombs, sometimes modelled like little houses, laid out in a grid pattern. Living cities only figure in the Old Kingdom (2700–2300 BC) when the Pharaoh commanded the building

Pyramids of Cheops, Chephren and Mycerinus, Giza

Kiosk of Trajan on the island of Philae (before relocation)

of a town to house men working on his pyramid tomb or on public works, as in the narrow grid of little box-dwellings at Medinet Habu. Egypt was vulnerable to penetration only up and down the Nile Valley, from the Mediterranean (as was ultimately to happen in the Greek and Roman conquests, which spelled the end of this empire) or down the Nile river from Nubia in the south. Even here, nature afforded some protection, for in Old Kingdom days the boundary was marked by two islands which could be defended, Elephantine and Philae, and by the first of six cataracts. Man added to nature with a series of forts and accompanying temples built on the Upper Nile. One of these, the dramatic fort at Buhen, had castle-like buttressed walls with a perimeter of a mile. It is now under Lake Nasser, the world's largest man-made lake, which backs up the Aswan Dam. When the dam was built, some of the most beautiful temples were moved from the encroaching waters. The Temple of Isis with its pylon gateways was moved from the island of Philae to Agilkia; and a little gem from the period of Roman occupation known as the Kiosk of Trajan was also saved. The little Dendun temple has gone abroad; it was taken apart and reconstructed in New York's Central Park. The most exciting rescue in engineering terms was raising the Great Temple of Abu Simbel up 210 feet onto higher ground. The architects of the New Kingdom had carved the temples into the sandstone mountain, so the temples had to be cut away and a steel dome, camouflaged to look like stone, was erected to recreate the original atmosphere. Today, the four enormous effigies of Rameses II, one headless, continue to sit, immense and implacable, intimidating invaders from the south with their basilisk stare as they have done for 3000 years and waiting for the rising sun to penetrate the temple at the equinox.

For both kingdoms the Nile below the cataracts provided a perfect waterway. Prevailing winds conveniently blew north to south and carried boats up river. During the Middle Kingdom (22nd–20th century BC), mud-slips were built so that boats could be pulled upstream to bypass the cataracts and establish access to trading posts and forts in Nubia. On the return journey, the big brown sails were furled and the current swept the boats swiftly home. Enormous blocks of granite from the quarries at Aswan were brought downstream on barges or rafts in this way to build temples and tombs, and by this route too came the rich traffic in spices, ivory and skins as well as gold and jewels from the mines in the interior of black Africa, over which the pharaoh exercised a monopoly.

The river also dictated much about the architecture. Both ordinary dwellings and buildings intended to last—tombs, pyramids and temples—were sited on the edge of the desert, beyond the high flood mark which was, of course, also the edge of the precious fertile strip, which in the growing season started so abruptly that one could stand with one foot on crops and the other in the desert. Within this area on the western bank, the land of the dead, were the causeways leading to the funerary temples and complexes and the villages for the workers in the Necropolis, the city of tombs with which in the New Kingdom period the cliffs of the Theban hills were honeycombed.

On the eastern bank, the bank of the living, were the wharves and boat-building areas, quayside beer- and eating-shops and beyond, the great temples, often with an avenue of spinxes leading up to them from the quay, along with the ordinary dwelling-houses, shops and workshops that made up the town. Most dwellings were of mud-brick and there are no remains today. But little flat, almost two-dimensional models, called 'soul-houses', found in the tombs suggest they were not very different from those lived in today. The houses of the noblemen were luxurious, with loggias and gardens, fountains, ornamental tanks for fish, used to keep down mosquitoes, and suites of many rooms, enclosed behind high mud walls. Entry was through a single door, and inside a rich man's house corridors led to the several living quarters. Details of a vizier's house painted on the wall of his tomb show three corridors. One leads to the servants' quarters, one to the women's quarters and the third to the main living areas, which included lofty reception rooms, the roof supported on columns painted dark red and bearing lotus-capitals, while the walls were covered in paintings of flowers and birds.

On both sides of the river, mud-brick walls protected buildings from unusually high floods, just in case the pharaoh and his priest-astrologers, who measured the rise of the Nile at nilometer stations along the bank, failed to predict the correct flood-level. By May the river returned to its natural level and cracked baked mud, turning from dark brown to grey under the fierce sun, lay where all had been lush only a few months previously. These cracked mud-blocks probably formed the building material for the primitive houses, until it was discovered that a stronger brick could be made by moulding the brick and incorporating straw and cattle-dung. But the fall of the Nile had a more profound effect on Egyptian architecture. For the next five months farming was not feasible, nor was there any point in it. The pharaohs had therefore at their disposal an enormous labour force of peasants, augmented by races enslaved in times of conquest. The pharaohs set them to work on the pyramids or tomb-complexes, which were their lifetime's preoccupation. Only the availability of such an enormous force can explain how the pyramids were built, particularly when we remember that stone was floated down the Nile

House of the North, Sakkara

Temple of Amun, Luxor

from as far away as Aswan and that in the case of the Great Pyramid of Cheops, for instance, two million stone blocks were used, some of them weighing fifteen tons.

The techniques available to them were really very simple. The Egyptians never learned to harden copper, so, although they had both saws and drills of copper, the tough granite of Aswan had to be split from the rock face, first by hammering vertical trenches into the rock with balls or hammers of a hard rock called dolerite and then by driving in wedges either of metal or of wood that was soaked in water until it expanded. The stones, some of which still show quarrymen's marks, were brought on the Nile to the pyramid site and dragged on sleds with papyrus ropes to the work site. The base was marked out and made level by filling a trench with water. After the first course of stones was laid on the level bed, an earth ramp was built, just as (we suppose) the Sumerians did for their ziggurats, and this was built higher with each successive course of stones. All the stone blocks must have been dragged up the spiral ramp by gangs of men, for there is no evidence that the Egyptians knew the pulley. They did, however, use levers, and they also spread a thin layer of mortar between the stones, more, it is believed, to float one stone up against its neighbour as the angle of incline increased than to hold them in place.

The first major monuments were mud-brick tombs, known as *mastabas*, for nobles and royalty. They began simply enough, with mounds of earth raised over pit graves in which the dead were laid, preserved in natron. The earliest remains of a royal mastaba of the Archaic period are at Sakkara, on a bluff of the desert overlooking

(opposite, top) *Painting of Great Temple of Abu Simbel*

(opposite, bottom) *Mural from the tomb of Menna, Thebes*

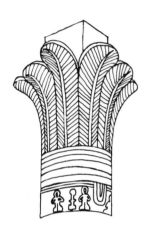

Memphis. These tombs were rectangular, the sides sloping inwards with an angle (known as a 'batter') of 75 degrees to a flat top. It is reasonable to suppose that, like the pyramids later, they were built up by step technique. They might rise to a height of 25 feet, containing an outer chamber, whose walls were often decorated, and an inner secret chamber holding statues of the family. The burial chamber itself was cut deep into the rock below—normally a single room, perhaps with store-room opening off. Beside the tomb a little funerary temple was built so that the priests could leave bread, wine and vegetables there for the departed spirit. These ancillary rooms gradually became incorporated into extensive walled complexes. When later in the Old Kingdom royal tombs became enclosed in pyramids, nobles continued to build mastaba tombs first in brick, later in stone.

About 2650 BC, during the Old Kingdom period, the stone mastaba that was being built across the river from Memphis for King Zoser (Djoser) of Dynasty III developed through several changes into a stepped pyramid, and at this point Egypt's unique contribution to architecture manifests itself. Thanks to the Egyptian cult of the individual, the name of the architect has been preserved for us—Imhotep, counsellor and vizier to the King and a man of inventive and original mind. He was priest, scholar, astrologer and magician, and so skilled in the arts of healing that 200 years later he was deified as the god of medicine. The funerary complex he built for King Zoser at Sakkara covered a vast area enclosed in a white wall 32 feet high, and incorporated, as well as the six-stepped pyramid towering 200 feet over the shaft that tunnelled deeply down to the burial chamber, eleven separate burial pits for other members of the royal family. Here, for the first time, we find features which were to become some of the mainstays of architecture.

First of all Imhotep used stone, translating into this strong medium the techniques previously used for building in wood and mud-brick. His is the first use of *ashlar*, or dressed stone, that is to say, stone slabs laid smoothly together so as to present a continuous surface, as distinct from *rubble* stonework, in which the stones are separately identified and picked out by the pointing which surrounds them. But of even greater importance was Imhotep's translation of the bundles of reeds, used in the vernacular buildings to hold up mud-packed walls, into stone architecture's basic component: the column. Left on one remaining side of the House of the North, an administrative building in the Sakkara complex, are three crisp, beautiful, 'engaged' (i.e. partially attached) columns, based on the papyrus reeds which grew in the marshes of Lower Egypt. The shaft imitates the triangular stem of the plant, and the *capital*, or block, at the top of the shaft on which rests one of the cross-beams that support the roof is here shaped like the open umbel-head of the papyrus. Egyptian architects repeated this conceit in the furled papyrus-bud capitals on the Temple of Amun at Luxor and in lotus-flower and palm-leaf capitals, and Greek classical architecture later adopted it in the fluted columns based on bundles of reeds, and in the capitals derived from native Greek plants such as the acanthus leaf.

Palm leaves and papyrus-bud capitals, Egypt

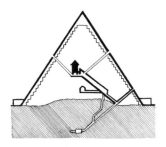

Section through Pyramid of Cheops, Giza

The great era of pyramid building in the Fourth Dynasty was probably ushered in by Huni, last pharaoh of the Third. He continued Imhotep's work by converting what appears to have been originally planned as a seven-step pyramid at Meydum into the strange and fascinating geometrical form we associate with Ancient Egypt: four triangular walls rising from a rectangular base and sloping upwards and inwards to meet at a point. The three best known are the pyramids of Cheops, Chephren or Khaefre, and Mycerinus. They stand in a group at Giza, with three little Queens' pyramids at their feet.

The pyramid was the pharaoh's bid for immortality. He did not build a great city to demonstrate his power, as Nebuchadnezzar did at Babylon, Darius and Xerxes did at Persepolis, as Alexander did at Alexandria, or Constantine at Constantinople. His intent was more practical and pressing. He believed that to gain immortality he must ensure the physical survival of his body, his earthly appearance, and the appearance of what life was like for him during his lifetime, at least in the form of models. Then, when his spirit had finished roaming the earth in animal form, his corpse and home would be there, ready for him to inhabit as his eternal home. For this, doors and cavity windows into the tomb-room were left open to allow the spirit to move freely and also to look through to keep a protective eye on his own corpse.

First the body must be embalmed—a long and complicated process, taking 70 days if properly done, and requiring the building of embalming chapels round the tomb. To perpetuate the dead man's appearance, death masks were made, like the famous gold mask of Tutankhamun, and portrait busts were ranked all round an entire funerary temple. Round the walls was painted the story of the man's life with charms and identifying hieroglyphs, and the rooms contained models of his house, garden, boat and the other possessions he wished to continue to enjoy in the afterlife. Frequently provision was made for the burial of wives, concubines and other members of the family.

Once the architects had provided for all this activity, the pyramid and its contents had to be safeguarded both from the severities of weather and from robbers in quest of the riches buried with the dead. Hence the entrances were concealed, usually at an unspecified distance up one sloping side of the pyramid. A shaft, whose degree of slope was arbitrary, led to the tomb chamber, and might have had a bend in it. The potential thief might also have been side-tracked by a labyrinth of corridors leading to galleries, used both for ventilation and for access to other tombs, if it were a family complex, or to store-rooms. Sometimes the thief would be deceived by fake entrances as in a maze, or by blocked-off access corridors or pits in the floor, which also served to collect any rainwater that had penetrated the tomb surface. The pyramid was built in advance to the level of the burial chamber, and only after the pharaoh's body had been put in position were the shafts for building access filled in and sealed off.

The threat of tomb-robbers was undoubtedly one factor in the change from pyramids to royal rock-cut tombs in about 2000 BC. From then on, the pharaohs of the New Kingdom cut into the 1000-foot

Temple of Amun-Re, Karnak

orange-yellow cliffs of the isolated Valley of the Kings in the Theban Hills—still in the Land of the Dead, the west bank of the Nile, but far enough from the funerary temples to preserve the secret location of the tombs. The entrance followed the pattern of the pyramids in that it was placed at a random height on the rock-face; from the door a funnel-shaped passage, down which the funeral sled could be pulled, was bored into the cliff to a T-junction; here, at the point where passageways led off on either side to the tomb chamber and to other rooms, was placed a statue of the dead man so that the morning sun could shine down the entry passage onto his face. A system of tilted bronze mirrors led light down to the inner passageways and chambers for tomb-artists to work by. The change from pyramids to rock-tombs seems to have foiled tomb-robbers, however, only in the case of Tutankhamun, who died young and was buried in his vizier's tomb.

The enigma of the pyramids is intensified by the contrast between the crafty irregularity of the internal arrangements and the extraordinarily simple external appearance rising from the desert—like sculptures in an exhibition. They are orientated precisely to the four points of the compass, and the geometry is amazingly exact. The four sides of Cheops' pyramid are almost exact equilateral triangles, built at an angle of 51–52° to the ground; and the base of Chephren's, although big enough to swallow up six football pitches, is a perfect square to within 15 millimetres. How, we wonder, did they arrive at this shape? The question is sharpened by the presence of two other geometrical forms the Egyptians appear to have invented in the New Kingdom

Winged solar disc

and Ptolemaic periods, the obelisk and the pylon. Perhaps the most impressive pylon gateway (enormous sloping or battered buttresses on either side of the opening) is of the fourth century BC at Edfu. One hundred feet high, it forms the entrance elevation to the Temple of Horus, son of Osiris and falcon-god, of whom the pharaoh was said to be a reincarnation. In the temples of Amun-Re and the moon-god Khons at Karnak, a suburb of Thebes, they erected both obelisks and pylons.

The likely answer to the puzzle is that these were not so much geometrical forms as abstractions from nature: they all derive from the worship of the sun, whose dominant presence in Egyptian lives made him the greatest god of all, in the form of Ra or the less austere Aton. The pyramids were stairways to the sky, and this is suggested by the habit of gilding the tips of both pyramids and obelisks with electron, and of inscribing winged solar discs on each face of the pyramids. Here we encounter the Egyptian dualism of light and dark: the relentlessly powerful blaze of desert sun taking concrete shape on the outside of the pyramid; inside, the sooty darkness which H.V.

Temple of Horus, Edfu

Pylon and statues of Rameses II, Temple of Amun, Luxor

Morton so vividly described when he visited the tomb of Cheops in 1937:

> It was one of the most sinister apartments I have ever entered, a really horrible place, and I could well believe that it might be haunted. The air was stale and hot, and the foul reek of bats so strong that I kept glancing up, expecting to see them hanging on the corners of the walls. Although this room [the burial chamber] is 140 feet above the level of the sunlit sandhills outside, it gives the impression of being in the depths of the earth. . . . It was indeed the darkness of the grave, and joined to the darkness was the silence of death. . . .

On the bank opposite the Western City of the Dead was the City of the Living. In the New Kingdom period, Thebes became capital and religious centre for the cult of Amun-Re, and was then the greatest city on earth, along with Karnak, with its massive temples and colossi and Luxor further south, possibly connected by an avenue of sphinxes. The building of temples and palaces reached its peak during the three dynasties of the New Kingdom, particularly in the reign of Rameses II. This was Egypt's imperial phase: the boundaries were pushed north and east as far as the Euphrates and southwards into the gold-rich lands of Nubia or Kush. Some temples were built over a long period,

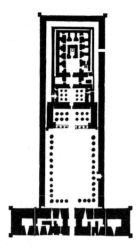

Temple of Horus, Edfu

with successive pharaohs adding further courts and halls, as happened at the Temple of Amun at Karnak. The extraordinary thing about this temple is the unity of the whole concept when one considers that the building started about 1400 BC, and the famous hypostyle (many columned) hall was added 400 years later, while the entrance pylon was the last of six and was not built until the Ptolemaic period (fourth century BC).

This temple was rightly classed as one of the wonders of its age. And it is fairly typical of the monumental massing of the temples: its great open outer court contrasting with the hypostyle hall, crammed with 134 columns with capitals carved like the open and closed umbels of the papyrus reed; outside the hall, its pylon gateway guarded by its colossal priest figures (a life-sized human figure between their feet reaches up only to their knees); its processional approach, the *dromos*, between rows of ram-headed sphinxes. We have some impression of just how breathtaking the temple must have been if we picture it on a ceremonial occasion; the courtyard and the hypostyle hall crowded with priestesses brought to dance and sing before the pharaoh; and the ranks of shaven white-robed priests ready to conduct the god-king into the inner sanctum.

Before Imhotep turned their attention to stone, Egyptians were highly proficient in working with wood, a skill probably developed for ship-building. We know they could make plywood of up to six layers, had mastered wood-inlay, and had developed most of the joints we use today, including mortice and tenon, for native woods like willow and sycamore yielded only narrow planks, which had often to be joined together. Building traditions more appropriate to timber than to stone continued in the temples; they used no arches or vaults, so in the hypostyle halls the great spaces spanned by stone lintels became a forest of columns lit through grille-windows above the central colonnade and light reflected back from the white alabaster floor paving, thus increasing their mystery as well as their grandeur.

The great temple of Amun at Luxor was the most stylish and elaborate; Karnak, in whose erection the Queen Pharaoh Hatshepsut played an important part, the biggest and most awe-inspiring. The temples of the Ptolemaic and Roman period, like the temple of the hawk-god Horus at Edfu or the similar temple at Dendera of Hathor, the goddess whom the Greeks were to identify with Aphrodite, were smaller. Many of the best temples were those associated with the tombs, notably that of Queen Hatshepsut at Deir el-Bahri on the west bank opposite Thebes with which it retained religious commerce on the Beautiful Feast of the Valley, when cult statues of Amun-Re were ferried across in the sacred barque from Karnak for ceremonies. The cool, well-bred horizontal lines of the complex, which includes valley temple, mortuary chapel and causeway, contrast impressively with the vertically scored precipice under which it is set; the limestone terraces of smooth post-and-lintel arcading, linked from level to level by massive ramps, are serene, elegant and commanding, without pomposity or aggression. This is surprising, for the woman for whom they were built, the only female pharaoh, had her share of both

(opposite) *Funerary temple of Queen Hatshepsut, Deir-el-Bahri, by Senmut*

pomposity and aggression. She usurped her son-in-law, Thutmose III (setting aside the odd crab-wise royal succession which passed through the female line to the man the pharaoh's daughter married), and took over herself. Thutmose, assuming his rights after her death, informed posterity of his feelings by knocking the heads off all the statues of the Queen in the valley temple.

Hatshepsut's temple is a satisfactory place to leave the Egyptian phase of our story, for we have only to set its picture alongside that of the Temple of Poseidon at Cape Sounion, Attica, to see that the Egyptian temples are of the same lineage as those of classical Greece. Indeed, although some of the Queen's columns are square, some are as much as sixteen-sided like an embryonic Doric column, a prefiguring of early Greek architecture that has been noted in some other Egyptian buildings, such as the fluted and tapered columns at the entrance to rock-cut tombs of the Middle Kingdom (2133–1786 BC) at Beni-Hassan.

However, before we move to Greece and Rome and through them follow the main current of Western architecture, we must step aside to look in the next few chapters at the cultures of the Eastern world, which, though often not much younger than the Middle-Eastern civilizations we have traced so far, made their own very individual contribution to our story.

4

The Holy Mountain and the Sacred Womb

It is difficult to decide at what point we should look at the so-called 'exotic' architectures of India, South-East Asia, China, Japan, and pre-Columbian American because chronologically their story does not parallel Western development. While the Western world romped its way through all sorts of styles and modes of building, those civilizations which did not pass away altogether—as did Mesopotamia, Egypt and Persia—often remained at the same level for many centuries.

In this part of the story we find ourselves in a vast area of peninsular continents hanging like a fringed frontal into the eastern seas from a wire of mountain ranges that continue from the Hindu Kush in the west to the mountains of Sechwan, China, in the east. Obviously there was a wide variety of available building materials and climatic conditions within such a vast area.

Nothing remains of early buildings in bamboo and thatch, although writings in Sanskrit speak of great cities, and the Muslim conquest of India in 1565 records, for instance, the destruction of a great palace complex in the Vijayanagara Hindu kingdom of the south. Wood was the main building material—softwoods, top-grade teak from Burma and *shisham*, poor man's teak, growing in the valleys of India, floated down from the forested mountain regions. The superb brickwork

Banteay Srei Temple, Angkor Wat

tradition of Mohenjo-Daro continued in the river plains of Bengal and the Punjab and in Sri Lanka and Burma. Then stone became accepted as a 'sacred' material for building the temples which comprise the surviving contribution to the story of architecture. In areas where stone was scarce, it was used as a facing material over rubble walls. Sri Lanka had no problem of supply and distinguished herself in temple building. India had sandstone and marble south of the Indus, and granite in the southern mountain plateau, the Deccan. But woodwork techniques were constantly employed in stonework, telling us much of the lost wooden buildings—even to the point of using carpentry joints, and the prevalence of all-over carving techniques on the temple facings is similar to the handcarving and poker-work we see on trays and boxes carved by Indian craftsmen.

The architecture of this area was spread and animated by two great and enduring world religions: Hinduism and Buddhism. Perhaps no architecture reflects more vividly the underlying philosophies of the

Carvings on the temple at Halebid, Mysore

people who built it than that of this wide area. If we take the Hoysa-lesvara Temple at Halebid with its tiers of elephants, lions and horsemen rising to a many-armed god as typical of Hindu architecture and lay it side by side with a Buddha in enlightenment after death from Polonnaruwa, Sri Lanka—his countenance bland and beatific as the lotus flowers on the soles of his feet—we become aware of the contrasting atmospheres of the two religions. The architectural provision required of the two religions shows a less emotional and more practical contrast; while Hinduism is a religion of individual daily devotion with public ritual confined to the priests, Buddhism is strongly community-orientated, leading to monasteries of cells grouped round courtyards called *viharas*, *chaitya* or assembly halls, and stupa-temple mounds round which gather pilgrims and large congregations. Hinduism, originally called Brahminism after its priestly caste, arose from a strange fusion. On one side was the dark, earthy Dravidian religion of the Indus Valley, writhing with cult images and fertility symbols; on the other the idol-less worship of the warlike pale-skinned Aryans, who invaded India by the passes in the north-west frontier about 1500 BC, about the time the Shang Dynasty was establishing itself in China.

A key to understanding the architecture is to be found in a reconciliation of elements in Hindu life which at times seems contradictory. We have to reconcile the erotic pages of the *Kama Sutra* and the pornographic fantasies we see translated into stone in the tortuous forms on many temple walls with the near-impossible asceticism of yoga—at its most intense in the holy *saddhu*, sitting motionless in the fierce heat, heedless of time or of the clamours of the flesh. But to the Hindu there is no paradox: all things are permeated by a universal spirit, Brahma; all are aspects of the same god. This Janus-face is constantly mirrored in the architecture of Asia—in abstract plans and symbolic outlines combined with a profusion of bulbous towers and all-over carvings, luxuriant as jungle-growth, frenzied with many-armed gods and gibbering monkeys and harshly streaked with parrots.

In 255 BC, Asoka, the third Mauryan Emperor of northern India, became a convert to Buddhism and established it as the state religion. It was based on the teaching of the 'enlightened one', Siddhartha Gautama, who, born in the fifth century BC into the knightly caste in a state on the northern Ganges plain, had preached an Eightfold Noble Path, whereby any man irrespective of caste might free himself from constant rebirths and achieve nirvana (ultimate liberation). Buddhism was one of two movements that broke away from the stranglehold of the Brahmin priests at this time, the other being Jainism, which is probably less important architecturally. Asoka was an active ruler and founded the first unified Indian empire by modelling his administration and military exploits on those of Alexander the Great. He also built the Royal Road—today's Great Trunk Road—from Patna to the northwest. In repentance for a particularly bloody campaign against Kalinga in east India, when 250,000 of the enemy were slaughtered, he turned to religion, ordering the first cave shrines (probably based on Persian Achaemenid tombs of the sixth and fifth

Statue of Buddha entering nirvana at Gal Vihara, Polonnaruwa

centuries BC) to be cut for the Jain ascetics in the Barabar Hills; thereafter he extended his empire spiritually, sending missionaries as far as the Hellenic world, Nepal and Sri Lanka.

Asoka's influence can be found all over India in the carving of ethical teachings on pillars and rock-faces, in rock-cut shrines and monolithic accessories to shrines, in thousands of tumuli or stupas (he is said to have erected 84,000 in three years) and in the ruins of a palace with an immense hypostyle hall at Pataliputra.

Underlying Buddhism, Jainism and Hinduism is the concept of the universe as a vast ocean in the middle of which floats the world. The centre of that world is a great mountain made of five or six ascending terraces of which mankind occupies the bottom one, serving guardian deities the middle tiers, and at the top are sited the twenty-seven heavens of the gods. It is amazing how often we can trace architectural forms and details back to this basic concept.

In the first place, it dovetails so exactly with the Hindu belief that the gods live in mountains or caves, a belief which prompted, when they came to build a temporary dwelling-place for a god on earth, what we may call mound and womb architecture. All Hindu temples are temple-mountains, and the classic Buddhist structure, the stupa, is not a building at all, but rather an enormous mound of earth, solid and impenetrable, which gradually became encased in brick or stone for increasing permanence.

Few stupas remain from early times. The Great Stupa at Sanchi, central India, in spite of much reconstruction and restoration in the nineteenth century, retains the basic form given it by Asoka between 273 and 236 BC. The present mound, which probably dates from the first century AD, presents the typically wide, shallow shape, 105 feet in diameter and 50 feet high. All the classic stupa features are here: the railings or carved stone balustrades to separate the sacred area from its secular surroundings, broken at the four points of the compass with high carved ornate gateways called *toranas* (which were to influence the Chinese *p'ailou* and the Japanese *torii*); ambulatories running round the mound linked by stairways to the flattened stupa top, where a shrine or altar is situated. All stupas are holy monuments and reliquaries, since, even if they do not house an actual relic from the Buddha's life, they mark a spot which he or his followers once hallowed with their presence.

The symbolism is laid out in copy-book fashion: the great dome of heaven revolves round the cosmic access, which is visually indicated by a pinnacle formed of umbrellas, symbolizing the soul's passage

The Great Stupa from the south-west, Sanchi

*Thuparama Dagoba,
Anuradhapura*

*Stupa of Swayambhunath,
Kathmandu Valley*

through layers of consciousness; the four gates ornamented with the Buddha's signs—the wheel, the tree, the trident and the lotus—face the four points of the compass. Railings demarcate the walkway—an important element—designed so that the worshipper may carry out the devotional exercise of passing clockwise round the shrine, studying carvings on the walls of the Buddha's life.

Many fascinating forms evolved from the stupa. The original shape was retained in Sri Lanka, as we see in the third-century Thuparama (reconstructed AD 1200) *dagoba* (for so stupas are called in Ceylon) in the ancient capital of Anuradhapura, where we can also see pillars from the ruins of the monks' cell-complexes. This city is distinguished by ruins as extensive as those of Babylon and Nineveh, and columns can still be seen from two of the palaces, the Peacock Palace and the Brazen Palace, which is reputed to have once boasted many storeys roofed in brazen tiles and, within, halls of pearl and gold and an ivory throne decorated with the sun, the moon and the stars.

In Pagan, Burma, there are still five thousand of the thirteen thousand bell-shaped temples that once ran for twenty miles along the Irrawaddy banks before the destruction by Kublai Khan. Some, like the Schwezigon Pagoda, are still plated with gold-leaf over the coating of hard polished plaster that encases the brick stupa. In the Swayambhunath Stupa in Kathmandu Valley we find the late Nepalese style:

on the square sides of the temple the curly, hooded all-seeing eyes of the Buddha gaze from beneath a helmeted roof of the thirteen umbrella rings of the Buddhist heaven.

So much for the mound. The opposite of temple-mountain architecture, womb architecture, is also a form of religious expression and is used by all three religions. Hindus, Jains and Buddhists all preserved the tradition of very early Indian architecture in cave shrines and assembly halls, hewn with staggering skill and hard labour from the living rock from as early as 200 BC until the ninth century AD.

Chaitya was originally a general term for a shrine, but is today most often applied to the Buddhist assembly halls often accompanying a *vihara* or monastic dwelling. The rock-cut chaityas were sometimes stupas in reverse: instead of a mound of earth rising up, a mound of earth was excavated from the hill. The walkway here forms a processional ambulatory similar to what one might find in a Christian church. It is separated from the hall by a row of columns of naked

Rock-cut Chaitya Hall, Karli, Deccan

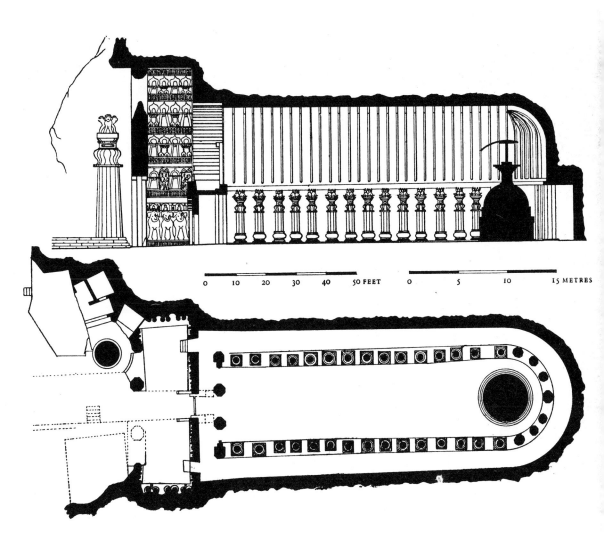

| 0 | 10 | 20 | 30 | 40 | 50 FEET | 0 | 5 | 10 | 15 METRES |

Temple of Ajanta (cave no. 19)

rock and forms an apse at the end. At Karli in the Deccan (78 BC) the pillars are squat with capitals like ribbed fruit—a detail that persisted in Indian architecture for a thousand years. The first-century chaitya at Bhaja, which was used by Buddhist monks, had a high barrel-vault as at Karli. In the apse stood a small stupa, surmounted by a telescoped umbrella finial, often carved from a column of rock rising directly out of the floor, and reproducing the crowning umbrella on a stupa. Chaityas were often lit by horseshoe windows, such as the one of about 250 AD at Ajanta, where there was a monastic university with over 23 schools and chapels cut into the rock. Ajanta, an overgrown ravine in central India, where jackals whine at dusk, boasts 29 caves, hollowed out across a long period from the second century BC to about AD 640, when the Chinese traveller Hiuen Tsang described them. The window traceries—the window bars, surrounds and grilles—of these cave-shrines resemble carved timber whether they are in fact made from wood or cut out of rock.

The Hindu version of the temple is different. It moves from architecture hollowed out of rock to buildings which are almost sculpture,

*Rock-cut temple, Kailasa,
Maharashtra*

*The five raths,
Mahabalipuram, near
Madras*

carved from the living rock upwards. For the Kailasa Temple (750–950), designed as a replica of Shiva's natural home, Mount Kailasa in the Himalayas, 2,000,000 tons of black volcanic rock are estimated to have been dug out. The lower storey of this temple was added later by burrowing still further into the rock and carving it out in the form of elephants, symbolizing strength and monsoons, which appear to be carrying the temple on their backs. In the monoliths at Mahabalipuram, near Madras, south India, single blocks of granite were cut *in situ* into chariots (*raths*) and life-size elephants, by the kings of the Pallava dynasty in the seventh and eight centuries. Only the entrance hall of the Temple of the Sun at Kanarak, Orissa (thirteenth century), was built, but its power consists more in the fact that the whole pavilion is sculpted as the sun-god's chariot than in its bands of famous erotic sculptures round the outside. Surya, an Indo-Aryan deity, daily circles the globe in his chariot, drawn by sometimes four and sometimes seven horses, and the red sandstone temple is given twelve wheels to match the signs of the zodiac and give the impression of motion. The interior of the ninth-century Elephanta Temple on Elephanta Island in Bombay Harbour has a carved cornice and squat pillars, with capitals resembling ribbed fruit, such as those at Karli.

The earliest ruins of a free-standing temple are in Afghanistan and date from the Gupta rule during the second century AD. The Hacchappayya Temple at Aihole in the Deccan (AD 320–650) is one of the first examples extant to emerge from its cave-womb and sit above ground. But the symbolism has not faded away—far from it. The womb is still there: the little dark unlit shrine called the *garbha griha*, at the heart of the Hindu temple on the ground floor, in which the god sits. This is the holy of holies, where only priests may enter to feed, dress and tend the god. In Orissa and other parts of southern India, a common pattern is to have a series of vestibules to the shrine, and these are laid out one behind the other on the same axis as the shrine chamber. Directly over the shrine and indicating its presence from the outside, is the *sikhara*, meaning a mountain peak, a spire-like roof. Round this axis, often forming a plinth base to the temple, is the *mandapa* or dancing hall. The sikhara is formed by receding courses of stone and is quite hollow: its sole purpose is to simulate a mountain and to indicate to the outer world the position of the sacred cosmic axis—an invisible rod of power—which connects cave and mountain. There is a great variety in the size and shape of the sikharas in different areas, but it is always in the sikhara, with its commanding height and impressive carving, that the god's dignity is demonstrated, rather than in the chamber for the cult image, which is poky, dark and airless. This is very apparent in the two remaining Shore Temples of the eight century that stand on the beach at Mahabalipuram, the larger facing east and the smaller towards the setting sun. Age has somewhat blurred the features of Shiva's Nanda bulls who guard the approach, but the pyramidal sikhara, ringed by three walkways, the floor of each providing a roof for the one below, is still very impressive.

The South Dravidian temple (from about AD 600 to 1750), found in the states of Madras, Mysore, Kerala and Andrha, is the only kind of Hindu temple that is not confined to accommodating the god's shrine and the priests who attend the god. It provides for community worship and daily life by a more complex grouping of courts and towers and mandapas covered by repetitive roof styles under either a series of sikharas or a series of stepped roofs rising around the ascending sikhara. Seventy examples remain with, typically, several courtyards set along the axis one behind the other, some of the inner ones with flat roofs, and each one entered by a tower gateway called a *gopuram*—shelved pyramids oblong in plan that grow smaller as they approach the central shrine. But the gopurams are certainly not self-effacing pieces of architecture: their receding stepped sides, writhing with figures, clustered with domed houses, represent the holy temple-mountain and are often patterned frenetically in an ascending order of creation from man on the bottom step to gods at the top.

The Great Temple of Madura (1623), which has long corridors supported by 2000 columns shaped like lions and galloping horses, is a good example of the South Dravidian type. It is virtually a small town, the original little shrines to Shiva and his consort Menakshi almost lost amid the later bustle of courts, halls and gateways, vividly proclaiming the union of sacred and secular in Indian art with busy bazaars, trumpeting temple elephants and worshippers washing themselves and their clothes in the lake-size Tank of the Golden Lilies.

The Shore Temple, Mahabalipuram, near Madras

Great Temple, Madura

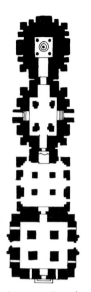

Lingaraja Temple,
Bhubaneswar, Orissa

What all the temples have in common is a walkway lined with sacred carvings, either immediately round the shrine within the mandapa or outside the temple. A Hindu temple is an object of veneration in itself, and it is an act of worship to move round it—clockwise from an eastern entry for a living temple, and anticlockwise from a western entry for a funerary monument like the great Khmer temple, Angkor Wat, in Cambodia. Another feature they have in common is that, however much they appear to go up into the air or to burrow into the ground, all the usable space is in fact at ground level.

This is not surprising in hot lands, where much of the daily life is lived in the open air. In silhouette and plan, temples varied from place to place according to local stylistic predilections, available materials and factors such as rainfall, which affected roof and sikhara shape and pitch. Whether the temple is of the simple northern type, composed of tower and vestibule surrounded by an ambulatory and then a high wall of about six feet to separate holy from secular ground, or of the more complex South Dravidian type with courts on an axis, the separate elements can be clearly distinguished from the outside. They may be linked together by passages, but they are planned as separate entities. Inside the temple the two main structures are a broad-based assembly hall for worship, frequently low and squat in silhouette, and a small square shrine room over which rises the sikhara. The Brahmeswara Temple at Bhubaneswar, a growing provincial capital in Orissa (which was built in the ninth century, a great period of temple-building in north-east India) shows these elements very clearly, as it does the three stages on the exterior: the plinth base, a band of ornate carving and the dominating sikhara. Brahmeswara is the greatest surviving Orissan-style monument from the seven thousand which once encircled the sacred lake; its sikhara rises like a corn cob, topped with a ribbed disc like a flat plush-velvet cushion executed in stone.

Whatever the type of silhouette, the temple is always an image of the cosmos informed by the life-giving spirit of God. Astrological advice was sought in order to decide when a temple should be erected,

Brameswara Temple,
Bhubaneswar

Angkor Wat, Cambodia

and the plans of some of the more complex, having the satisfying symmetry and mystical perfection of a mandala, are geometric diagrams of the cosmos and the process of creation. The stupa at Sanchi with its railings and gateways on the compass points states it with absolute simplicity.

Of the many beautiful expressions of Asian art, we must pick out two spectacular buildings which make an unforgettable impact—Angkor Wat in Cambodia and the Buddhist temple-mountain Borobudur in Java. Both have the advantage of impressive natural settings. Borobudur stands against a background of volcanoes, whose shape it mirrors; it was originally carved out of a mountain. Angkor Wat rises out of jungle, islanded from the trees by a moat two-and-a-half miles long. Suryavarman III, King of the Khmer empire, and Deva-Raja (god-king), 113–50, built here as a dynastic monument the world's largest religious complex, so enormous that pilgrims attempting the ritual circumambulation find that they have let themselves in for a twelve-mile walk. The centre of the temple rises in five terraces to a height of 215 feet, and is crowned with 5 fir-cone towers, symbolizing Mount Meru; it is reached by a raised road and cruciform entry platform.

'To enter by causeway and lilied moat', says Rose Macaulay, in *Pleasure of Ruins*, 'was to be caught into some delirious dream'. The visitor moves from one terrace to another, up twisting or straight, steep flights of stairs from which grasses grow, finding a route through the maze of courts and long corridors, whose walls sway gently with Apsaras, the dancing nymphs, 'and always the musing god', until eventually he looks down on 'a roof of forest that surrounds the

Temple of Borobudur

nearby city of Angkor Thom.' For after the fall of the Khmer empire, the forest rushed back, engulfing the cities of the kingdom. The god's snake symbol, transformed into a balustrade that wraps itself around the temple enclosure, was throughout the centuries rivalled by more constricting snake forms—the creeping roots and branches of fig and banyan trees. This stupendous piece of architecture remained stifled in their vicious embrace not for a mere one hundred years like the palace of the Sleeping Beauty, but for five hundred. However, sooner or later, Prince Charming must come; and in 1861 he appeared in the guise of a French naturalist, Pierre Loti, who, while hunting for a rare tropical plant, stumbled on and gave the kiss of life to the prize of Khmer art. Painstaking work had by 1973 restored much of the temple to its former glory. Alas, since 1975, under the military supremacy of the Khmer Rouge, its lovely terraces have become once more prey to neglect and rain, fungi and vines; and few gods can still muse, for vandalism and pilfering have robbed most of them of their heads.

The temple of Borobudur, the Buddhist *pièce de resistance* of about AD 800, has the fascination of the elemental. This is partly due to its origin as an outcrop of rock, partly to its enormous size; seen from below, the massed masonry of its carved terraces dotted with niches containing Buddhas seems not man-made, but rather a natural cliff of crumbled rock, pocked by hermits' caves. The whole is an image of the soul's journey to nirvana, for pilgrims must, as at Angkor Wat, pass along long corridors, ever upwards and inwards, through the nine stages of self-abnegation in the approach to enlightenment. From the plinth the pilgrim passes through four square enclosed terraces to three open concentric terraces, where sit, inside 72 bell-stupas of chequered lattice, 72 buddhas—some, who have lost their bell-lids, visible from the waist as if sitting snug in their bath-tubs—until he achieves at the apex, the little enclosed and pinnacled stupa in which, no pilgrim could doubt, must surely lie, eternally waiting, the mystery at the very heart of existence.

Buddha in one of 72 stupas,
Borobudur

5

Puzzles and modules

The architecture of the Far East shows extreme individuality, compelling and memorable, stemming from a culture that is cool, aloof and self-sufficient. Aloof, of course, as seen from the West. Geographically, China turns her back on the West and looks East, to Korea, Japan and the rising sun. Behind her, on the west, massive mountain barriers separate the Far East from the rest of the world.

Our knowledge of her early architecture is patchy, partly because of her tradition of building in wood—a highly perishable material—and partly because both Chinese and Japanese have shown no inclination to enshrine pomp and circumstance, whether worldly or heavenly, in monumental and permanent architecture. But in the 1970s hundreds of imperial tombs of the Ch'in dynasty (221–206 BC) were uncovered from the orange earth of the Yellow River valley. Among them was the tomb of the conquering Ch'in king who united China and took the name of Ch'in Shih Huang Ti, which means First Emperor of China. This man not only built a new capital and the Great Wall of China to repel Mongul incursions, but also in the course of 36 years dragooned some 7,000 conscripts to create an underground 'spirit city' containing dummies of those who at an earlier period would have attended the Emperor to his tomb—600 terracotta figures, six feet high (were the Chinese a tall race in 200 BC?), each with a different face as if modelled on individual soldiers. There was also a model of the Ch'in idea of the heavens with sun, moon and stars moved by machinery, and, most informatively for us, a layout model of the Ch'in kingdom. Here are the Yellow and Yangtse rivers reproduced in mercury and made to flow by some mechanical contrivance into an ocean; and here are the buildings of the old capital reproduced in pottery—farms, palaces and pavilions.

These tomb models have substantiated the picture of early Chinese wooden architecture which historians had previously deduced from wooden buildings in Japan traditionally reputed to be rebuilds at many removes of Chinese buildings, due to an obliging Japanese habit of building replicas on adjacent sites every 20 or 30 years. Shrines of the sun-goddess of the ancient pantheistic Shinto religion of Japan, of Ise and Izumo are cases in point.

It is however relatively easy to put clues together and come up with something that approximates Chinese society of 3,500 years ago, because China appears to have evolved her sophisticated culture early and in isolation, and then chosen to pursue only those technological developments which suited the national temperament, remaining relatively static in many areas until the present century.

The persistent use of wood had, by the nineteenth century, threatened to replace a land of jungle with a landscape bald and

Pottery house model from Han tomb

denuded. It was not that the Chinese did not know how to use brick. From the third century BC they used brick arches and vaults in tombs. Buddhism brought with it in the second and third centuries AD the Indian and Burmese traditions of brick and stone building, exemplified in pagodas such as the Liao dynasty brick pagoda in Manchuria (907–1125), in the *p'ailou*, the striking triumphal arches used as city gates, and in the bridges which, in this well-watered country, have always been features of great beauty. There is superb brickwork, too, in Kublai Khan's palace, its Ming successors, and in many fortresses.

But undoubtedly it was wood that they found most pleasing. The wooden trabeate or beam structure, which developed first in China and was then passed on to Japan, is one of two distinctive features of Chinese architecture. The second was a body of rules—a sort of kit of unwritten planning by-laws—strickly adhered to, which governed the planning of any town or building, controlling siting, orientation, plan and even colour. These laws stemmed not only from physical, social or political requirements, but from a philosophy of design which embraced harmony in nature and what the oracles had determined was 'propitious', called Feng-shui. They were about the use of space, the eternal theme of architecture, and about creating spaces; and space was all-important in Chinese philosophy—more, some commentators think, than time, and certainly more than structure. But we must look at structure first if we are to have an image of the buildings.

No doubt it was the plenitude of wood that originally prompted its use in the early building types. In the northern areas along the River Amur, the earliest dwellings were not so much caves as holes in the ground over which a roof was set, supported by tree-trunk pillars driven into the ground. Early Japanese buildings were similarly created with a thatched roof resting on the ground (Jomon culture), and in the later Yayoi culture with a tent-shaped roof held by a ridge-pole between two forked sticks perched above a wattle-and-thatch wall that looked like a natural grass mound. This has remained the vernacular farmhouse pattern in Japan. In southern China, South-East Asia and Indonesia, the likelihood of flooding prompted the raising of wooden buildings on to piles; this has remained the vernacular type in these areas until the present day.

What was to become the classic Chinese structure was developed in the middle Yellow River Valley—a wood-frame building on a platform. Earthquakes, fairly frequent in China and endemic in Japan, may well have influenced the evolution of this structure. What was wanted was not solid walls, which could be cracked and rent apart by any upheaval in the earth's crust, but a structure which at best might be able to ride the heaving earth like a boat, shifting and settling back into position, and at worst, would be disposable, easily rebuilt after devastation. Possibly the base platform could act as a raft.

A good example of early Chinese architecture is the Chil-Song-Gak (Hall of the Pleiades) in Bo-Hyan-Su Temple in the Myohyang Mountains (Diamond Mountains), Korea, built during the seventh and eighth centuries. Here are the three basic elements of Chinese and Japanese houses: a raised platform, a wall-frame and a roof. Typi-

Izumo Shrine, south-east of Tokyo

cally, the podium was solid, there were never any cellars, and could be made of stamped earth—in later versions often faced with brick or stone—or of pounded clay, rubble or uneven stones as in the Korean example, or even of laid brick or ashlar. On this the wooden frame of the house was erected. This is the first time in our story that we have found a national building type that is on the frame principle, that is, the roof is supported on a frame with corner pillars; the walls are later in-fill. In the wooden houses of the Far East we can see the structural principle exemplified in naked simplicity, with the minimum of obscuring cladding.

The Hall of the Pleiades has solid stumpy tree-trunks as corner pillars, which is typical of the early type of architecture, and a single lintel beam (architrave), which usually became double in later versions of the classical building type. Columns of pine or cedar were generally set on protective bases of stone or bronze that were to become increasingly elaborate in carving or engraving. Also for protection from weather or termites, the pillars were painted with lacquer or an oil and hemp mixture which had brick dust mixed into it; from this may have come the custom of painting columns and brackets all in one colour, frequently a vivid red. On the columns was set the distinctive lintel structure which supports the roof. There were no chimneys: heating was normally by portable stove, and the smoke escaped from the side or from under the ridge of the roof. This was no problem in the humid heat of the south, where the walls were filled in by mere decorated screens, often only half-height; even in the bitter north, where timber walls might be forty inches thick, it was customary to leave a gap below the roof-line. Window glass was often of paper, which could be rolled up like a blind to let in the breezes on a hot day. For in these lands, exposed to the sun for much of the year, windows existed as air-vents rather than to let in light. In Japan, both outer and inner screen walls might be of paper.

The roofs were remarkable. They did not use the triangular tied construction of the half-timbered houses of mediaeval Europe. The Far East never used the diagonal reinforcing strut; diagonal wood strips on the surface such as appear on the Han tomb farmhouse model are purely decorative. The wide eaves of Chinese and Japanese houses are supported on a trabeate pyramid (*trabis* is Latin for a beam). As well as the purlins on which the rafters rest, the lintel beam between the two corner columns supports short vertical members which carry a lintel of shorter size. This pattern may be repeated with lintels of decreasing length up to the roof, the weight being forced back down on to the two original pillars. To help carry the weight, or to allow for sideways expansion and to achieve greater eaves overhang (the classic method of providing a shaded balcony or courtyard area where the family might sit out of the sun or rain), extra pillars would be added at the sides, each carrying its own post-and-lintel construction.

The additional columns provided galleries and aisle-like spaces inside. To meet the needs of architects who wished to extend the eaves overhang without cluttering the interior with columns, however, a

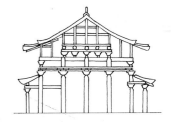

Chinese beam frame roof

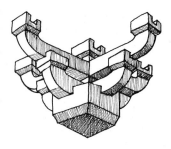

Kou-tung brackets

system was evolved of cantilevering the overhang outwards on clusters of brackets known as *kou-tung*; these were works of art in themselves, locking together like Chinese puzzles. Attention was further drawn to the brackets by the tradition of painting the beams and the rafters they supported in gay colours. The inspiration for these *kou-tung* may have come from Persian sources by way of India. Their importance was emphasized in the Sung era, the Silver Age of Chinese culture, when, following the publication of a master-builder's manual in 1103—*The Methods and Design of Architecture* (*Ying tsao fa Shih*) by Li Chieh—a module for the spacing of pillars and beams (previously often charmingly irregular), based on the bracket size, was established for use throughout the empire. When a new module was put forward in the seventeenth century by the Ching's Palace Office of Works, it was again based on the bracket arm.

Altering the angle of brackets made possible the marvellous undulating swags of Chinese roofs, and combined with a chosen roof-shape—gabled, hipped, half-hipped or pyramidal—created fascinating outlines. From the Han dynasty (206 BC–AD 220) onwards, eaves hang in catenary curves and have curved ridge lines and hip seams; sometimes they sport serrated edges like dragons' teeth and exuberantly winged corners hung with little bronze bells. The ridge pole was considered so important that a special ceremony took place when it was set in position. For good measure, tiles might be grey in the north and elsewhere blue or green or purple or yellow. Yellow was the imperial colour, and a bird's eye view of Peking in Ming times might have established the social status of different areas according to roof colour.

The pagoda is sometimes considered the characteristic form of the Far East. Certainly, practically every town in China boasts at least one pagoda, often sited to block the entry of evil spirits into the town from the north-east—the 'direction of the devil'. But in fact the typical Chinese building pattern was one-storey, or at the most two-storey, rectangular buildings grouped round courtyards. It is interesting to note that, unlike most countries where sacred structures set the standard 'quality' pattern for the national style, temples in China and Japan were built in the style of ordinary domestic housing. This reversal of sacred and secular may be typical of the mentality of the Far East, perhaps accounting for the sacred nature of Japan's domestic tea ceremony.

It has been suggested that the pagoda, which was generally attached to a temple, may have developed from the model of a typical house in the Han tomb—a rectangular hall with above, in the centre, a single, first floor study-room, to which the master might escape for serious thought, topped by a granary attic. Another plausible explanation is that it developed under Buddhist influence—a type of sikhara or pyramid of Buddhist umbrellas. However, the tiered *lou* was already an ancient form in China, and can be traced back to models of watch or water-towers in the Han tombs. Very likely it evolved from a combination of all three.

We can trace this evolution through three pagodas. First, through

the twelve-sided pagoda of the temple of Sung Yueh, Mount Sung, Honan, the oldest surviving brick building in China, dated AD 523, and highly reminiscent of an Indian temple. Second, through the lighthouse-like Sung dynasty Enemy Observation Pagoda (Liao-ti T'a) of AD 1001–50, a watchtower for the frontier between the Liao and Sung territories at the K'ai Yan temple, Ting-hsien, Hopei. Not until the pagoda of the Fo Kung temple, Yung Hsien, Shansi, of 1056 do we find the form completely sinicized. An all-wooden pagoda, it has the uneven number of floors which was to become *de rigueur* (usually seven or thirteen) The Chou belief that heaven has nine layers caused nine to be favoured in the Chou period. In the Fo Kung temple we have five floors, indicated on the exterior by jutting roofs, with the intermediate galleried floors unexpressed. Originally the pagodas were shrines or reliquaries attached to Buddhist monasteries. They

Pagoda of Sung Yueh Temple, Mount Sung, Honan

Enemy Observation Pagoda, K'ai Yan Temple, Ting-hsien, Hopei

housed an image on the ground floor and were hollow above, like the Indian sikhara, or sometimes contained a giant image that went up through several floors or carried a series of images on galleried floors.

For all the similarity in form, the Chinese pagoda never had the mystical significance of the sikhara as a vertical axis round which the cosmos turned. The Chinese were concerned with the cosmic axis— but for them it was horizontal, on the ground. The points of the compass were crucial, their separate identities linked with colours, animal symbols and seasons. Black stood for the north, winter and night—death of the day and the year; and from this direction—not surprising when one thinks of the cold winds from Mongolia—evil came. And so from as early as 6000 BC Chinese towns and houses were laid out on a north/south axis, the towns on a grid with the main street running north to south, the house doors facing south, the *good* direction of the Red Phoenix and the summer sun. The west was seen as white autumn, the white tiger at the evening of the day and the year, white peace and white mourning robes at the end of life. The importance of ancestor worship in the ancient religion therefore makes the south-west corner of the house the sacred area: no utilitarian offices were placed here.

But there were 24 cardinal points to be contended with, in addition to the main compass points, when siting a house, grave or town. Diviners were consulted as to the local forces of good and ill luck (harmony with the 'cosmic breath') by an ancient 'science' called *feng shui* (literally, 'wind and water'). These are still consulted today, even for a project as up-to-date as the revolutionary Hong Kong Shanghai Bank in Hong Kong of 1982-3. *Feng shui* not only dictates the site in relation to hills, roads and streams, and the building's orientation, but also the position of the doors (one Singapore bank constantly lost business deals until it changed its entrance), the relationship of house-blocks within a compound, and even the number of rooms in a house (three, four and eight bedrooms are unlucky and must be avoided).

After the site was chosen, a wall was built, again, often in association with *feng shui* to block evil influences from an unpropitious direction. Walls and the privacy they give are important to the Chinese. Fittingly, the first emperor, Ch'in shi Huang Ti, joined into the Great Wall of China all the stretches of wall along the northern frontier that feuding neighbouring clans had built against each other. It is a superb example of interaction between man and his environment as it loops its way, following the natural contours of the hills, 2,383 miles from the Gulf of Pohai to Chia-yu-kuan in Kansu Province. Completed in 210 BC, the Wall was maintained by successive emperors and finally given the refacing we see today by the Ming dynasty (1368-1644) from the fifteenth to the sixteenth century.

Both structurally and symbolically, the wall is the important distinguishing characteristic of Chinese architecture. In the first place, the defensive wall explains the puzzling lack of defensive castles in a country whose long history was patterned with fighting between clans and feudal overlords. The nobleman's town was his castle. The Ch'in

capital of Hsien Yang was planned to hold 10,000 people, and the *Great wall of China*
Imperial city at Peking was built big enough to harbour within its
walls the entire population of the city if need be. Ch'in unification in
the third century had brought about feudalism, and towns became the
bureaucratic and administrative centres. This system of walls for
bureaucratic identity, privacy and defence was repeated from macro-
cosm to microcosm: the country was walled, each city was walled and
had its own god of wall and moat, each dwelling within the city would
normally consist of several buildings within a walled courtyard to
house the customary extended family, which might comprise one
hundred relatives. Indeed, the word for 'wall' and the word for 'city'
were the same.

Peking, the northern capital, epitomizes the system. Its fortunes as a capital oscillated until in 1552 the Ming emperors built a new wall, 9 miles around with 7 gates, to take in the southern suburbs, which had developed under the pressure of a population explosion. This gave the city its four famous walled enclosures, and also put within the outer enclosure the Temple of Heaven (Ch'i Nien Tien) of 1420, built, as was the custom, in the open air on a mound to the south of the capital city. Moats and bastioned walls encircled the Outer City to the south and the Inner City to the north; inside the Inner City were the walls through which one had to pass by the Gate of Heavenly Peace (T'ien-an Men) into the great public square which formed the entrance courtyard to the Imperial City. To penetrate to the heart of the complex, the Forbidden City—the box within a box—another wall had to be breached by the Meridian Gate (the Wu Men), the horseshoe canal crossed by the central of the five bridges, and the gate-house buildings, guarded by the Emperor Chi'en Lung's great bronze dog-lions, passed through by the Gate of Great Peace (the T'ai-ho Men), before the podium, on which the Palace of Great Peace itself is set, could be attained. One is reminded of those ingenious boxes within boxes which the Chinese excel in carving out of ivory, and which hold a sort of mystical anticipation that within and within and within one may penetrate to the seat of power and majesty.

Thus enclosed, each part of Chinese society could keep itself to itself, forging relations with the outside world on its own terms. The same aloofness informs the planning of city and house, which is conceived from the inside looking out, and not, as in our Western streets, each house proudly showing off its position, station and beauty to the passer-by. Clues to the status of a house-owner can in fact be picked up from its compass position within the city or within the street-block or *fang* within the city grid; and once inside, there are factors like the height of the platform on which it stands and the number of inner courtyards which indicate status. Under the Ming dynasty imperial legislation fixed the number of bays of a single-halled dwelling— 9 for the Emperor, 7 for a prince, 5 for a mandarin and 3 for a citizen. But what can be seen from the street are blank walls. Houses look inwards to their inner courtyards, so there are no windows to be seen in the walls rising above the entrance courtyard, and even the view through gateways is blocked by 'spirit walls'— screens set just inside the entrance to obstruct the passage of evil spirits, who can move only in straight lines. However, the top of a flowering tree may be glimpsed in the entrance courtyard, and the spirit walls themselves are often very beautiful—carved in geometric or natural patterns of crazy-paving or 'cracked-ice', with lotus flowers or bamboo wands, or perhaps painted white with a single good-omen character in black.

Frequently the entrance court is approached through a side gate, but no impressive façade greets the visitor—simply one long wall of the house with the doorway placed in the centre (never in the gable wall). All houses must for good luck have a back door as well as a front door, and the two must not be in line, again to foil evil spirits.

(opposite) *Temple of Heaven, Peking*

*View from Meridian Gate,
Forbidden City, Peking*

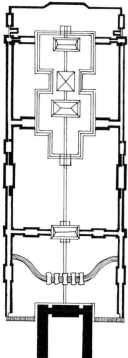

Forbidden City, Peking

*Kinkaku-ji, The Temple of
the Golden Pavilion, Kyoto*

Rules of etiquette decide from this point whether the visitor will be invited further in to discover for himself the symmetrical division of the house into the bright (*ming*) public rooms to the front and the cool dark shady (*an*) apartments at the back, which are the private family rooms. This layout, no doubt in part caused by the need to create cross-draughts within the interior, reflects a certain element of Chinese formality and privacy: steps to left and right, which lead, respectively, the host on the east and the guest on the west separately towards these back rooms, give the guest a clear understanding that he penetrates to the inner sanctum on the host's terms and may not make himself free of the house.

Gardens have been a feature of Chinese architecture from long before the building guidelines were set down in the *Ying tsao fa Shih* in 1103. The T'ang Emperor Wu even turned the imperial gardens at Chang'an into something of a wild-life park, enclosing it in 100 miles of wall and importing rhinoceros from India to roam among hills, lakes and woodland. The watered and wooded landscape surrounding the Summer Palace six miles north-west of Peking is dotted with

The Long Walk, or Corridor, at the Summer Palace, Peking

Pavilion through the Moongate, Han Shan Ssu Temple, Soochow

charming and idiosyncratic architectural features—pavilions, pagodas, covered walkways round the lake promontory, bridges, gateways, steps. Here waters spout, purr and tinkle, leaves rustle, paths
meander, water-lilies sway gently on the surface of lakes like full
moons—'Now sleeps the crimson petal, now the white, Nor wakes
the cypress in the palace walk; Nor winks the gold fin in the porphyry
font . . .' All is a dreamy fantasy misted in almond blossom.

In palace as in humble dwelling, the building is rectangular and
formal, the garden free. The macrocosm/microcosm duality persists.
The house is a small version of the Chinese view of the world: an open
five-sided box with a lid for the sky. The garden is a miniature version
of nature, of mountains reduced to rocks, forests to plants and mosses,
rivers and oceans to brooks and pools. There are no straight lines: all
is sinuous, and sloping to foil those myriad evil spirits, which can only
move in straight lines. In the same way, the decoration between house

Yin/yang symbol

and garden—gates, balconies, screens, railings, steps—abandons the angular geometry of the house for rounded and flowing lines and the patterns of nature—cracked ice, jointed stems, tasselled fronds, ferns uncurling, bamboos quivering.

Commentators have associated the contrasting styles of house and garden with the two great indigenous Chinese philosophies, Confucianism and Taoism. The founders of both were seeking for a principle of unity in life during a turbulent period of Chinese history. Confucius was a government official (Kung Futzu) in the fifth century BC and preached a civil servant's solution to the problems of life. Conservative and authoritarian, he respected the traditions of the ancestors (*li*) and advocated a Way (*tao*) of social order and peace, brought about by rational and competent administration. We can trace the effect of his philosophy in the united empire of the Chin, which succeeded the years of the Warring States in the establishment of a bureaucratic feudalism so strong that it lasted until 1911, and in the order, hierarchy and exact geometry that characterizes houses. In contrast, the garden reflects the Taoist concern for the life of feeling, intuition and mysticism. It is a movement away from rationalism, order and symmetry to freedom, experiment and contemplation.

China has an ancient legend that in the beginning the Supreme Lord sent out two opposite forces, the *Yin* and the *Yang*, to share control of the universe. In the Chinese house and garden we see the two polarities reconciled and shown to be complementary.

When we turn to Japan we find that so great was the effect of Chinese culture that much of her architectural story has already been told. Japan, a string of rocky volcanic islands lying out in the Pacific, 125 miles from any mainland, was, until recently, very isolated. Her history has alternated between periods of native rule and culture and occupation from abroad. The original Neolithic Jomon culture and the indigenous Shinto religion were first disturbed by Yayoi immigrants from China, who came by way of Korea from the first to the

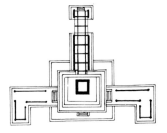

Phoenix Hall of the Byodoin Temple, Uji

Phoenix Hall of the Byodoin Temple, Uji

fifth century AD; and hard on their heels came Buddhism. The highest architectural expression of this import of Chinese religion is probably the Amida Hall of the Byodoin Temple above the river at Uji, south of Kyoto (then known as Heien), usually called the Phoenix Hall, because its plan is shaped like a bird. Dated eleventh century, its frontage was copied from a T'ang palace, and its rich embellishments of gold, silver, lacquer and mother-of-pearl show the sumptuous Chinese/Japanese/Buddhist style at its height.

After the fall of the T'ang dynasty in China, Japanese vigour reasserted itself; the Emperor moved his capital to Heien, and from the eighth to the twelfth century, the first indigenous domestic architecture appeared in the form of rambling country houses for the lords who headed the clans. The usual pattern was a series of rectangular buildings connected by corridors, set down irregularly in a landscaped garden with pools and islands.

Pagoda of Yakushi-ji
Temple, Nara

Continuous clan skirmishing, culminating in a century of civil wars, resulted in the transference of power from the Emperor to a military commander who bore the title of *Shogun*, or Commander-in-Chief. From the twelfth until the nineteenth century the chief power resided in the Shoguns with their private army, the Samurai. The architectural consequences of the power of the Shogunate and of the introduction of gunpowder were the marvellous garrison castles, which in Japan replaced the Chinese walled city system of defence. Often moated and set on high platforms of dressed granite or stone to resist fire, a major threat to their log superstructure, and with a curved batter to resist earth movement, these impressive buildings have towns huddled at their base, and they are clearly in command of the surrounding countryside.

In the 1630s, Ieyasu of the Tokogawa Shogunate, expelled all foreigners, closing the borders to traffic upon pain of execution. Christianity, which had come in with the Dutch, Spanish and Portuguese explorers in the sixteenth century, was crushed. Japan entered the so-called Floating World period, a time of middle-class affluence and a golden era for the arts; music, puppetry, *No* theatre, *Haiku* poetry, painting, and woodcuts, especially of blossom and of Japan's volcano, Fujiyama. In the next two hundred years of prosperity, the population soared to thirty million and the standard of literacy was high. By 1854, Japan was ready to resume relations with the outside world and eventually to take her place as one of the world's leading technological nations.

What are the distinctive features of Japanese architecture? The Chinese type of building originally adopted was the rectangular building set on an open platform of wooden stilts; to this the Japanese added an external verandah, often called a fishing gallery because, wherever possible, dwellings were sited on the edge of a pond or lake, and fish, a staple part of Japanese diet, could thus be obtained fresh. The original tent roof persisted for at least two thousand years, with its characteristic V-shape at either end of the ridge pole. But the most general roofshape is a combination of gable and half-hip in which the gable eaves curve backwards slightly to disappear behind the wrapped-round hip, achieving from the front a strange silhouette like a farmer's broad-brimmed hat.

The Japanese pagoda with its five linear roofs is more refined than Chinese versions. The roof-shape here, tauter, slimmer, hovers with wide wing-span over the building. In some cases, the eaves' overhang is as much as eight feet. Roofs, sometimes of unequal size, are stacked on a shady square-core tower like discs on a spindle and topped by a high, thin finial called a *hosho*—the sacred crowning gem, so spindly that it appears to trail away in the sky like the cry of a wild bird. The silhouette often resembles a calligraphic character or the pine trees that typify Japanese scenery. On the East Pagoda of the Yakushi-ji at Nara of AD 680 the roofs are alternately narrow and wide, with an entry-door on the lower of each pair. However, only the door on the ground floor provides access: those above and the galleries surrounding the floors are sham. The five roofs of the pagoda of the Horyu-ji

Double roof, half-hipped

Himei-ji Castle

Kasuga Shrine, Nara

at Nara subtly decrease in size as they go upwards, in a proportion of 10:9:8:7:6. Castles have the most exciting roofs of all, because the Japanese managed to solve the intricate structural problems involved in piling up storeys with gables facing watchfully in different directions. Perched above the water and with their white-plastered rendering, the castles suggest the movement of a cluster of great white seabirds about to lift off from a rocky perch so that it is no surprise to discover that Himei-ji Castle of about 1570 in the Hyogo Prefecture is known as the White Heron.

The Japanese skill in woodwork surpassed even that of the Chinese. They had much practice, both because of the need for rebuilding after earthquake and hurricane, and because for many centuries before the permanent capital was fixed at Nara in AD 710, the imperial court was peripatetic, and craftsmen had to evolve buildings finely jointed and carefully slotted together to allow rapid dismantling and re-erection. Even early gateways to Shinto shrines, the equivalent of Chinese *p'ailou* (which were called *torii*), exhibit masterly workmanship in their twin-beamed simplicity; as does the earliest extant wooden building in eastern Asia, the *Kondo* or main hall of the Horyu-ji at Nara, which was built for Buddhist monks by Japan's early hero, Prince Shotoku. The brackets carrying these enormous eaves are robust and beautiful.

The Chinese preoccupation with symmetry was early shaken off. Precincts started off adhering to a north/south axis, but when the Horyu-ji precinct had to be rebuilt after a fire in 670, the architects incorporated an existing mortuary chapel in the Golden Hall (the Kondo) and set the pagoda, which holds a clay sculpture tableau of the Nirvana of Buddha, next to it. In 733 the Hokkedo was added onto rising ground within the temple precinct. Like the Kondo, it was a basic single-unit building, with the typical early unevenly spaced pillars, but it was gentler and prettier, with the older pattern of shallow roof in silvery-grey tiles and gently curving eaves.

Where the tradition of orientation was maintained it was for practical purposes. To cope with the overpoweringly strong afternoon sun from the west, the long side of the house would be on the east/west axis, with the living-room facing south or south-east; in addition, it was common to have a seasonal change of living areas and to move into the darker parts of the house in high summer. Eventually, the movement away from Chinese models passed beyond finding their own axiality to a distinctive taste for asymmetry. A taste for variety of façades developed and led to an interest in the natural qualities of materials and the lovely contrasting use of surface texture, which was to form part of the Japanese legacy to modern architecture. Typical is the 1397 Golden Pavilion, Kinkaku-ji, in the Kitayama Palace grounds. Permutations of the pleasure given by the different detailing and surfaces on each storey are multiplied by the reflection in the lake.

Interest in texture was promoted by the Zen Buddhists, a sect whose rise to importance coincides with the rise of the Shoguns. Their insistence on simplicity influenced the economy of line, colour and detailing in modern Western architecture. It also complied with one ancient ritual of Japanese architecture: the use of a module. The house itself, the size of internal areas and the screens which created the bays along the elevations of a house were established by a module of six feet by three feet, the size of a rice-straw floor mat, the *tatawi*. Originally laid side by side loose, mats were later actually set into the floor, and eventually, after 1615, standardization of the module was formalized when the capital moved to Edo, today called Tokyo. By that time the early pattern of corridors joining separate buildings had long since given way to corridors formed by paper screens. After the twelfth century, runners were fixed to the floor to allow these screens to be pushed aside so that new areas could be opened up or, in summer, so that the whole side of the house could be opened to the garden. The Japanese do not have traditional furniture: they sit back on their heels and eat from trays, and sleep on mats. This has two effects. Life is lived at a very low level: ceilings can be low, and the beauties of the garden are admired from a couple of feet above the ground. But the second effect is more important: it gives the house-space an enormous flexibility. Houses usually had two raised areas—the chief one, for living and sleeping, was furnished with floor mats, and shoes were removed before it was entered; the other, floored in wood, was used for corridors, verandahs and lavatories. A lower, unfloored area normally supplied hall, bathroom and kitchen areas. The Japanese thus possessed a traditional architecture which was the envy of the West: a system so flexible that it could retain individuality while lending itself to the mass-production of building components.

The tea-houses built for *cho-no-ya*, the tea ceremony, epitomize the cool economy of Japanese module architecture as do their flower arrangements of a single spray of blossom set against a white wall. Tea-drinking was originally associated with Zen Buddhist monks,

who drank tea to keep themselves awake during contemplation. A
Zen priest called Shuko prevailed upon his friend the Shogun Yoshi-
masa to build him a special little tea-house in the grounds of the Silver
Pavilion in Kyoto. Tea-houses were thus based on a monk's simple
study, contemplative, pure, beautiful. Walls and door panels were
white or else translucent to let in the light reflected from the ground,
the chief source of illumination under those deep eaves, mats covered
the floor, and furniture was confined to shelves and an alcove displaying an important work of art—perhaps a painting or a bowl or a
single flower arrangement—and to the tea-making equipment itself.

*Tearoom of the Shokintei
House, Katsura Imperial
Villa, Kyoto*

The spirit of Japan we find distilled in the tea-houses is also present
in the gardens. Zen Buddhism in particular affirms the need to be at
one with nature, and gardens, whatever their size, were important.
Like Chinese gardens, they represent the world in miniature, but here
art more particularly contrives nature. You do not walk in a Japanese
garden, but view it from the gallery or verandah. And so, as with the
flower arrangement, great painters were employed to design gardens,
such as So-ami's sand garden adjoining the tea-house of a Kyoto
temple. Like the black-ink paintings of which the Japanese were so
fond, sand gardens should be a study in dark and light—rock forma-
tions created from carefully searched-out *art trouvé* (to split a rock

would be to violate nature), white sand raked into hillocks and wave patterns, miniature trees, water in lakes, ponds or little waterfalls according to the space available.

From the sixteenth century onwards, the Chinese influence is apparent in the art and architecture of Europe. But in the long run it has been Japanese architecture that has proved more influential. Among the features that the world has drawn from Japan are the standardized building components based on a module; the rethinking of internal space with fitted carpets and floor cushions; the use of bean bags or bed-rolls to replace furniture; space made flexible with screen dividers; the use of untreated natural materials producing contrasting textures (linen, wool) within a narrow range of colours (white, black and natural wood), which often accentuated the structure; and finally the interchange between house and garden architecture, which assumed a full role in European architecture in the twentieth century.

Ryoanji Temple Garden

6

Ritual of Blood

In the sixteenth century Charles I of Spain sent his conquistadores to the New World, where they found strange civilizations dating from the first millenium BC. When, after landing on the Mexican Gulf, they pushed their way through rain-forests, thickset with thorns, and infested with mosquitoes, to the Aztec city of Tenochtitlan, the site of Mexico City today, there was plenty of reason for native Indians and Spaniards to stare at each other with wild surmise. The apparition of the Spaniards fulfilled a prophesy among the Indians: the Aztec emperor Montezuma II and his men believed they were witnessing the second coming of Quetzacoatl, the plumed serpent god, who, it had been predicted, would come again, white and bearded and majestic from the East. They were riveted by the strangeness of the armed warriors with flashing steel, popping firearms and thunderball cannons, mounted (most fearsome of all) on monsters with thudding hooves, tossing manes and lashing tails. For these people possessed neither iron nor steel and did their fighting with poison-tipped arrows and weapons of bronze and obsidian. Moreover, the Pre-Columbians never discovered the wheel and had never seen a horse. Indeed, in this country, unlike in the high Andes of Peru, where llamas are sometimes used as pack animals, man was the beast of burden—a tradition so deep-seated that even today building workers often prefer to shift massive stones on their backs in great woven baskets supported by headbands, rather than use wheelbarrows or trolleys. As for the horse, it was of course a historic meeting, indeed the start of a centuries-long love affair.

And what was there to stop the Spaniards in their tracks? The area which they invaded, south of where Christopher Columbus had landed some twenty-seven years earlier in 1492, was the isthmus that connects North America with the west coast of South America; and in this region (which today comprises Mexico, Yucatan, Honduras and Guatemala) and an area on the Pacific coast of South America (comprising modern Peru and the fringes of Bolivia and Chile), the ancient civilizations in the Americas were in their final phase. The Spaniards, pushing their way inland through Yucatan, may have first stumbled on some of the enormous stone heads, eight or nine feet high, which the ancient Olmec race had left behind, along with remains of the two classic Meso-American architectural forms, the pyramid and the ball-court; and may have caught glimpses of the crested temples of the Maya, marooned among the tufted trees.

At last, under the terrible blue-ribbed volcanoes of Mexico, they were stopped in their advance by a people far outnumbering their own handful of troops and quite unlike any they had come across before: dark, pulsing, powerful and warlike. These were the Aztecs,

Teotihuacan, looking down the 'Street of the Dead' from the top of the pyramid of the Moon

From Codex Mendoza, Bodleian Library, Oxford

migrant tribes who had come into the area, slaughtering as they went, searching for an eagle that would be sitting on a cactus, eating a snake—the sign, according to their vicious humming-bird war-god, Huitzilopochtli, which would identify the place where they had to settle. The symbol, which now graces the Mexican flag, was spotted on an island on saline Lake Texcoco. And so, on two neighbouring islands, they founded their cities of Tlatelolco and Tenochtitlan, where Mexico City spreads itself today, using a light, local volcanic material called *tezontle*—a sort of dull red pumice stone—so that the city foundations should not sink into the marshes of the lake.

The Spaniards must have been impressed by Tenochtitlan, laid out in 1325, as was characteristic of the Meso-American cities, on spacious town-planning principles which would be acceptable today, with vast plazas surrounded by temples and palaces raised on great pyramidal mounds, the different areas linked by traffic on the canals and by bridges connecting great sweeping causeways, wide enough to take eight conquistadores riding abreast; with fresh water brought in by special canals, and gardens lush with flowers. But there was a stench in the air, and even the bloodthirsty Spanish soldiers recoiled from a rose-red city dyed with human blood. Blood often figured in the ancient worship of the jaguar and of Quetzacoatl, the Feathered Serpent, which was common to most Meso-American tribes. Sometimes the worshippers indulged in ritual bloodletting, sometimes in the sacrifice of animals and, occasionally, of humans. It was for such ceremonies that the standard city centre had developed: vast squares for public assemblies, religious dancing and games, laid out before pyramid temples, up which great flights of steps soared to the god's little house at the zenith. There would often be a statue of the god at the top of the steps, and here the priests performed the public rites of sacrifice, tiny figures impressively close to heaven on a plinth that towered over the packed piazza of frenzied worshippers.

The Aztec ritual was particularly bloodthirsty, for Huitzilopochtli had to be supplied with a diet of human hearts, cut still beating from the victims' breasts, if he was to permit the sun to continue to make its daily pilgrimage across the sky. And so the processing priests descended, pulled their victim up the great flight of steps, and bent him backwards, priests on either side pulling arms and legs taut, over the sacrificial stone which stood before Huitzilopochtli's image. 'Thereupon,' says a Spanish chronicler, 'they gashed his breast open ... seized his heart ... then rolled ... his body over, cast it hence, bounced it down.' From the top of the 91 steps of the Castillo they threw the hearts down into the lap of Chac, the cruel rain god.

Until recently it was thought that all that had remained of the cities were descriptions in letters and reports back to Spain that had been preserved in the royal and monastic archives. But in recent years, excavation of tunnels for a transport system and for sewers and electric cables in Mexico City has yielded exciting finds which tie in with the Spanish accounts. On the site of the final Aztec defeat in the Plaza of the Three Cultures, the Temple of Tlatelolco in red igneous rock stands beside a Spanish church and monastery. Close behind the great Baroque Cathedral of Mexico City, with the vast square of the *Zocala* behind, the foundations of the Great Temple of Tenochtitlan itself have been unearthed, the temple whose consecration in 1487 involved the sacrifice of a great many victims, variously estimated at 10,000 and at 80,000, ritually slaughtered four at a time, from sunrise to sundown, for four days.

Warrior column from temple at Tula

Castillo, Chichén Itzá

Whether the ancient Meso-American cultures developed autonomously has long been a matter of dispute. There may have been tribal movements from east to west, from North Africa across the Atlantic, from Peru to the Polynesian Islands, which would explain puzzling similarities in such wide-flung cultures, including their architecture. It could explain why a mere handful of tribes, all from this middle belt, developed such advanced civilizations while to north and south the Indian tribes remained at a primitive stage. It could explain why, when the tribes to north and south made huts of branches and leaves, these people, like the Mesopotamians, used adobe bricks of mud and straw to build square houses, which sometimes showed sophisticated features such as several floors, gutters, streets, sewers and aqueducts. It would explain why in jungle or desert coasts they brought stone long distances to build stepped pyramids.

Pyramid of the Niches, El Tajin

Caracol Observatory, Chichén Itzá

Their land-surveying, calculation of time and astronomy probably excelled those of Babylon and Egypt. Tunnels and angled holes in their observatories for siting the rise and fall of celestial bodies give some clue as to how astronomical calculations were made. At Monte Alban, the Zapotec 'city of the gods', there is a boat-shaped observatory with a central siting tunnel that dates from between AD 500 and 700. At about the same time, before AD 600 at El Tajin, the Gulf Coast capital, the Totonacs built the Pyramid of the Niches. Archaeologists gave it this name when they excavated it in the 1950s because they thought its many recessed window embrasures, one for each day of the year, had lost their statues. But we now understand that the niches had astrological significance for the Indians. Seen in plan the pyramid bears a strong resemblance to the mandala plan of Borobodur. But we are not suggesting cross-influences here; the mandala does appear to be a universal symbol, full of subconscious meaning and satisfaction to human beings. The Caracol (Snail) Observatory at Chichén Itzá dates from the time of or before the resuscitation of the late Maya city by the Toltecs in the early ninth and tenth centuries. The snail is a tower ten feet high, with two circular viewing tiers around the core spiral staircase which gives it its name; set on a series of stepped terraces, it is the only circular building so far found to have a classic Maya vault.

El Castillo, Chichén Itzá

Amerindian complexes distinguish themselves by the grandeur and spaciousness of their public areas, which are set apart from the domestic quarters of the city. Even the buildings of the lowland Maya, characteristically long and low here where they are sited on open ground and do not have to rise above jungle, are still set on high platforms. The 330-foot long Palace of the Governors at Uxmal, for instance, stands on a man-made esplanade 43 feet high. It is estimated that 2,000 men, working three years, each consisting of 200 working days, would have had to shift between them some 1,000 tons of building materials a day in order to create the esplanade. The pattern for the central ceremonial area was established in Teotihuacan, north-east of present-day Mexico City. Founded in about 100 BC, by the first century AD it was bigger than imperial Rome. Here, temples piled one against the other are set around an area reserved for dancing and cannibalistic feasting.

Palace of the Governors, Uxmal

Corbelled doorway, Palace of the Governors, Uxmal

One of the first Meso-American colonnades is to be found in the other Toltec capital, Tula. Here the pillars tell the story of Toltec conquest: those at the temple doorway are the standard Quetzacoatl pillars with the snake's head, spikily fanged and feathered, at the base, and the tail holding up the door lintel, while at the front are enormous pillars in the shape of inexorable Toltec warriors, wearing feathered headdresses and breast-plates shaped like butterflies. At Chichén Itzá, the Toltec influence is seen in the colonnades and porticoes that connect ceremonial areas.

Also in Chichén Itzá is the largest and grandest example of another Meso-American ceremonial space: the ball court. The object of the game was to knock a solid rubber ball (there was plenty of rubber about; the Spaniards referred to the Olmecs as the 'rubber people') of about ten inches in diameter through stone rings set high on the walls of the court, using the hips, elbows and thighs. Murals on the walls of the courts showing that the vanquished team was sometimes ritually sacrificed bear out the religious importance of the game, also suggested by the siting of courts near temples, often with a connecting way to a viewing platform for the priests and dignitaries.

In contrast to the grand exteriors, the interiors of buildings were cramped, windowless and dark. The little temples set atop the soaring pyramids were exact copies of the adobe huts in which peasant Maya may still live today. Even the palaces, for example the Palace of the Governors at Uxmal, lack windows and were lit by natural light through the doorways and had dark narrow rooms assembled, it appears, on a unit basis, sometimes in double rank, as at Uxmal, more for the occasional show than for everyday living, which was conducted out of doors.

There are particular details that can be used as clues to distinguish between the ruins of one Meso-American tribe and those of another. Characteristic of the Early Maya cities, which have in the last century been disentangled from the stifling embrace of the jungle, are the steep pyramids crowned by little square temples with corbel-vaulted roofs surmounted by a plumed ruff of stone standing up behind their roofs, known in Spanish as *cresteriá*. Often this protrudes above the vegetation and gives the whole pyramid the appearance of a raised orna-

The Great Ball Court, Chichén Itzá

mental throne—a seat of authority. The god presumably looked out from his little house over his jungle kingdom. It was made possible by the abundance of tropical hardwood which, used for the lintels, was tough enough to support such a superstructure.

Nine was the sacred number for the Amerindians, and many pyramids have nine basic stages. The arrangement of steps varies. Some

View of the Great Plaza from the North Acropolis, Tikal

climb in sheer flights to the top—as in the Castillo, Chichén Itzá, where four flights of stairs, in perfect symmetry, sweep up the four sides of the pyramid; on other temples the steps are arranged in a series of shallow swooping flights which often fail to correspond to the stages of banked earth and rubble that form the actual temple mound—as in the Pyramid of the Magician at Uxmal. This pyramid shows another Maya feature—corbelled vaulting, in which only the last two jutting stone-courses meet under a great cross beam whose weight stabilizes the structure. This sort of vaulting is also found at Palenque along the façade of the Multiple Court and in the crypt chamber of the priest-king in the temple of the Inscriptions, the only Meso-Amerindian example of a burial pyramid, which is entered by a triangular door from a staircase built within the walls. Arrow-headed corbelled openings occur also in the later Puuc-style buildings of the northern Maya, for instance in the arcades connecting the two wings to the central block of the Palace of the Governors at Uxmal.

The well-preserved friezes around the buildings of the dry lowland Puuc area are remarkable not only because we know they were executed with only bronze and obsidian tools, but also because they are so varied. The smooth warm dignity of the Turtle House at Uxmal, almost classical Greek or Egyptain in its simplicity, contrasts

Turtle House, Uxmal

System M Pyramid, Monte Alban

with the band of decoration on the Governors' Palace, in depth almost half the Palace's total height and conferring a curiously arresting, boxy, beetling appearance. Different again are the complicated repetition masks of Chac, the rain god, that decorate the Codz-poop or Palace of the Masks at Kabah, near Uxmal, where the assembly of thousands of identical segments would have been impossible had they been so much as half an inch out.

In the Mexican isthmus, in the ancient capital of Teotihuacan and later cities, buildings are distinguished, in addition to the use of standard proportion and silhouette, by rectangular panels called *tableros*, which emphasize the stages of the stepped pyramid: the *tablero* is normally cantilevered forward over the sloping wallface known as the *talud*. The silhouettes suggest that the Meso-Americans had a good eye for incisive outlines and contrasts of light and shade created by the brilliant sunlight. The same features are displayed in Oaxaca, the area stretching northwards from the southern Mexican coastline, in the very beautiful south façade of the Palace of the Columns at Mitla, a Miztec city of about 1,200 inhabitants, its long, low lines and crisp geometrical friezes reminiscent of Puuc-style Maya, and in the Pyramid of Quetzacoatl at Xochicalco, near Cuernavaca, with the feathered serpent squirming all over it.

At El Tajin, in the Pyramid of the Niches, flying cornices jut over hollow recesses to produce a marvellous chiaroscuro effect. The builders' intention may have been less to fulfil an aesthetic demand than to use the niche frames to reinforce the structure and keep the central core of packed earth in place. Traces of red, blue and black paint remaining on the pyramid suggest that most Pre-Columbian temples had a layer of brightly coloured plaster, made from burned limestone laid over the facing stonework or adobe mud-brick, and in some cases murals were painted onto this background.

Finally, we must look at the contribution made by the architecture of Peru, which is different from that of the isthmus cultures. The chief distinguishing feature of Inca architecture is its large-scale masonry, built in courses and tightly jointed without any mortar. Some of the most skilful masonry in the world can still be seen in the lower walls of some streets in Cuzco, one-time Inca capital; and the scale of the pieces in this cyclopean jigsaw can be judged from seeing a herd of llamas feeding or a man standing below the three-tier ramparts of Sacsahuaman, the fortress which stands guard above the capital. This masonry was probably achieved by hoisting the great blocks up on rollers with liana ropes, and swinging them backwards and forwards until they ground into place between their fellow mammoth stones.

But masonry is not the only Inca achievement. Today, as you climb higher and higher into the Andes at altitudes so great that guards on the train offer the passengers oxygen, you can see evidence of Inca fortresses and their network of communications—roads and bridges over chasms and ravines—waterworks, and agricultural terraces, superbly carved in serried ranks from precipitous canyon sides. They were made possible by the existence of a highly regulated and no doubt tyrannical feudal society, in which the young and fit were

Macchu Picchu

annually conscripted to contribute to public works. In return for this service, a virtual welfare state operated, providing insurance against famine, sickness and old age.

One hill fortress, Macchu Picchu, which may have been the sanctuary sought by the Inca king, Manco II, from the invading Spaniards, is considered by many one of architecture's most breathtaking achievements. The excavations are not complete, but houses, stairs, courts, temples, granaries and graveyards have been identified as well as a novitiate convent for the maidens known as Virgins of the Sun, who served in the Inca temples. As if aware that they could not improve on nature's grand conception, the builders tucked the city into an inaccessible saddle between two majestic cloud-wreathed sugar-loaf peaks. Far below this garrison of sheer living rock, the river Urubamba snakes its way. Solid and void defy definition or delineation. Ghost houses enveloped in mist and snow materialize out of the very mountain, for man has incorporated the rocky outcrops into the house walls in a grey-green osmosis of man-vegetation-mineral, of past and present, of living and dead, of earth and heaven. Macchu Picchu not only epitomizes the piercing excitement of architectural experience, but also in the interaction of man and his environment provides a fleeting glimpse of some elemental reality.

7

The Landscape of the Gods

With the architecture of ancient Greece we return to the mainstream European tradition. One of the most aesthetically perfect bodies of work in the Western European tradition, it was also the foundation of many subsequent styles in different parts of the world. It therefore occupies a unique place in our story, and we must look at it carefully and ask how it took shape. Its growth and development forms one of the most entrancing episodes in architectural history. It has a logic and inevitability about it, like the drama that the same civilization was able to invent and perform.

To the traveller approaching Attica by boat and seeing the white columns of the Temple of Poseidon at Cape Sounion for the first time (not one of the earliest buildings; it dates from about 440 BC) the immediate impact, with the ruins gleaming above the blinding blue sea, is of the landscape and the light. The land, with its unexpected humps and hills, its moments of drama, its untidy olive groves and bleached grass, is evocative, moody and memorable. The light, praised by everyone from Plutarch to John Henry Newman, who speaks of its 'special purity, elasticity, clearness and salubrity', must have played a crucial part in the evolution of the classical orders of architecture. The clear, dazzling sunshine makes for strong shadows and encourages clean, powerful forms in the landscape. And the materials were there to make that possible—the local limestone, at first often covered with a marble stucco, and then marble itself.

Against that background there emerged the most impeccable architecture, the expression of an exquisite, mature national consciousness.

Temple of Poseidon, Cape Sounion

Like that consciousness, it took its shape gradually. For Greece was not, for most of its history, one country. With its mountainous mainland and scattered islands it began as a group of city-states, usually in rivalry with one another. What brought the culture—and the architecture—to a climax was the supremacy of Athens. In the golden age known as the Hellenic period (800–323 BC), the city-state was established as the basis of society, new cities were founded and Athens emerged as the supreme power after decisive victories over the invading Persians. The zenith was reached in the fifth century BC with an astonishing flowering of philosophy, art, literature and drama. The Parthenon, which we shall discuss in some detail, was one of the supreme achievements of that period.

As we have already seen, the region that later became Greece saw its first civilization in the island of Crete, which reached its peak at the palace of Knossos. That was the Minoan civilization (3000–1400 BC) and its great buildings were every bit as complex (literally labyrinthine in the haunts of the Minotaur) as those of any other state at the time. It was succeeded by a culture at Mycenae and Tyrins on the mainland, possibly less elegant architecturally but, especially in the Fortress of Mycenae, lowering over the Argive plain from its menacing heights, more warlike and formidable. The military aspirations of most of the Greek states continued. Alexander the Great, even though he was tutored by the philosopher Aristotle, made his mark as a ferocious warrior of incomparable vigour and genius, and did much to destroy the inheritance of the great early civilizations; certainly the Persians saw his bloody victories as the destruction of art and ordered life. That makes it all the more remarkable that Athens was able to witness such a flowering of culture in the fifth century. Architecturally, the story moves from the fortress to the market-place, from the citadel to the agora. A Greek philosopher remarked that high ground was the place for aristocracy and low ground the place for democracy. What took the place of the fortress was the temple, which in Athens reached the pinnacle of perfection; what completed the market-place were social and communal buildings that brought people together to talk, argue and trade. What brought unity to Greek architecture was the column and the lintel.

Discarding the arch, even though they knew about it and could have used it had they wished to do so, the Greeks concentrated on perfecting the constructional element that most perfectly suited the climate, materials and society that used the buildings. For it was a society that used—and therefore saw—architecture not as interior rooms, but from the outside. Both the temples and the other buildings of the agora or market-place were exterior architecture. They put all the fun and the refinement on the outside. For it was not in the dark and inaccessible interior that things happened; the interaction between men and gods happened in the open air, where the welcome fingers of the breeze played through the slim colonnade as if on a lyre, where a shaft of light emphasized the clarity of an Ionic column, and the hide-and-seek of sun and shadow was petrified into a moulding.

Before we can go any further we must therefore look at the temple, starting with one built in a manner that was to become the first of the three major styles that have been used ever since throughout the world—the Doric Style.

If we look at a Doric temple and mentally pull it apart, we can immediately identify the primitive structural elements we saw being put together by the Egyptians or the Persians. We see how the bundles of reeds tied together to form door-posts or roof-supports have become fluted Doric columns. We see that these columns go down into the earth—a base was a refinement which was only to make its appearance with the Ionic style. The flat block of wood placed on top of the reed bundle to carry the roof structure is there still as the *capital*. This is the feature of a column that we look at first to check which order of Greek architecture—Doric, Ionic or Corinthian—the architect is using in the building. During three centuries (seventh to fourth century BC), the wooden beams that span the space from column to column (the joints occurring over the middle of the capital) changed to blocks of stone which form the *architrave*. Sometimes a wide capital will carry two parallel blocks of stone, as we can see if we walk between the columns and look upwards in the so-called Theseion (the Temple of Hephaestus) in the Agora at Athens (445 BC). About twenty feet was the maximum span possible, so anything wider meant that additional columns had to be inserted. Above the architrave is the decorative frieze, composed of *triglyphs* and *metopes*. We can easily appreciate that the triglyphs (meaning three slits)—protruding blocks scored with three grooves—originated as the ends of the cross-beams of the roof. In between these beams-ends the Greeks hung decorated terracotta plaques, and in stone temples the surface of these spaces (the *metopes*) were carved with figurative scenes. Finally, in a timber-frame building a narrow projecting course of stones called the *cornice* framed the base of the triangular pediment which filled in the gable end under the wide, sloping eaves.

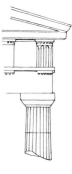

Greek order: Doric

Wood persisted as a roofing material, even in the stone temples, and its susceptibility to fire offers a convincing explanation of why so many temples, such as those on the Acropolis, have been left to us as roofless ruins. However, stone roofs do occur, becoming more common in the Hellenistic era (323–30 BC) which followed the death of Alexander the Great. The Temple of Hephaestus has a stone ceiling coffered (that is, cut away between the stone beams so that it looks as if made from upturned empty boxes) to lighten the great weight of the stone. The city of Alexandria must have been largely stone-roofed, for Julius Caesar attributes to this the fact that his troops did relatively little damage in taking the city.

Greek order: Ionic

The Greeks did not use mortar, but made the bed for the stones slightly concave and ground each stone into position with sand to produce hairline joints in a manner similar to that later adopted by the Incas in Peru. The short drums, of which a column was made up, were fitted together with a central wooden (and later iron) dowel: iron clamps fixed with molten lead linked blocks of stone together, and iron bars were used for strengthening as, for instance, in the architrave of the Propylaea on the Acropolis. The carving of friezes

Greek order: Corinthian

and columns was enormously extended once marble had come into general use for temples from about 525 BC. The glowing Pentelic marble from quarries near Athens was used for the temples on the Acropolis. Yet the Greeks were not content with that material. They painted figures and details in what we would find garish colours—red, blue and gold—just as the eyes, lips and nipples of their bronze statues were inlaid with coloured stones.

The classic temple plan of the fifth century BC did not become much more complex in structure than the megaron, the hall of a Mycenaean chief. The statue of the god replaced the hearth, and the row of pillars down the centre, necessary to carry the roof, was reorganized to form a colonnade right around the outside of the rectangular building. The entry was usually between the customary six columns on the short side, and through the open door the statue would face the rising sun. Often, an entrance porch was screened off by a second rank of six pillars, and, to balance the porch, there might be a treasury, entered from the back, at the other end of the temple.

We begin to find what distinguishes these temples from what had been built before—the throne-room at Knossos, Darius the Great's palace at Persepolis, the Temple of Khons at Karnak—when we come to examine the three types of *orders* under which, as we have already noted, Greek temples can be grouped. The term 'order' is really quite a good one, because it not only implies the organization of the components of the temple, but it also suggests the satisfying relationship and proportion that these components bear to each other and to the whole. The first two, the Doric and Ionic, evolved in the first half of the fifth century BC, the Ionic slightly after the Doric. The third, the Corinthian, came in at the very end of the classical period and overlaps with Roman.

Earliest and simplest, the Doric temple, with no base, plain capitals and undecorated grooving along the shaft of the pillar, appeared between 1000 and 600 BC in mainland Greece, the lands settled by Dorian invaders from the Balkans. The stocky, silent grandeur of the Doric pillars in the earlier Temple of Hera, Paestum (530 BC), can be contrasted with the precision of detail and the serene simplicity that

Temple of Hera, Paestum

give ineffable dignity to the later Doric (490 BC) Temple of Aphaia at Aegina.

The Ionic temple is usually found in the islands and on the coasts of Asia Minor, the areas settled by Greeks who had fled from the Dorians. Its columns are slimmer, lighter and more delicately sculpted and can be readily identified by volutes on the capitals that look like rams' horns or a scroll lightly rolled up at either end. A glance at the total profile of this order reveals how much more complex it is than the Doric. The slender column is set on a tiered and decorated base; the flutings along the column are scalloped at top and bottom, and are separated from each other by a narrow flat fillet; metopes and triglyphs have disappeared, but the frieze and pediment are likely to be fully carved. The steps to the *stylobate* (the plinth on which the temple stands) are less massive than with the Doric—and therefore easier for the worshipper to climb. The Ionians had a treaty port on the Nile Delta, and this contact with the enormous Egyptian temples influenced the magnitude of the Hellenistic Ionic temples by comparison with the Attic Doric. The Temple of Artemis (Diana) at Ephesus, for instance, was so large that Antipater in the first century BC included it in his list of the Seven Wonders of the World.

The Corinthian capital, shaped like an upturned bell surrounded by serrated leaves, on the one hand evaded what had always been a problem with the corner pillars of the Ionic, namely that the capital is made to be seen from the front; and on the other, offered possibilities for elaborately carved symmetry, which was to find great popularity in the lavishness of the Roman Empire. But undoubtedly it has a charm of its own when used delicately as in the Choragic Monument of Lysicrates in Athens. The earliest use of the Corinthian capital is probably in the Temple of Olympian Zeus in Athens, begun in the days of the tyrants in the sixth century BC, but not completed until the first century AD by the Roman emperor, Hadrian.

But for classic examples of the first two orders, we need go no further than the Acropolis. Today the rock is approached by an impressive flight of steps, broken in the middle by a path for animals on their way to the sanctuary to be sacrificed, but these date only from

Choragic Monument of Lysicrates, Athens

Temple of Nike Apteros, Acropolis, Athens

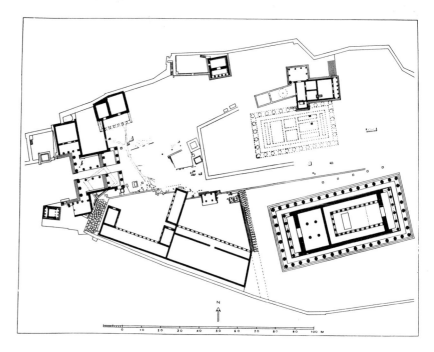

Roman times. The ancient Athenians crossed the agora diagonally by the processional way and then zigzagged up a path to the great entrance gateway, the Propylaea. With wings jutting forward on either side, the Propylaea opens its arms to pilgrims from the west. Isolated on a bastion to the right of the entrance is the tiny temple of Nike Apteros (the Wingless Victory), the sole survivor of the small

Parthenon, Acropolis, by Ictinus and Callicrates

temples which originally ringed the rock. It was built by Mnesicles in about 427 BC and uses Doric on its outer columns, Ionic on the inner, in a fittingly restrained manner so as not to pre-empt the glory that burst upon the worshipper as he passed through the gate into the sanctuary. Here an important aspect of the layout can be seen. Nothing is direct, everything is in perspective, at an angle. Greek architects put symmetrical buildings into unsymmetrical and irregular places and manipulated the levels of the ground so that the sense of unity was experienced by moving around the site, like the Panathenaic procession on its main feast day, rather than by viewing buildings separately from a stationary position.

Caryatid Porch, Erechtheum, Acropolis, Athens

The temples of the Acropolis, dedicated to the guardian deities of the city, were totally destroyed by the Persians. But Pericles, after the victories at Salamis and Plataea (480–479 BC), was inspired to devote some of the war-fund collected from the Greek city-states to rebuilding the temples under the supervision of the sculptor Phidias. A sculptor as overseer made sense at the time, because the temples were in some ways exhibition halls for sculptures of deities or even of victorious athletes, and sculpture was considered the superior art. And so the pilgrim's first encounter would have been with Phidias' bronze statue of Athena, by all accounts so big that the sun flashing on her helmet was used by sailors at sea as a beacon by which to set course for Piraeus. Phidias' statue retained the site of its predecessor outside the wall of the earlier temple.

The statue no longer stands on the Acropolis, and today on entering the temenos, or sacred enclosure, the eye is drawn to the right of centre, to the highest point on the rock, where stands the Parthenon. In ancient times a second statue of the goddess Athena by Phidias, this time of gold and precious stones, stood within the temple itself. Today, it is possible to clamber into the ruins over the stylobate, without troubling about doors, but in the fifth century BC the temple turned its back on the Propylaea, and pilgrims had to walk round the outside to the entrance orientated towards the rising sun on the eastern side. To the north, beyond the site of the Parthenon's predecessor, is the little temple of the Erechtheum, which in its day played a bigger part in the ritual than the Parthenon itself. Because the temple steps down the hillside on two levels, a continuous colonnade was impossible; but it makes an ingenious use of the Ionic by rising through two levels on the side where the hill falls away, and being half-height on the adjacent façade. Most unusual of all, and a detail much disputed, is the porch, where a row of powerfully built maidens, known as Caryatids, replace the columns.

But we must pause at the Parthenon, not simply because it is the best-known of all Greek buildings, but because it has been the subject of meticulous study which has revealed some of the mathematical secrets of its perfection of form and proportion. Built between 447 and 432 BC by Ictinus, Mnesicles and Callicrates under Phidias' direction, it obeys the canons for classic Doric proportions generally adopted after the sixth century BC, except that the customary six columns on the east and west ends have been increased to eight. But

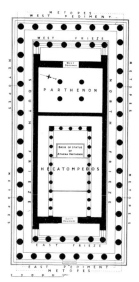

Parthenon

its power to enchant and satisfy lies in the subtleties of line and proportion. Even in its own time these refinements were legendary.

When, in the nineteenth century it was measured in detail, it was discovered that there is scarcely a straight line in the whole structure: every surface is hollowed or swollen or tapered in such a way that the eye can slide along its contours unobstructed by any optical distortion, so that nothing jars, all is harmony. Most Greek buildings of this golden period use *entasis*, the device whereby tapering columns are given a slight swelling about a third of the way up to counteract a tendency of the eye to see them as curving inwards from either side, the most extreme and bulgy example being the Basilica at Paestum. But on the Parthenon this exercise in *trompe l'oeil* is not limited to the columns. All the horizontal lines (such as the architrave and the stylobate), which, left to themselves, would appear to sag slightly in the middle, are similarly corrected; the corner columns are thicker and stand closer to their neighbours, so that they will not appear spindly against the sky, and, furthermore, they tilt inward slightly at the top to avoid an illusion of falling outwards; the triglyphs are spaced progressively further apart as they reach the centre front and back, so that they will not create hard lines by being directly over a column. The design of the Parthenon called for meticulous measurement; precision in calculation; mastery in masonry; and a unique fineness of perception and response. The result is breathtaking.

Still in Athens, let us look down from the Acropolis at the city as a whole. The ordinary dwelling-houses at this time were an undistinguished huddle of windowless single rooms giving onto courtyards linked by narrow twisting alleys, under the hill. It was where people congregated that interesting architectural events happened. Especially impressive was the open space, the agora, which, officially the market-place, gathered around itself the meeting-halls used for government and law. Here, democracy was born. It was a very limited democracy (indeed, the Roman system made for greater equality) since the right to vote, to be elected to the assembly and to hold public office were denied to women, to slaves, on whom the Athenian economy depended, and to foreigners, irrespective of how long they had lived or worked in Athens. But here was established the principle of

Acropolis, view of the agora and Mount Lycabettos

representative democracy and with it free speech, a principle which was to affect education and the advance of thought in the West. Here Pericles made his famous oration. Here, under the colonnades of the *stoas*, (sheltered promenades lined with shops and offices which became the characteristic feature of the agora) loitered the philosophers and their disciples—Socrates, Plato, Aristotle—who were to lay down the foundation of philosophical enquiry for the Western world.

The *stoa* was a simple but enormously influential invention of the Greeks, which took the principle of the column and lintel, but linked them together to form a long colonnade which had many uses. It was a method of grouping together a lot of shops and workshops, which would otherwise have looked like a random collection of sheds and huts, and of giving them a dignified unity. It provided a space for people to sit in or walk under in the shade, where they could talk and barter their goods. And if it had an upper storey it could provide offices and other rooms. It was the major unifying feature of the agora. The two-storeyed Stoa of Attalus, under the Acropolis, was built in about 150 BC. It has been restored by American archaeologists as a museum and gives a very accurate impression of how a stoa must have looked. Other stoas were scattered around irregularly to north and south of the Athenian agora; in later Hellenic-planned towns both agora and stoa are geometrically defined and orderly in layout.

Other important buildings were the assembly hall, the town hall, the gymnasium, the stadium and the theatre, which played a significant part in the life of the Greeks. In Athens a theatre, dating from the early sixth century BC, lies to the south of the Acropolis on the site of successive wooden theatres. Primitive banks of seats, taking advantage of the lower contours of the rock, were not replaced by stone seating until after the earth and timber seats collapsed in 499 BC. While temples were not required to cater for public worship, theatres were. They were associated with the frenzied rituals in honour of Dionysus and had to be large enough to include a circular or semicircular stage, or *orchestra*, for the chorus and the dancing involved in the rituals, an altar for the libations with which performances commenced and space for a vast seated audience. It was here that Aeschylus, Sophocles, Euripides and Aristophanes presented their plays, laying down the

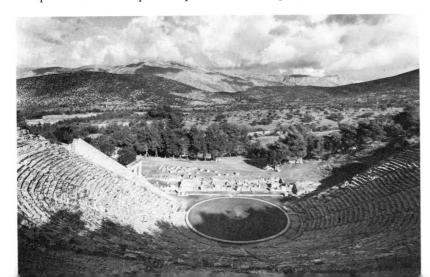

Theatre at Epidauros

pattern for Western drama and theatre.

In the Hellenic-planned towns, the theatre tended to be outside the town proper. The bowl-shape which had been found to be acoustically effective did not fit into the grid plan; and it was moreover the Greek habit to hunt out a site where the natural contours of the ground could be readily converted into an amphitheatre. And they had to be very big. The theatre at Epidauros, built by the architect Polykleitos in about 330 BC, could hold 13,000 people and the acoustics are so perfect that any whisper from the circular orchestra can be heard in any of the seats; an effect partly due to intensifying the bowl shape by making the rake on the upper set of seats steeper than on the lower, partly to the ingenious use of resonators in the form of large pottery urns beneath the stone rows of seats. I have been to a performance of Oedipus the King at Epidauros and it was one of the most unforgettable experiences I have ever had.

The other major building type was the stadium for games. Stadia, which had to be at least a *stade* long (200 yards) for the races, were also placed outside the town walls. The Athenian stadium of 331 BC could accommodate 60,000 spectators. The embankment of earth around the narrow stadium at Olympia, the little town in the Peloponnese, which established, from the eighth century BC onwards, the competitive games every fourth year, provided standing room for 40,000 people. In addition to the stadium, all Greek cities had gymnasia where the local young men trained as an essential part of their education—a principle which we see firmly entrenched in the English educational system. Salamis in Cyprus has good examples of both theatre and gymnasium, the latter remodelled by the Romans.

All these types of building were represented and grouped into a synthesis in the new planned cities of the Hellenistic period. Some were rebuilds on higher ground of cities which the Ionian Greeks had originally sited on estuaries of rivers which had since silted up; others, in Asia Minor, were founded after Alexander's conquests. The common pattern, attributed to Hippodamus of Miletus (fifth century BC), was for the city to be laid out on a grid plan below an acropolis, with a central agora, thoroughfares crossing the town, and separate zones scheduled for commercial, religious and political life. Hippodamus himself laid out Piraeus, the port of Athens, which is five miles from the Acropolis and connected to the city by a walled road known as the 'long walls'. Miletus was similarly planned in 466 BC after the Persian Wars. Priene and Pergamum are examples in Asia Minor. Gracious living made its appearance in these cities; streets were wide and paved, temples large, theatres, gymnasia and council chamber spacious enough to accomodate all adult males with the right to vote; sanitation was improved and some private houses became more imposing.

The Greek genius for bringing man, nature and the gods together in an awe-inspiring unity is to be found at its most dramatic at Delphi. Delphi was the most sacred of the sacred sites of ancient Greece. For it was the sanctuary of Apollo and the place of the oracle. Like many a successful sacred site, it was a magnet for pilgrims; and as in many

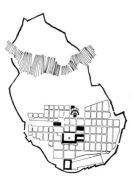

Priene, Asia Minor

Theatre and Temple of Apollo at Delphi

others the behaviour of the locals in making as much money from the faithful as possible was often disgraceful. But as a total experience of landscape and buildings cunningly, never obviously, sited (for as we have seen in Athens, the Greeks never produced elementary axial symmetry in their landscapes, whatever they did in the buildings within them), Delphi is a masterpiece of imaginative layout, every turn and corner of the route carefully considered as to its emotional impact on the pilgrim.

The first building that a traveller would see after climbing the ragged hills from Athens was the Tholos, a circular temple whose architectural purpose was to turn the attention towards the slopes of Parnassus, where the shrine of Apollo was constructed (mostly from the sixth century onwards). The Sacred Way leads upwards from the sanctuary, never in a straight line, but turning back upon itself past the Athenian Treasury (the first Doric building constructed entirely of marble), zigzagging, so as to give a succession of carefully contrived views, to the Temple of Apollo, which stands proudly in its Doric majesty upon a huge level plinth of cyclopean stones. Then, ever upwards, to the Theatre (early second century BC), which is acoustically superb, with a dramatic view across the fierce ravine below. Still further up and to one side is the Stadium. It is a magical place—as it was intended to be. And the magic is made by the unity and coherence of the buildings with the land.

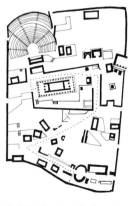

Delphi, showing the Sacred Way

*View of the Old Forum from
the Campidoglio, Rome*

Hadrian's Villa, Tivoli

8

The Authority of Competence

Under the Roman Empire, architecture, buoyed along by new techniques, achieved a prowess that, in some areas, European architecture was not again to reach until the seventeenth, eighteenth or even nineteenth century. But this is not apparent at first sight, particularly if we have just been looking at Greek architecture and our eye is attuned to Greek proportions and orders, because, content to leave matters of art to the Greeks, the Romans borrowed many of the external trappings of that older civilization's very external architecture. So, viewing the Old Forum of Rome from the West, we might at first see this as a straight translation of an agora.

It is only when we come to examine some of the buildings in detail that we realize how superficial are the similarities between the two peoples. Where the Greeks sought for man's harmony with the universe, communed with the abstract, and expressed their cosmic consciousness in art as fine as man's purest ideals, the Romans had no time for such idealism. They were a robust practical people with sharp logical minds, who excelled in the making of laws, in engineering feats and in administering territories. The harmonies they sought were not of the spirit nor among the celestial spheres, but in their immediate home circle and in the territories they had conquered. Their religion revolved around the family, with lamps burning before household gods, the *penates*, in the *atrium*, or hall, of their villas; the virtues that they extolled the most (along with physical courage) were *pietas* (loyalty to parents and ancestors) and *gravitas* (responsibility). They considered the Greeks effete. They were convinced that the Roman way of life alone was right, as we see from the following quotation from Vitruvius, a military engineer in the service of Julius Caesar in the first century BC, who wrote the only extant treatise on architecture before the fifteenth century.

> But although southern nations have the keenest wit, and are infinitely clever in forming schemes, yet the moment it comes to displaying valour they succumb because all manliness of soul is sucked out of them by the sun. On the other hand, men born in cold countries are indeed readier to meet the shock of arms with great courage and without timidity, but their wits are so slow that they will rush to the charge inconsiderately and inexpertly, thus defeating their own devices. Such being nature's arrangement of the universe, and all these nations being allotted temperaments which are lacking in due moderation, the truly perfect territory, situated under the middle of heaven, and having on each side the entire extent of the world and its countries, is that which is occupied by the Roman people. *Ten Books on Architecture*, Book VI.

The legendary origins of this conceited race are strangely romantic, involving the illustrious but illicit union of Mars, god of war, with a vestal virgin, and the subsequent rescue of their abandoned twin sons by a she-wolf, whose bronze statue stands today on the Capitoline Hill in Rome, the spot where one of the twins, Romulus, founded the city. That was, reputedly, in 753 BC, the year from which the Romans counted their dates (*ab urbe condita*); but in fact neither bronze nor city is likely to have existed prior to 600 BC. Indeed, by that time, when elsewhere in the world great things were afoot—Buddha teaching in India, Confucius in China, Jimmu, the first emperor of Japan, ascending his throne, Judah undergoing the Babylonian captivity, and the Persians sweeping all before them and yet to encounter the Greeks—Rome was little more than one among many village-states in mid-Italy. Then in 510 BC she took her first step towards greatness by expelling the tyrannical Etruscan kings and declaring herself a republic. The national temperament now began to show itself in systematic conquest, first of her neighbours so that by the third century BC she dominated Italy, then a land of city-states; in the third and second century BC, the three Punic Wars secured North Africa and Spain; by the first century BC, Rome possessed the entire Hellenic world, and when Augustus established the empire, all the known world was theirs, and the Mediterranean truly was the sea at the centre of the world.

Victory achieved, the vanquished were not forced to bury their national identity and customs; these could be retained with Roman citizenship, provided they were prepared to accept Roman law, taxes, military service and an undemanding religion. In race and religion toleration was probably greater than under the vaunted democracy of the Greeks. Even in regard to class: although aristocratic patricians dominated the Senate, plebeians had an established right to constitutional office; and although the slave-labour force—swelled each time that territories were conquered—had no political voice, there was a kind of apprenticeship system towards citizenship.

'The Roman Empire', says A.N. Whitehead (in *The Aims of Education*, chapter V), 'existed by virtue of the grandest application of technology that the world had hitherto seen: its roads, its bridges, its aqueducts, its tunnels, its sewers, its vast buildings, its organized

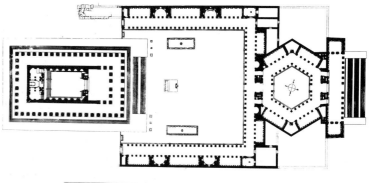

Temple complex at Baalbeck

merchant navies, its military science, its metallurgy, and its agriculture.' It meant the dissolution of political and commercial frontiers, and a supply of commodities from abroad. It meant running water in homes, public lavatories, sometimes arranged in groups, where everybody sat on marble seats between sculpted dolphins, reading and chatting for all the world like gentlemen of leisure at their clubs; it meant hot and cold public baths to relax in, fora for law and politics, circuses for chariot races and gladiatorial fights or for watching Christians being eaten by lions; and theatres for drama, of which the most popular were not intense tragedies like those of classical Greece, but slapstick like Plautus' works.

It is therefore not surprising that the architecture built by such a people was directed to immediate practical purposes rather than to aesthetic satisfaction. The Romans were ready to leave matters of art to the Greeks, and leaned heavily on Greek forms and tastes when buildings of serenity, dignity and power, suitable to a great empire, were called for. These qualities are apparent in the series of new fora built by successive emperors to accommodate increasingly complex social, legal and commercial needs. Augustus initiated the first by building a new forum in contrast to the accumulation of buildings that had grown piecemeal round the old one: he set a colonnaded stoa along both sides of a great rectangular space, closing the vista at the end with a Temple to Mars. Although the original inspiration was Hellenistic, the Roman imprint quickly appears. Buildings are not sited in response to the natural environment, in mystical communion with the contours of the place; instead, there emerges a new concept: planned space enclosed by architecture. The new fora are less concerned with individual temples than they are with the total design, conceived as awe-inspiring set-pieces that demonstrate imperial power. A series of geometric shapes unfold as one walks through the forum at Baalbek, Lebanon; and in Augustus' forum at Rome, contrived views and vistas are enclosed by a temple façade.

In the Flavian amphitheatre known as the Colosseum, the architecture was distinctively Roman. While the Greeks used their theatres exclusively for drama, the Romans required amphitheatres to stage, in addition to drama, fights between men and animals, and hairpin-shaped arenas where they could race their chariots. Many are still standing. The one at Orange, in the south of France, of awesome proportions, is particularly well preserved, although the wooden awning that sheltered the stage, supported at the front by two great chains fastened to high masts rising from corbelled piers at the back, no longer exists; those at Arles and Nîmes in Provence, are still used for bull-fights. But the Orange amphitheatre is unusual for, like the Greek theatres, it is at least partially hollowed out of the hill. And here we have the basic difference between Greek and Roman forms. The Greek concentration on the exterior is, in the theatre, turned inside out: the theatre has no outside, being sited in a natural hollow below a hill, usually outside the main city. Its sloping seats were built into the hillside, and nature provided her own backdrop of hills or sea for the players on the stage.

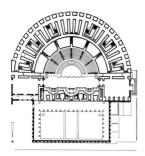

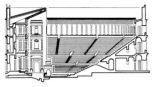

*Plan and section of theatre
at Sabratha*

In contrast, the Colosseum, built by the Emperors Vespasian and
Domitian between AD 70 and 82, stands in the city centre, elliptical in
shape, on level ground. For amphitheatres such as this both an inside
and an outside architecture were required, and for drama even the
backdrop must be man-made, like the *scaena*, now reconstructed
behind the stage in the Roman theatre at Sabratha in North Africa of
about AD 200. Once inside the Colosseum, whose enormous auditorium could seat 82,000 spectators, and which continued to be used for
animal games until the sixth century AD, we can gaze upwards at the
remains of four tiers of seats, and downwards, through where the
floor of the arena once stretched, to a web of circulation passageways;
and we are left in no doubt that this is internal architecture of the
most complex design. Vaulted passages between the wedges of seats

Theatre at Orange

*Interior of the Colosseum,
Rome*

Colosseum, Rome

Temple of Bacchus, Baalbek

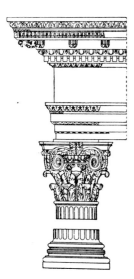

Composite order

(all worked out mathematically) at each level gave speedy access to seating and, moreover, speedy exit, so that the auditorium could be cleared quickly in case of fire. Below stage, cages and detainment areas for beasts and criminals were provided by passageways closed by portcullis gates, and mechanical lifts and ramps were used to bring performers up to the arena floor.

It was, clearly, a much more sophisticated and intricate construction than a rectangular temple dependent on columns holding up lintels. What gave us the idea that the Roman amphitheatre was a straight translation of the Greek? If we return again to the outside, we immediately see what it was that deceived us: the four floors of the Colosseum present a copy-book façade of the Greek orders: Doric on the ground floor, Ionic on the second, Corinthian on the third, and pilasters running along the top storey. But what we now realize is that the orders play no part in the structure: the supporting members are built into the bodywork of the building, and the columns are simply a decorative device applied to the front.

The Romans made much use of the orders, their favourite being the Corinthian with its florid, luxuriant possibilities. Whether there is truth in the story that its designer was inspired at a banquet by the sight of a goblet wound round with acanthus leaves, there is a certain feeling of Bacchanalian revelry about this order, which is taller than either Doric or Ionic and seems in accord with the enormous size of some of the temples, such as those (now ruins) at Baalbek, Lebanon. Here the smaller of the two is bigger than the Parthenon. The Romans adopted two more orders into their repertoire—the *Composite*, a combination of Ionic and Corinthian, and the Etruscan, or Tuscan, a stumpier version of Doric. But characteristic of Roman architecture is the use of non-structural columns, frequently wholly or partially embedded in the walls—a device known as *engaged* or *semi-engaged* columns; sometimes the columns are flattened and squared off and are then called pilasters.

The device is clearly exhibited in another Roman architectural type: the triumphal arch. Often sited at an entrance to a forum, they were

Triumphal Arch of Septimius Severus

*El-Deir (Monastery)
Temple, Petra*

erected to commemorate victories. They had to be wide and grand
enough to allow a victorious army to march through in procession
between cheering crowds, driving before them carts laden with booty
and prisoners in chains. The lettering on the arches, detailing the
victories of Titus, Constantine or Severus and the gratitude of the
Senate and the people of Rome to the mighty ruler, is so clear and
impressive that it forms the basis of the typefaces of the Renaissance
and our own times. Whether the form has one arch, as in the Arch of
Titus on the edge of the Forum, or is designed in triple motif (small,
tall, small), as in the Arch of Septimius Severus, the massive architrave
on which the dedication is carved is carried like a banner, as unflinch-
ing as if held aloft by a legionary marching into battle.

Because the orders and classical motifs were no longer required
structurally, the way was opened to playing with the forms decora-
tively. Interior decoration in Pompeii foreshadowed Baroque caprices
in mock marbling and painted architectural vistas. One of the most
attractive of these architectural whimsies, thought to date from the
second century AD, is the miniature round temple set between the
sides of a broken pediment on the upper floor façade of the rock-cut

El-Deir (Monastery) Temple, in Petra, one-time caravan trading city, cut into the rose-red rocks of the Arabian desert.

The Romans did not have to rely on the post and lintel structure of the Greeks because they had developed a much more effective method of support in the true arch. They did not invent it: the true arch may go back as far as 2500 BC in Egypt, and we have an extant example in the tomb of Rameses II at Thebes of about 1200 BC. The Romans were not a particularly inventive people—probably less so than the Greeks. But perhaps the superior comments of Vitruvius have some justification: the Greeks had ideas, but often failed to carry them into practice, as if they did not choose to soil their hands with the practical. The Romans' command of abstract geometry and theoretical science might have lagged behind that of the Greeks, but they had no inhibitions about putting others' knowledge to practical ends. And so, while the Greek mechanics and hydraulics remained on paper as ingenious toys—steam-operated doors to temples or oracles, or penny-in-the-slot holy water dispensers—the Romans set their knowledge to improving everyday life.

The same with structures. They speedily perfected the timber tied-truss roof construction, which the third-century Greeks had done no more than toy with. Their attention then turned to the true arch which, unlike the corbelled arch, where stones jutting from either side meet in the middle, is held together by pressure on the wedge-shaped stones, called *voussoirs*, radiating around the arc. During building the arch was supported by a temporary scaffolding called *centering*— usually a wooden structure or a mound of earth. A series of arches with padding in between to form a tunnel produced a barrel vault, and where two barrel vaults met at right angles they formed a *groin vault*.

The exploitation of this structure went hand in hand with the development of concrete. The properties of volcanic soil mixed with lime to make a waterproof concrete were early recognized on the volcanic island of Thera (rechristened Santorini during the fourth Crusade), but the best substance for concrete-making was *pozzolana*, a red volcanic soil from Puteoli (today Pozzuoli), a port near Naples. The Romans used several kinds of concrete aggregate, collectively called *caementum*, which varied from a random collection of stone and brick rubble and even potsherds to carefully organized layers of brick and pumice such as tufa, particularly suitable for the dome or the upper part of a structure where lightness of weight was called for. As a rule they poured concrete into a permanent framework or casing, preferring this to removable shuttering, which leaves an exposed concrete face, and is unfortunately often used today. The framework might be in traditional squared blocks of stone (*opus quadratum*) or a rough stone frame (*opus incertum*); if the framework was of brick, the bricks were either laid diagonally to form teeth for the concrete to cling to (*opus reticulatum*) or were triangular in shape, laid point inwards (*opus testaceum*).

The combined arch/concrete structure, by rendering pillars unnecessary, opened up a new world of spatial design. The imagination flowered in structures which were not to be emulated until the architects of the Renaissance read the manuals of Vitruvius or used classical models. For instance, the dome of the Pantheon, the temple of the gods built by the Emperor Hadrian between AD 120 and 124, with a diameter of 143 feet, remained the widest dome until the nineteenth century. It is built in concrete between permanent frame walls, 23 feet thick, that are brick on the outside and marble facing on the inside. Here was a temple, in direct contrast to the Greek temples, designed to be looked at from the inside as well as the outside. An even, diffused light penetrates everywhere, and it is a moment before one realizes that, since there are no windows (from the outside the whole building appears solid), the light must be flooding in from the unglazed hole, the *oculus*, or eye, in the centre of the dome. The dimensions are exactly planned; the dome is a perfect circle, its radius is equal to its height, and it starts its ascent at a height equal to the radius of the drum which forms the body of the temple. The upper parts of the dome are made from volcanic tufa, for lightness, and are cut away in panelled coffering, itself cut back in frame after frame, a device which is both decorative and structural. The oculus cleverly dispenses with weight at the top of the dome. But there is another clever way in

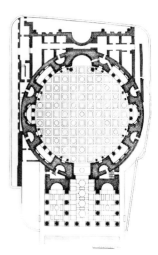

Pantheon

which the dome is supported. If we look at the building from the inside, we see that the dome springs from the second storey, but if we look from the outside, we see that there are three floors indicated on the outer wall: the dome is, in fact, set inside the drum, which forms the main body of the temple, and one storey of drum rises up around it on the outside, forming a buttress. The Romans made much use of buttresses, and every type of buttressing occurs in the Pantheon. The entrance portico, screened from the interior by Corinthian columns, was reconstructed from the remains of a little temple, built by Agrippa, Augustus' son-in-law, in 25 BC.

The power of arch and concrete to act on the environment spread to all areas of everyday life—roads, bridges, aqueducts, harbours, theatres, housing, water-supply and drainage. Water was usually piped underground, but where pipes had to emerge to cross a valley, aqueducts carried it along arched bridges, which, like those that carried roads, are among the most beautiful functional pieces of architecture in existence. Augustus' aqueduct at Segovia, Spain, has 128 arches of white granite 90 feet high. The water supply to Nîmes, France, which was twenty-five miles long, includes the famous Pont du Gard, AD 14, with its dry-stone masonry, still standing as an eloquent tribute to Roman engineering.

Civilizations before the Romans had, of course, known of sanitation. Terracotta pipes led water into terracotta baths, and running water passed below lavatories in the Palace of Knossos in 2000 BC; Sargon I of Assyria (721–705 BC) had jugs of water by his lavatories; Sennacherib (704–681 BC) and Polycrates of Pergamum both constructed aqueducts. The Romans, however, planned drainage for whole cities. The main drain into the Tiber, the Cloaca Maxima, built by the Etruscans before 510 BC, was the only major sewer in Europe until the seventeenth century.

Inside the houses of the affluent (*domus*), water ran from taps, bath-water was led along pipes from boilers on the top of furnaces

Pont du Gard, near Nîmes

and there were individual lavatories. Heating was largely by braziers of coal carried from room to room; but in cold areas like Britain and Gaul, and for country villas and public baths, the *hypocaust* was used, that is, the floor was raised up on brick pillars, and heat and smoke from slow furnaces beneath rose into the rooms through patterned slits.

Life was less luxurious for the working people who inhabited the 46,602 *insulae*, or high tenement blocks, listed in the census of AD 300. They were lucky if there was a common lavatory on the ground floor, and they had to collect water from a tap in the street. The lot, however, of men, in particular, was much ameliorated by the high standard of the public services. Public baths were either free or cost very little, and were often in sumptuous buildings. The public baths of the Emperor Caracalla in Rome, today used as an opera house, were surrounded by gardens and gymnasia, and boasted a round room with a dome which was divided into a hot room (*calidarium*), a medium-hot room (*tepidarium*), vaulted and lit from the clerestory, and an open-air swimming-pool (*frigidarium*).

Insulae were often three or four storeys high and may even have reached five or six at one stage. Those at Rome's port, Ostia Antica, although now in ruins, show the common arrangement of arcaded shops on the ground floor. The pattern was taken up during the Renaissance by designers of palaces for merchant princes, and it is still being followed today. As in tenements today, inhabitants of insulae were prey to exploitation, and Juvenal, writing at the end of the first century AD, talks of how landlords arrested the collapse of their property by shoring it up with 'gimcrack stays and props' and 'papering over great cracks in the ramshackle fabric'. They were also

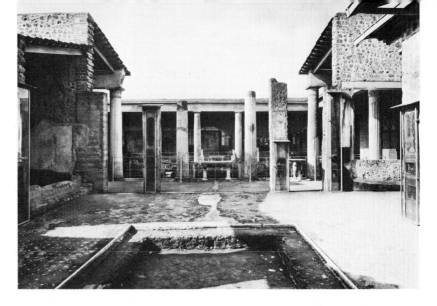

House of the Vetii, Pompeii

easy prey to fire, so that, says Juvenal, 'By the time the smoke's got to your third-floor apartment (and you still asleep), your heroic downstairs neighbour is roaring for water and shifting his bits and pieces to safety. If the alarm goes at ground level, the last to fry will be the attic tenant.' According to Tacitus, after the fire of AD 64 the height of the insulae was limited to 70 feet and party walls were forbidden; instead of timber, the use of fire-resistant stone from the Alban Hills was recommended, and flat roofs on the porticoes to give fire-fighters access became obligatory. When the burnt-out city was rebuilt, arterial roads like the present Via del Corso were cut through previous built-up sites to act as firebreaks in future emergencies. A fire corps, whose officers held army status, had already been created by Augustus when a fire in AD 6 had destroyed a quarter of the city.

The standard of living of the rich far exceeded the bare physical needs and safety precautions of the poor. The eruption of Vesuvius in AD 79 set a death-mask of molten lava over the commercial city of Pompeii and its seaside companion, Herculaneum. All was transfixed—paved streets, fountains on mosaic walls, where water once spouted from lions' heads, shops and taverns, graceful houses with mural paintings, delicate mosaic floors, fan-lights, architraves over doors and colonnaded peristyles.

The rich used their country villas as refuge from noisy Rome. Set in small self-supporting estates, they were usually run, in the master's absence, by a bailiff and a staff of freedmen and slaves, and included arable land, olive groves, vineyards, orchards, barns, granaries and workshops. Entered into inconspicuously from the road, Roman villas (like Chinese dwellings) looked inwards to the atrium, a mosaic-paved courtyard with a central pool, a pluvium, used for bathing or simply to hold goldfish. The pluvium also served to collect rainwater from the pitched red-tiled roofs which surrounded the atrium and jutted forward a little for shade. From the atrium opened the dining-room with three long couches placed along three sides of a table (for the Romans ate in the reclining position), the study, the library, the guest and owner's bedrooms, and the lavatories. Sometimes the formal rooms were grouped around the atrium, and the family lived in two-

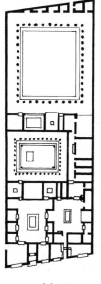

House of the Vetii

storey quarters to one side. Larger houses extended around an open courtyard with a Greek peristyle, and this, like the formal garden which most villas possessed, was laid out with grass, fountains and statues, bay hedges, rose and vine trellis-walks and perhaps, even a dovecot. Just how much thought and pride were put into the design of these country retreats can be gleaned from a letter from Pliny the Younger to a friend whom he is trying to entice to his villa at Laurentum, not far from Rome. Among its attractions are a D-shaped courtyard enclosed by colonnades, a dining-room with folding doors, windows all round, and a view of the sea from three sides, a library with bookshelves, a winter bedroom with underfloor heating, a sun-parlour, rosemary and box hedges along the drive, a garden where mulberries and figs grow and a terrace filled with the scent of violets.

As for the palaces, inhabited by god-like emperors, it is scarcely surprising that their opulent apartments and grounds should put us in mind of Imperial China. At Spalato (Split, Jugoslavia), Diocletian built a palace to retire to in AD 300. Modelled on a legionary fortress, it is almost a city in itself, entered into from a street on one side, its grounds extending to an arcaded frontage and wharfs on the Adriatic. Hadrian's Villa at Tivoli was virtually a little kingdom. What remains of its seven miles of gardens, pavilions, palaces, baths, theatres and temples may still be seen.

In the public sector, a new type of lofty hall, the *basilica*, first appeared in the city in the Basilica Porcia of 184 BC and grew popular under the Empire and was used to house the increasingly sophisticated legal and commercial activities. Made sometimes from stone, sometimes in brick and concrete, which allowed large spaces uncluttered by columns, a plan evolved for big assemblies. The pattern was taken up by the Christian church and established as the norm in the early Christian and Byzantine era. Usually rectangular, the length twice the width, the basilica divides into a main hall (the nave) and single or double side-aisles screened with columns. The roof was normally timber, and, since the main nave rose above the side aisles, light entered through a row of clerestory windows on both sides of the upper walls of the nave. A semi-circular apse at one end held the tribunal, sometimes raised, for the seat of the presiding magistrate. In what is left of the Basilica of the Emperor Maxentius, completed by his successor Constantine (AD 310–313), we can appreciate how impressive the simplicity and grandeur of the barnlike confines of the basilica form must have been to the Romans. There were two apses in this basilica, the second added by Constantine, and the roof was deeply vaulted in concrete hexagonal coffering between brickwork ribs.

The basilica carries us architecturally across the divide between the Western Roman empire and the Eastern empire of Byzantium with its new religion, Christianity, which was to become the chief architectural inspiration for the next ten centuries. Constantine and his basilica provide the bridge, for, before his death in AD 337, he had started to build a church to St Peter, in Rome, and had transferred the imperial capital to Constantinople.

Palace of Diocletian, Spalato (Split)

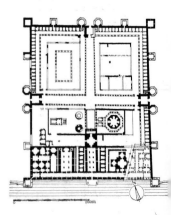

Interior of 4th-century catacombs, off Via Latina, Rome

Basilica of Constantine, Rome

9

The Worshipping Community

Early Christian architecture picks up from where the Romans left off, with the basilica. It was to become the stock Western church type for the next 900 years and led directly to the subsequent architectural phase, the Romanesque. But, as we have seen, it started as a secular hall of justice, and not as a religious building at all. In fact, during the first centuries, the Christians built no churches. Poverty and the need to hide from persecution were not the only reasons for this. The whole ethos of Christianity at this stage was in direct opposition to the combined trappings of state and religion to be found in the pagan temples, where gods and emperors were worshipped side by side. A bricks and mortar establishment held little interest for the early believers; their concern was with the promised second coming of Christ, and they lived in daily expectation of meeting him in the street or market-place.

The Acts of the Apostles give us some idea of how they shared this period of waiting, wherever possible living together in a community. Since most of them were ordinary working people, their cells were likely to be over a workshop belonging to one of their number or in an average vernacular house—a succession of rooms opening off a courtyard. A similar attitude towards the community led to the development of the catacombs. Christians, believing in the resurrection of the body, did not adopt the Roman custom of cremation; they liked to be buried beside their brethren, if possible near the grave of an apostle, often under tombs simply made from slates stuck into the ground. As the graveyards filled up, they hollowed out the earth to create catacombs in which passages were lined with tiers of alcoves for the bodies.

But Christian remains are not the only ones that were scarce at this period; we have very few secular post-Roman remains at all. As the Empire went into a long drawn-out decline, masonry structures of all sorts—temples, roads, bridges—became neglected, fell into disrepair and were eventually used for quarries. It was the period facilely called the Dark Ages, the period of the crumbling of the ancient Roman Empire, when Europe was subjected to incursions of Germanic tribes collectively called barbarians, a name long before coined by the Greeks for all foreigners whose uncouth speech sounded to them like 'Ba-ba-ba'. Angles, Saxons, Jutes, Franks, Huns, Goths and Vandals infiltrated the Roman provinces, bringing about a racial and cultural restructuring of the civilized world other than the Far East.

As with any large institution, erosion came from both outside and within. In the third century, Diocletian abandoned Rome as the capital and moved to Nicodemia, about fifty miles from Byzantium; later emperors were to establish capitals at Trier in Germany and at Milan.

Byzantine capital from Ravenna

In 402, harried by Goths and by malaria from the surrounding marshes, Honorius moved the Western capital from Rome to Ravenna, a move of architectural consequence. Eight years later, Alaric the Goth did indeed sack Rome, but it was at Toulouse that the Goths preferred eventually to set up their capital. By 475 Rome was finally occupied—and the Western Roman Empire crumbled.

In 285 Diocletian appointed a co-emperor for the East, and although Constantine briefly reunited the empire in the fourth century (as Justinian was to do again in the sixth), the division was finalized when, on Theodosius' death in 395, the imperial possessions were shared between his two sons—Honorius, who would rule the West from Rome, and Arcadius, who would rule from Constantinople, Constantine's city on the Bosphorus. In 476 the last Emperor of the West, Romulus Augustus, abdicated, so Western Rome went as it had come—with a Romulus.

The Christians, heroically defending their new faith, might be seen as an internal cancer, eating away at the Empire. But in some ways the new church and the old empire appear to have nursed each other through the centuries of barbarian invasion. Once the Christians had grasped that Christ's message was not only for the Jews, but was for the whole world, they found a ready-made international vehicle in the Empire. And after Constantine declared Christianity the official imperial religion in AD 313, Rome found in the Church a refuge and sanctuary for her classical traditions. Not surprisingly with Europe in the melting pot, there was a long period of ambivalence between the old and the new religions, and exclusively Christian forms took some time to appear. A baptismal font in Tuscany shows pre-Christian gargoyles and Celtic interlaced ornament as late as the eighth century. Constantine, who thought of himself as the thirteenth apostle and dedicated his new city of Constantinople to the Virgin Mary, nevertheless set up a statue of Delphic Apollo in the Hippodrome, and a temple to Rhea, mother of the gods, in his new market-place.

Interior of Santa Sabina, Rome

Interior of S. Maria delle Grazie, Grado

To compound the confusion, after Theodosius in 380 had declared all religions other than Christianity heretical, temples were taken over lock, stock and barrel as Christian churches, or looted to build new churches. The Corinthian columns of the nave of the basilica of Santa Sabina in Rome (422–432) for instance are antique.

Basilicas became increasingly used to house the choirs and big assemblies that were part of the religion that was now official. But at first the simple Christians persisted in using the basilicas for communal living as if they were rooms in their house-churches. They would curtain off the side-aisles and use them for discussion and the instruction of catechumens who, until they had received baptism, were denied participation in the eucharistic rite. Since the eucharist was originally part of a communal meal, the altar-table was placed anywhere in the basilica—in front of the apse, where the Romans had placed their pagan altar for the sacrifice which initiated the conduct of business, or even in the centre of the nave, but not in the apse itself. The apse from where the tribune, assessors and praetor had once presided, later came to have stone seats built around it for the clergy, with, in the case of cathedrals, a central throne for the bishop.

Interior of S. Maria Maggiore, Rome, by Pope Sixtus III

In the East, less harried by barbarian invasion, there was more time and leisure for theological controversy and liturgical changes, and the clergy more and more took over the nave. Sometimes, particularly in Syria, the nave had a raised semicircular chancel, called a *bema*, with railings around it, for the clergy to sit on during the early part of the Mass. The congregation was pushed out into the aisles, which became increasingly wider to accommodate it, a tendency which eventually resulted in the cruciform church characteristic of the East, and into galleries built over the side aisles. In the West, the plan and shape of the older basilican hall was retained as the liturgy became formalized. The chief variation at this stage lay in whether the nave arcading adopted the classical trabeate style, where a series of lintels rest on the pillars, as in S. Maria Maggiore, Rome, which dates from the classical revival of Sixtus III (432–40), or was formed by arches resting on the pillars, as in Santa Sabina on the Aventine Hill in Rome, allowing nave and aisles to interpenetrate in greater light and freedom. This second type became characteristic of the churches of Ravenna in its period as capital during the fifth and sixth centuries, and remained popular in Italy beyond the twelfth century.

The first surge of building for the new creed came after 330 when Constantine, the first Christian emperor, transferred his capital to Byzantium, an old Greek trading colony on the Bosphorus, and laid out a whole new city with roads, civic spaces and a blaze of churches. One of his first acts as Emperor was to hand over the Imperial Palace of the Lateran in Rome to the Bishop of Rome, and to build alongside the church of St John Lateran, a basilican church modelled on the basilican audience chamber he had built at Trier, Germany, when he was Western Co-Emperor there. In the Holy Land, he built the Church of the Nativity in Bethlehem over the reputed site of the cave in which Christ was born. Its atrium, or front courtyard, is now part of Manger Square, where today buses park. He replaced the customary apse at the end by an octagonal chapel, and pilgrims could peer down through an *oculus*, or eye let into the floor, into the sacred cave below. This octagon was replaced in the sixth century by a sanctuary with a trefoil apse off it. Today, entering the church by the low door, placed either

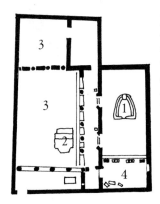

Church of Qirbizé, North Syria: 1 Bema, 2 Cistern, 3 Courtyards, 4 Iconostasis

for defensive purposes or to prevent animals straying in, it is easy to be swept by, without being aware of it, through the dark cavernous stretches of Constantine's church with its dull-red Corinthian pillars on the way to the birth-cave with the star let into the floor.

In Rome, the first church of St Peter, built in about AD 330 over a graveyard on the site of the Circus of Nero, had an impressive nave 400 feet long and five double aisles, all ending in arches which led onto the first recorded transept or cross-aisle, placed across the head with one central apse off it. The transept was designed so that pilgrims could revere the tomb of the apostle—a typical *aedicula* of the period, composed of a slab on two small pillars before a wall niche. This plan was to live on, notably in Carolingian and Frankish architecture in Tours (995) and in the church of St Rémi, Rheims (1000), but it is that first transept which is particularly important.

There are two distinctive features about these early basilican churches. First, they eschewed the complicated technology of vaults evolved by the Romans for their baths; possibly for the sake of cheapness, they reverted to the simple construction of slim walls—brick-faced concrete in Rome, stone or brick elsewhere—and columns holding up wooden roofs. Second, they were normally placed on the outskirts of the town, except in Constantinople where Constantine was building an entirely new city, either because the poor Christian community could not afford highly priced sites in the built-up areas or because of their desire to build over the burial place of a saint, and the graveyards were outside the boundary walls. We find churches like Sant' Agnese fuori le Mura, Rome, built in 630 to replace Constantine's basilica of 324, and St Paul's Without the Walls, one of the best early examples remaining, more ornate than Santa Sabina, with a plan like old St Peter's, which was burnt down but rebuilt in replica

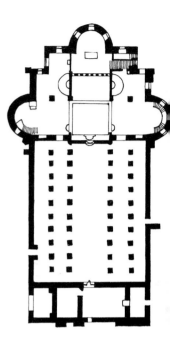

Church of the Nativity, Bethlehem

Interior of Mausoleum of Galla Placidia, Ravenna

in 1823. Twin towers on the façade, which we tend to associate with Romanesque churches, appeared amazingly early. A carved ivory casket of about AD 400 symbolizing Jerusalem, the holy city, shows twin round towers, and they were quite common in Syria from the fifth century onwards. The bell-tower, or *campanile*, which features on the sixth-century churches of Ravenna, was also developed early. That of S. Apollinare in Classe, erected by Justinian on the site of a temple to Apollo, is one of the earliest examples of a round tower.

The exterior of the basilican church tended to be simple and austere, perhaps to prepare the humble penitent for the vision of heaven awaiting him inside. Here the muted colours of Roman-style pavings, built up through the marbles of the pillars, gave way to a burst of mosaic covering the walls. In Ravenna the mosaics were at their most fabulous during the extensive building programme of Justinian's reign. Galla Placidia's little Mausoleum (420), which houses her tomb, and where her husband and her brother the Emperor Honorius are also buried, has a deeply spiritual character that is created by the blue mosaics, whose patterns follow the lines of the structural arches, and by the golden glow from the alabaster windows.

The particular intensity of light and refraction in Byzantine mosaic comes from the fact that the cubes are of glass covered with a thin layer of gold leaf or with another colour, and finished off with a top film of glass. Commencing in the brick and plaster basilicas, where the design of the mosaics was necessarily repeatedly interrupted by the angularity of the structure, this wall-clothing was to become fully liberated in the Byzantine structure of arches and domes. At one with the structure, the patterns could now flow untrammelled from the floor up over the walls, swelling and ebbing over the arches, and

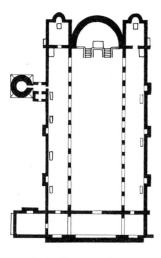

S. Apollinare in Classe, Ravenna

S. Fosca, Torcello, showing double squinches

gathering to a consummation in the central dome, usually in a great figure of Christ, pale-faced with sad and compelling eyes—a countenance of power, wordlessly teaching the lesson of Eastern mysticism: Be still and know that I am God.

Between the early Christian basilica and the domed church of the Byzantine period there was a third type of church linking the two forms—the centralized church. This type commenced as a mausoleum, or shrine. A rotunda was built over the shrine of the Holy Sepulchre, Jerusalem, by the end of the fourth century. St Peter's, built as a shrine and not a church, had originally no altar; its place was taken by the transept, which provided circulation space for pilgrims to the tomb. Inspired by Roman classical mausolea or polygonal audience halls like the so-called Temple of Minerva Medica in Rome or the rotunda incorporated into Diocletian's palace at Spalato, the suitability of the circular or octagonal form for assemblies around a sacred object began to be appreciated. In square or rectangular churches as well as in circular ones, this centralized plan was often indicated on the exterior by the fact that the roof was raised over the central space, either as a timber pyramid or as a dome. We see this in the mausoleum of Constantine's daughter, Constantia, in Rome (converted into a church, Santa Costanza, in 1256), which is a rotunda with an outer encircling aisle, while the roof of domed brick is held up over the central tomb-space by an inner girdle of pillars which, in effect, forms an inner dodecagon.

Constantine's Church of the Holy Apostles in Constantinople, which no longer exists, represented by all accounts the next phase in development: the amalgamation of the congregational basilica with the centralized shrine. As thirteenth apostle, his tomb was to stand in

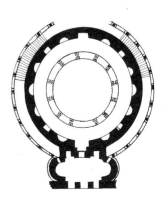

Santa Costanza, Rome

the central space, surrounded by twelve columns to symbolize the twelve apostles; and from this centre not one but four great naves were to project in the form of a cross. A similar plan was used at Qal'at Sim'an in north Syria, where an eight-arched octagon was built round the pillar-like hermit's cell, in which the eccentric Saint Simeon Stylites squatted for thirty years. Four churches, each with a nave and two aisles, radiated in cross-form from the octagon; and the whole sanctuary complex, complete with porticoed monastery, was pitched between the quarries that provided the stone and the ceremonial gateway from which a sacred way ran down to a pilgrimage town of hostelries and convents.

In the Eastern Empire (which, at this stage, included Greece and the Balkans, Anatolia, Syria and Egypt), the Greek-cross plan with four arms of equal length was to become standard. It was theologically acceptable, since the Eastern church laid great emphasis on the cross, just as it insisted on the observance of a hierarchy in its wall-paintings—the saints at the bottom, then the Virgin Mary, and the Trinity or Godhead at the top, in the dome. It was also liturgically suitable. There was no need for vast choir and congregational areas in the Eastern liturgy, which was largely carried out by the priest behind a screen, while the people worshipped individually, perhaps by candle-light before ikons, pinned onto iconostasis or ikon screens, in the dark, mysterious spaces of the church. The shrine-like plan, where the cross arms projected from the central space—square, circular or octagonal—was not however the only plan; frequently the entire cross was contained within a square or rectangular plan, or else the arms were quatrefoil apses contained in a square, circle or octagon. And this form of a cross within a square was structurally useful because of the support that the exedrae, or areas opening off the central space, gave to that space and the dome it was likely to support.

The revolutionary aspect of the Byzantine dome was that it was set on a building of square plan. Domes had been built before, on the Roman baths and on the massive circular walls of the Pantheon. There are even domes on square tombs of saints in Persia, but since these are tiny buildings with a small dome span it was possible to rest the dome on an octagon, simply made by throwing a stone bridge diagonally across each corner. Such a solution would not serve for a dome of heavy weight, so instead a pyramidal wooden roof was often used as, for example, on the Martyrion of St Byblas in Antioch Kaoussie. San Vitale in Ravenna side-stepped the problem with an unusual structure of light pots fitted together. Then some unknown genius in Sassanian Persia was inspired to replace the corner lintel with an arch, known as a *squinch*; the earliest known example is from the third-century palace at Firuzabad. The eleventh-century church of S. Fosca at Torcello used two squinches, one above the other, to bring the vertical walls upwards and inwards to carry the round drum supporting the dome.

Squinches did not, however, provide the answer, especially where, as in a cruciform church, the dome would rest not on four solid walls but on the four arches which gave entry to the arms of the cross. The weight of a large and heavy dome not only bears down with crushing weight on the supporting pillars, but it also tends to push those pillars outwards. The solution, called a *pendentive*, came by resorting to the elementary technique of building out brick courses to make a beehive dome. Each beehive shape would start at the corner junction of two supporting arches, but stop when level with the top of the arches, forming curving triangles (the pendentives) that met in a ring poised on top of a canopy formed by the pillars and the arches; on this ring the dome would rest, thrusting the weight back down onto the massive corner piers. The dome could now vary in size, sometimes, as in Hagia Sophia, pierced all around with windows.

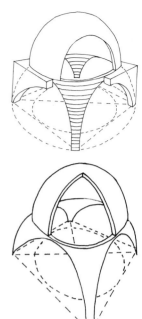

Setting out of dome with pendentives

It is difficult to exaggerate the effect of that invention. What the pendentive achieved can be appreciated if we compare the Pantheon, the Romans' greatest domed building, with the interior of Hagia Sophia, the Byzantine masterpiece, built by Justinian to replace Constantine's church, which had been destroyed by an earthquake in 532. The uniform suffusion of light in the Pantheon illuminates its containing, igloo-shaped walls, strong, smooth, clear-cut mouldings, exact triangular architraves over the niches—all calculated with the mathematical precision one would expect from an empire which had sorted out and organized the known world with admirable efficiency. Structurally it played safe by incorporating every form of buttressing known to Rome. In contrast, Hagia Sophia shows the ability to take a risk, essential to the pioneering of a new structure. The demand for our admiration is not dependent on a recitation of the statistics of this great building—that it has a square plan with a nave and galleried aisles; that it has a shallow central dome almost as big as the Pantheon's and only eight feet smaller than St Paul's, London (which has

Hagia Sophia, Istanbul

Interior of Hagia Sophia, Istanbul

forty brick ribs and is held up by four arches on massive piers); that the dome is buttressed on either side by a semi-dome of the same diameter, each with three little satellite domes to support it; that on the exterior the building is austere but for the rocket-like minarets added at the four corners when it became a mosque after the fall of Constantinople to the Turks in 1453—all such details seem irrelevant compared with the impression that one is a tiny creature in a living space. Such breathtaking architecture could only be achieved by a revolutionary structure. In the course of the construction adaptations had to be made, and at one stage the architects, Anathemios of Tralles and Isidore of Miletus, told Justinian that they doubted that it would hold up. Justinian, with the courage of faith or architectural perspicacity, told them to continue to build the arches till they met, when they would support each other. Hold up it did. A historian of the time, Procopius, speaks of how the parts have been 'fitted together with incredible skill in mid air and floating off each other and resting only on the parts next to them, producing a single and most extraordinary harmony in the work.' In his inaugurating sermon, Paul the Silentiary said the dome appeared to be 'suspended from heaven by a golden chain'. As for Justinian, when he saw the masterpiece, he stated, 'O Solomon, I have outdone thee!' While in the Pantheon light limits and defines the enclosure, here shafts from the forty windows around the drum below the shallow, floating dome, pouring through arches from apse windows or piercing unexpectedly from the triforium above the galleried side-aisles, mingle and interfuse in a way that makes it difficult to distinguish space from light. Where the Romans hid their arches in the structure of concrete walls and vaults, the Byzantines opened up arches into apses, dome or semi-dome, giving the impression that, rather than building up walls and roofs to mark off and enclose stretches of usable space, the architects have tunnelled into space itself.

Hagia Sophia is now a museum, and in spite of the admirable work done by the Byzantine Institute of America in replacing the veined marble that clothed the walls leading to the galleries, some of its former splendour has disappeared under the whitewash with which its Turkish owners obliterated the human figures forbidden by Islam, leaving their Cufic script still painted around the domes. Yet the glory remains.

This first Byzantine masterpiece was never surpassed. But the style it established took on a new and more homespun quality—less filled with light, more dark and cavernous with candles catching the gilt of mosaic or ikon—and spread from Sicily in the south (there are famous mosaics at Cefalù, 1131, Monreale, 1190, and Palermo) through Italy, Turkey, Bulgaria, Armenia and north into Russia, where, cut off by Mongul invasions from Byzantium, the Russians built their own brand of the style as late as 1714, in the Church of the Transfiguration on Khizi Island.

Each area developed its own version. Typical of Greece and the Balkans were the monasteries at Daphni and Hosios Loukas, with the cross-plan expressed on the exterior by separate pan-tiled roofs over the different sections. A late flowering of the style is seen in the fourteenth-century churches at Mistra which tumble down a hillside above the plain of Sparta. A fantastic elaboration of it is in the 20 monasteries on precipitous Mount Athos in north-east Greece, where no female—human or animal—has been permitted entry for one thousand years. Since Greece was at this period an unimportant outlying province of the Empire, its thirteenth-century cathedral at Athens is the smallest in the world—35 feet by 25, the Little Metropolitan and a midget Byzantine gem.

In the fifth century, refugees from the barbarian hordes crossed the Adriatic lagoons and created Venice as part of the eastern Byzantine empire; so it remained for 500 years. In the ninth century some of her merchants returned from Alexandria with the body of St Mark the Evangelist and built a shrine for it, replaced in the eleventh century by

Monasteries on Mount Athos

St Mark's Cathedral, Venice

the present St Mark's Cathedral. The Greek architect based his Greek-cross, five-domed church on Justinian's Church of the Holy Apostles in Constantinople, which no longer exists. In spite of spangled additions to the outside, including bronze horses looted from Constantinople, Gothic crockets or mini-spires and religious mosaics in semicircular lunettes, it has retained something of the magic of Hagia Sophia. The façade builds up in three tiers of semicircular shapes: on the ground floor, five magnificent doorways, deeply imbedded in the surface between a two-tier paling of little pillars; on the floor above, five rounded gable ends hold the lunettes, each with a quizzical ogee eyebrow (a moulding made up of a convex and concave curve) that remind us of Venice's Eastern affinities; on the roof, the shape is echoed in the lead-covered domes with their garlic-bulb finials. Inside it is entirely sheathed in a molten skin of gold mosaic.

For Armenia, on a high plateau east of the Euphrates, the Byzantine period was her finest hour. Today abandoned to grassland, Ani, the capital, was once known as the city of a thousand churches. The reputation of her architects was such that in 1001, after the dome of Hagia Sophia had been destroyed in an earthquake, the architect of Ani cathedral, Trdat, was asked to restore it. Armenia was the earliest country to adopt Christianity as the state religion in 301. There is a childlike quality in the primitive carvings of biblical scenes on the walls of their churches and in the conical caps fitted over domes that reminds us of early-Christian wall-paintings.

As for Russia, her distinctive contribution to the Byzantine style is the onion dome, which swells outwards before curving inwards. This appears to have evolved in the twelfth century in Novgarod, the farthest north the style had penetrated, where shallow domes tended to give way beneath the weight of winter snow. The early wooden churches, set up by Prince Vladimir of Kiev after he established Christianity as the state religion in 988, have perished. The first masonry church, Santa Sophia in Kiev (1018–37), built originally with one large dome to represent Christ and twelve smaller apostle domes, *Cathedral at Ani, by Trdat*

St Basil's Cathedral, Red Square, Moscow

was during the seventeenth and eighteenth centuries so elaborated with extra aisles and domes that it is not easy today to see its original form.

It is difficult to reconcile solemn Red Square, Moscow, with the gay and skittish appearance of its cathedral, St Basil's, built by Ivan the Terrible in 1550–60 in thanksgiving for his victories. Its central tower, scalloped with upraised eyebrows, is clustered around with a collection of smaller domes, which must have been individual enough when they were first built, but which, since they adopted many-coloured tiling in the seventeenth century, present an appearance of Oriental extravagance one expects from a fairground.

10

The Order and the Sanctuary

It was the critics of the nineteenth century who first recognized and gave a name to an architectural style that reached its zenith in western Europe during the eleventh and twelfth centuries. They called it Romanesque because its structural basis was derived from ancient Roman construction. Its builders were not concerned with the classical elements, such as the orders; although they might pick up and incorporate the odd classical bit as the early Christian architects had done. But in those places (usually in Italy) where quasi-classical details were specially designed, there is a distinctive character that belongs neither to the original classical period nor to its revival in the Renaissance. This can be seen in the Corinthian columns of the basically basilican church of San Miniato al Monte in Florence (1018–62), or in the cathedral at Pisa, where the tiers of delicate arcades on the west front culminate in a little temple-end. The Roman in Romanesque lies essentially in its foundation on the strong Roman vault. It is generated by an obsession with security; each building, whether castle, or church or abbey, is a stronghold, a fortress. Indeed, the purpose of all buildings at this time was semi-defensive, a tradition carried on beyond this age of disturbance, as we can see in the sheer brick sides of the Gothic Albi Cathedral, built as part of the city's fortifications and a shelter for the entire population in the time of strife between church and heretics, the Albigensian Wars.

One of the extraordinary things about the Romanesque is that both secular and religious buildings seem to have gained dignity from their ambivalent inspiration. The fortress-like quality is not surprising when we remind ourselves that this was the first settled and cohesive building programme to appear in Europe out of seven hundred years of turmoil. What had happened was that in the course of the several

Cathedral, Baptistery and Leaning Tower, Pisa

Albi Cathedral

*Reliquary of St Foy,
Conques*

centuries that preceded the millennium, those barbarian hordes we saw in the Dark Ages devastating cities and destroying culture had undergone a transformation. They had not only settled down, but had gradually become peoples whose leaders, in partnership with the Church, were to establish a new order—Mediaeval Christendom.

The first to become 'establishment' were the Franks, when Pope Zacharias approved the election of Pepin as King in 751. Then Charlemagne revived the lost idea of empire—a political entity embracing several peoples—by uniting the western Frankish kingdom. He was a shrewd man. Although he could hardly write his own name, he brought the learned monk Alcuin from the cathedral school at York across to Tours to set up a school where a new generation of Frankish rulers could be educated in the classical culture which had been preserved through the writings of Christians like St Augustine and Boëthius. The Pope crowned him Emperor on Christmas Day 800. Wandering minstrels of the eleventh and twelfth centuries sang of his valiant deeds in their *Chansons de geste*. He was canonized in 1,166.

Contributions to the new age by the one-time barbarians are patterned through the new culture. The workmanship of Frankish, Lombard and Visigoth ornament—wide bands of gold studded with enormous gems—found its way into the devotional furniture of the mediaeval Church, in the cross, chalice, reliquary and tabernacle doors. The grandeur and barbarism are exemplified in the tenth-century reliquary of St Foy in the pilgrim church at Conques, Auvergne. The casket enshrining the remains of the little martyr who refused to give her body to a lewd and pagan emperor was, ironically, honoured by being decorated with the gold mask of a fifth-century emperor's face by Pope Boniface.

One late group of barbarians, the Norsemen of Scandinavia, made a remarkable contribution to the emerging culture, not least in architecture. From Charlemagne's time their cruel-prowed Viking ships had preyed along the coastlines of Europe and, as we know now, had even crossed the Atlantic to North America. They applied their skill in using naturally curved tree-trunks for the prows of their boats to the *cruck*, the combined timber-post and roof structure, of England

San Miniato al Monte, Florence

Durham Cathedral

Cefalù Cathedral, Sicily

and northern Europe. In all the places where they made firm settlements—Normandy in 911, England in 1066, Southern Italy and Sicily—they established a distinctive and influential form of Romanesque known as the Norman style, seen at its best in Durham Cathedral, built mainly in the twelfth century.

At the same time a strong independent tradition flourished in the Celtic fringes which had remained unaffected by the European mêlée. From Ireland, which had been converted to Christianity through the Roman occupation in the fifth century, Christianity flowed back to the Continent by way of the British mainland. From Ireland came inter-woven decoration on stone crosses and churches, illuminated gospels (for example, the Book of Kells), and, of course, missionaries—Columba, Aidan, Alcuin and Boniface. The little Anglo-Saxon church of St Lawrence at Bradford-on-Avon, Wiltshire, dating from the cultural renaissance under Alfred, victor of the Danes, whose beautiful ashlar stonework may well have been reused Roman masonry, is an example of the Christian tradition that had existed in England for 600 years before William the Conqueror arrived from Normandy.

There was also the Saracenic influence. The tide of Islam's advance had swept as far as central France when Charles Martel, Charlemagne's grandfather, stemmed its flood at the Battle of Poitiers in 732. Even at the time of the First Crusade (1096), the Moors still occupied southern Spain—in fact the Kingdom of Granada remained a Muslim state until 1492. We can see this influence in the Moorish capitals in the cloisters of Segovia and, combined with Norman, in the Cathedral at Cefalù, Sicily.

The Western Empire—France, Germany, Italy, England and Northern Spain—was assuming a more settled identity. The inspiring principle was supplied by the Church. The system which unified and controlled society was that developed by the Normans and expressed in their dominant building types. That was the feudal system. If the abbey was the expression of the Church, the castle was the direct expression of feudalism.

The feudal system was, in many ways, a harsh one, in which life was poor and coarse for the serf at the bottom of the social ladder and not much more refined or sensitive for his lord. They were probably both illiterate, for book-learning was the prerogative of the clergy. The labourer lived in a hut of brushwood or of wattle and daub, a construction wherein thin strips of wood, woven together like a basket, were covered by a mixture of dung and horsehair and finished with whitewash or plaster. The lord's hall, the forerunner of the manor house and the castle, was also primitive: one great room, heated from a central hearth with louvred smokehole above, and furnished with sleeping-benches around the walls. The servants would bed down round the fire with the dogs.

Change came as daily life became more civilized. Chimneys began to be built in the outside walls of castles. Then stairs led out of the hall to upper quarters for the family, and, later still, kitchen and servants' wings were added. Lighting was primitive, perhaps mercifully so, since, until the thirteenth century, when soap became more common, people were not very clean. Insufficient water supplies and

Church of St Lawrence,
Bradford-on-Avon, Wiltshire

sanitation contributed to the lack of hygiene. The towns had the worst of it. By the eleventh century all the ancient aqueducts in Rome had ceased to function. The aqueduct which the Emperor Julian had built for bringing water to Paris was destroyed by the Norsemen in the ninth century. Not until the monasteries, always carefully sited by spring or stream, started to channel fresh water in and sewage away, and Greek and Arab medical texts were brought back from the East, was anything practical done about these vital matters.

Two other phenomena are crucial to an understanding of the Romanesque. The first was the passion for pilgrimage. Trade routes had already opened, but it was religious enthusiasm that made the heart of the community beat. It was manifest in visions, miracles, legends, saints and relics, wreathed in superstition and clothed in beaten gold encrusted with gems, each of which had a mystic significance; and it pumped the traffic of the time—monks and friars, pilgrims and crusaders—through the arteries of Christendom. With that traffic went the spread of Romanesque architecture, of wide naves and broad transepts that afforded space for the daily ritual and processions to a shrine. Local pilgrimages (like the Canterbury pilgrimage that Chaucer so vividly portrays) provided opportunity for social encounters, and, since saints were the heroes of the day, to visit the shrine of à Becket at Canterbury or St Foy at Conques and actually see the relics must have provided the glamour and excitement that a fan today gets from hearing his pop idol live in concert. And some pilgrims went a long way, to Rome or Jerusalem. After the Arabs had been forced out of the Basque region, the popularity of the shrine of the apostle James at Santiago de Compostela in north-west Spain provided a new magnet and the Cluniac Benedictines organized a fan of routes crossing France diagonally, from St-Denis and Vézeley and Le Puy and Arles.

The second phenomenon was the Crusades, the attempts by Kings and barons and their retainers, urged on by popes and bishops, to recapture the Holy Land from the Turks. The Crusaders, some of whom spent ten years away, brought back from the East not only the impact of walking on the soil once trodden by Christ, but also tales of

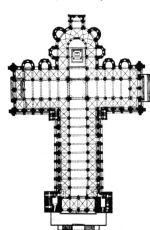

Santiago de Compostela

Krak des Chevaliers, Syria

the sun glinting off scimitar and coats of mail, the sharp smell of sweetmeats and danger, Greek scientific texts preserved in Arabic, Saracenic decoration and the techniques of siege. Their tombs were given pride of place in many a country church, where their effigies lie proudly with legs crossed to indicate that they once participated in that great adventure to the glory of God. The orders of the Knights Hospitallers and the Knights Templar were expressly founded to protect the Holy Land from the Saracens. They left in their wake not only handsome churches, monastic buildings and pilgrims' hostels, but also marvellous robust castles like the Krak des Chevaliers in northern Palestine, spoken of by a contemporary as 'the bone in the Saracen's throat'.

The key building in the spread of devotion was the abbey. And the creators of the abbey were the religious orders. Neither St Benedict, who, from his cave in Subiaco at the end of the fifth century, founded the first monastic order, nor St Bernard of Clairvaux (1113), the ascetic Cistercian reformer, who was said to have averted his eyes from a sunset for fear it would distract his thoughts from God, nor St Francis, born in 1181, who wanted his wandering friars to sleep on the forest floor with their brothers the birds and the beasts, could be considered a patron of the arts. Yet, as their orders spread and became richer, abbey churches soared upwards all over Europe. The Benedictine Abbot Hugh of Cluny (1024–1109), who built a new abbey church (then the largest church in Christendom), was superior over several hundred abbeys. The Abbey of Cluny, founded by William of Aquitaine in 1909 and given by him to St Peter and his successors the popes, was responsible for building most of the churches on the pilgrim routes on plans similar to Hugh's abbey and became very powerful, particularly from 1309, when the popes moved to Avignon. The abbot at Cluny played for the Romanesque a role similar to that which Abbot Suger's church at St-Denis was to play for the Gothic.

Monasteries were often sited just outside the city gates, generating a little suburb, with shops of their own, by their social importance in providing work, medical care, education and even sanctuary for hunted criminals. They were the power-houses of inventive talent. The Cistercians, the biggest farming order, initiated the agricultural developments of the time, especially in grain production, sheep-rearing, dry-stone walling techniques, water wheels and land drainage. Workshops were attached to all abbeys, where masons, carvers, joiners and engineers worked on the inspiration, experimentation and building techniques that were to blossom into the Romanesque style.

The earliest-known drawing of a great abbey, the Benedictine abbey of St Gall in Switzerland, was made in the year 820 and illustrates the scale and complexity of the buildings inhabited by these great communities. These communities played a central role in the economy of the times, in agriculture and in industry. In their churches and associated buildings, they reflected the dominance of the Church. From about 1000 the power of the Church increased, until by 1500 it informed all aspects of life. 'Shortly after the year 1000', wrote a monk of that time, Raoul Glaber, 'all Christian peoples were seized with a

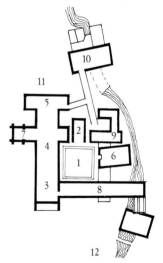

Plan of Fountains Abbey, Yorkshire: 1 Cloister, 2 Chapter House, 3 Nave, 4 Choir, 5 Chapel of Altars, 6 Refectory, 7 Tower, 8 Lay Brothers' Quarters, 9 Cells, 10 Infirmary, 11 Cemetery, 12 Guest Area

great desire to outdo one another in magnificence. It was as if the world shook and cast off its old age, everywhere investing itself with a white mantle of churches.' Like daisies in May, white-stone or lime-washed, they spread over the green fields of Christendom in a surge of relief that the millennium celebrating Christ's birth or death had not, after all, brought the predicted end of the world.

The typical abbey church was cruciform in plan, liturgically orientated with the altar at the east, the direction of the rising sun, and the main door at the west, in keeping with the contemporary obsession with symbolism. The east end was sometimes built up with the altar over a crypt and, in a pilgrim church, had a *chevet*—an ambulatory with chapels opening off it—behind the altar, whose pile-up of roofs with semi-conical caps would fittingly emphasize the position of the altar on the exterior. The same pattern was apparent in monastic churches, where crypt or chevet chapels provided space for a large congregation of priests to celebrate Mass daily, as gradually became the custom. Some churches had a tower over the crossing, but the German pattern developed a second transept, as, for example, at St Michael's, Hildesheim (1133–72), and would often have two towers dominating a massive west façade, known as the *westwerk*.

Characteristically, on the churches of Burgundy, the west front is decorated by massive sunken portals and is richly sculpted with figures spilling out from a Christ-figure on the tympanum over the main doorway to cover the entire front, in a manner now recognized as typical of the Romanesque. Such a church is Notre-Dame la Grande

Plan of St Gall by Eginhardt

Notre-Dame La Grande, Poitiers

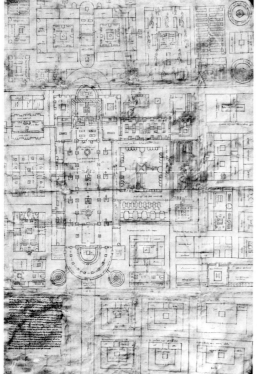

at Poitiers. We know who carved the tympanum of Autun Cathedral by the signature 'Gislebertus hoc fecit'. It portrays Christ in Judgment, with the damned writhing in a frieze below his feet, and nearby, the Magi being roused by an angel while they lie asleep under a semi-circular crochet blanket.

Sculpture of the Three Kings sleeping, Autun Cathedral

Stone is the usual material, but many Italian churches adhere to the local custom of using brick with marble facings, as in San Miniato in Florence. We can recognize a Romanesque building (whether it be a cathedral or a castle) by its massive and sheer stretches of stonework—ashlar on churches, roughstone on castles—covered with masons' marks telling the 'lodge' or workshop where the mason was trained. This suggests that skill in stonework was prized. Stonework, whether plain or carved, was slit by relatively few window-openings, a feature that creates the fortress-like appearance of the style. It is in direct contrast to the Gothic architecture of the second half of the Middle Ages, from the twelfth century onwards, where a new structure brought in walls almost entirely of glass.

Perhaps the classic feature of the Romanesque church is its semi-circular shape, the shape of the round-headed arch and its extension, the barrel vault, which was adopted from the ancient Romans as the mainstay structure of the period. It runs through plan, three-dimensional structure and even decoration—in the section of a round, smooth pillar, in the chevet with its semi-circular chapels bulging off it, in the semiconical caps to roofs.

In Aquitaine this geometrical shape appears in domed churches, the domes set over square bays, which may indicate cross-fertilization from the East. On the exteriors, it is to be found in the pilaster strips and blind arcades, often interlaced, which first appeared in Lombardy. They are therefore sometimes called Lombard bands, and act as decoration and as a form of buttressing. Even in the castles, round towers appear bulging from the corners, just as the side-chapels bulge from the chevets, and again the motif is structurally valid since the round towers make crossfire possible and the rounded corners make it more difficult to undermine the wall.

The motif is petrified in the barrel vault, which is the structural basis of Romanesque architecture. It is at its most beautiful in the tunnel-vaulted nave of St-Sernin, Toulouse, the largest surviving pilgrim church on the route to Santiago de Compostela, built between 1080 and 1100. However, barrel vaults are heavy, requiring massive walls and buttressing; two vaults intersecting at right angles to form a groin vault can be particularly clumsy. Experiments in Lombardy towards the end of the eleventh century led to a general adoption of vaults. The ribs were first calculated and built like the spokes of an umbrella, defining and emphasizing the groins, with infilling in between. The vault probably came to Burgundy from the East. We have already noted its use in Persian palaces. Autun Cathedral, for instance, was probably based on the Benedictine monastery at Monte Cassino of 1066–71, on which workmen from Amalfi, a city which traded with Baghdad, were employed. Because this structure sits best over a square plan, the nave or aisle was divided into square compartments by *diaphragm* arches. The roof of each compartment consisted of a groin vault. Where the arch of the nave was particularly high, two bays of the aisle were allowed for each groin vault. This structure may be recognized as one walks down the nave, even before one looks up at the roof, because the aisle arcades are alternately a pillar and a heavy stone pier to carry the weight.

By the end of the period the evolving structure was explicitly stated in the fabric of the building—in contrast to those early Roman models, where brick arches and vaults are hidden, embedded in the concrete walls. Possibly the enfolding arc of the vault, embracing like a mother's arm, appealed to an age sufficiently troubled to look for security. Spiritually, as well as physically, man was safe within the church.

In the castle, the same feature is also apparent. Here the watchful towers protruding from the sheer defensive sweep of the round keep, or *donjon*, make an aggressive and defensive gesture that reflects the reasons why they were built. However, in feudal society their function was not only military, it was also administrative. The castle became the seat of local government.

Between 1066 and 1189, the Normans built twelve hundred castles. The original castle form was the motte and bailey, the motte being a mound, sometimes a natural hill, often an artificial one, encircled with a ditch or moat, on top of which stood a timber structure which could be anything from a lookout post to a wooden dwelling, according to the space available. Looping from the motte's foot and connected to it by a wooden bridge was the bailey, a wide area protected by ramparts and earthworks. The bailey acted as parade ground and storage area, and would include retainers' houses, stables, and even armouries, depending on its size. The Norman development was to transmute the flimsy wooden dwelling on the motte top into a strong stone keep. The earliest examples are rectangular, holding a common hall and private chamber side by side on the first floor over the ground-floor storage area. After 1125, it became a round tower, with

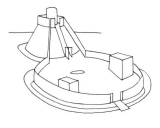

Castle with motte and bailey

Worms Cathedral

Interior of St-Sernin, Toulouse

the private chamber above the great hall. Later examples had circular or octagonal keeps with more complex plans. In some remains, such as the keep at Rochester Castle, Kent, of about 1130, the crucial well-shaft which supplied the water from top to bottom of the keep can still be seen.

Feuding families in Italian city-states would build their houses in the form of towers, solid at the base with single apartments on the upper floors, and sometimes a warning bell added on top. San Gimignano in Tuscany bristles splendidly with eleventh-century examples of such defiance. At Bologna, where once forty-one towers stood, two remaining towers, the Gli Asinelli at 322 feet and La Garisenda, draw attention to themselves by leaning together at a dangerous inclination only a little less than the famous bell-tower, or *campanile*, at Pisa. The slants of these towers are almost certainly due to inadequate foundations, a common fault at this period, and the probable reason why, of the English Romanesque cathedrals, only Norwich has retained her tower intact over the crossing. However, they provided the security required of them at the time, and given that the Bologna towers have been leaning since 1119, they have not done so badly after all.

Keep of Counts of Montfort, Houdan

But ultimately a castle indicated the beginning of a town, often, like the castle, a walled one. Most existing city walls date from between 1000 and 1300. The castle and the church towers would rear up above a wonderfully varied roofscape that resulted from the fact that the house fronts (the better ones arcaded) were not aligned but scattered along narrow twisting streets that looped up and down over untamed contours. There seems to have been little sensitivity to spatial planning, and anyway civic pride expressed itself in processions in honour of a patron saint rather than in town-planning. But the castle, like the abbey, was at the centre of an emerging society which we will see in some of its more glorious moments in the Gothic. We must at this point, however, examine the Islamic architecture that developed in the East at the same time as Romanesque in Europe.

Tower Houses at San Gimignano by Guelph and Ghibelline families

Dome of the Rock,
Jerusalem

Interior of the Great
Mosque, Cordoba

11

The Flowering of the Desert

For nearly two hundred years after 1096 the Christian knights of Europe fought the Muslims to retain the holy places—Palestine, where Christ had lived, and Constantinople, where Constantine had established the seat of the first Christian empire. Yet when you go there today it is the architecture left by Islam that is the more impressive. And that is all the stranger because the Muslim religion originated from a nomadic Arab people who lived under black tents in the desert and had, before religious fervour drove them to seek to conquer the world, few architectural pretensions. To trace that story and try to explain what happened there is no better place to start than Jerusalem.

Ever since Jerusalem was built, between AD 688-692, the golden cupola of the Dome of the Rock rising above the Western Wall and the creamy-brown rolling panorama of the city have commanded the attention of pilgrims, whether they were Jews, Muslims or Christians, and from whichever direction they approached over the hills. Close by, down some steps but on the same axis, Caliph Walid, son of Ibn el Malik, who built the Dome of the Rock, started in 710 to build the El Aksa mosque, rebuilt many times since, and at present having a dome of silver. They are two of the oldest Islamic buildings still in existence. They stand upon a naked white podium, with dark, tufted trees at its perimeter, that lies between the congested houses and tunnelled bazaars of the Old City on one side and the rising terraces of the Mount of Olives on the other. The podium is in fact the levelled-off top of Mount Moriah up which Abraham brought his son Isaac for sacrifice. It is also known as the Temple Mount, because Solomon's temple was built against one side of it.

Neither their exposed position nor their architecture is entirely typical of Islamic buildings, which tend to be hidden behind high walls and to concentrate on their interior arrangements. But they represent a tradition in its early evolutionary stages. The Dome of the Rock is used as a mosque today, but it is primarily a shrine, holy both to Jews and to Muslims. It is built around the hollow rock from which Mahomet is said to have made his leap to heaven in about AD 639. Structurally it is Byzantine. Its octagonal plan was suggested by the shrine of the Holy Sepulchre, which already stood in the Old City, not far away. A double ring of columns provides an outer ambulatory resembling those of the Roman-based Byzantine tombs and shrines, such as, for example, Santa Costanza, Rome. It is roofed with a shallow pitch, made imperceptible from the outside by the device— later carried to extremes on Persian gateways—of carrying the wall up sheerly into a parapet to provide an uninterrupted surface for decoration. Originally glass mosaic, the decoration, dating from the sixteenth century, is now a sheath of blue and gold ceramic tiles. The windowless drum, also faced in tiles, is supported by an arcade of antique pillars and carries the double-skinned wooden dome, clothed on the outside in gilded lead originally, today in anodyzed aluminium. The columns, gleaned from ancient sites, do not quite match and have been wedged between makeshift block-like bases and capitals. Islamic whimsy is a probable explanation for this, since the columns in the Great Mosque at Cordoba, Spain (about 785), are classical columns sawn off and jammed in in the same way. Early examples of the pointed arches, a recurring motif in Islamic architecture, are to be found in the screen wall.

The style of the El Aksa Mosque, despite much rebuilding, reveals its Christian origins; nevertheless its atmosphere is that of a mosque. This is Islam's holiest shrine after Mecca and Medina, and more accessible than those two. For, the Prophet's Mosque in Medina and Islam's central shrine, the Ka'aba, a strange cube-shaped building housing the sacred black stone—a relic of pre-Mohammedan worship—are forbidden to non-Muslims. The El Aksa consists of one long carpeted prayer-hall, and has typical timber bracing-beams cutting at capital level across from arch to arch of the arcade. It also has crosswise arcading so that worshippers may kneel on the floor facing the *qibla*, or wall orientated towards Mecca.

In Damascus, another city to take its turn as Muslim capital, the Great Mosque, the earliest mosque to survive intact, preserves other features typical of the mosque in its development phase. In 706, the Caliph al Walid took over a *temenos*, originally a Hellenistic sacred precinct containing a temple and later harbouring a Christian church, and turned it into a congregational mosque. The caliph made use of the existing square towers and turned them into the first minarets. The pierced stone patterns on the window grilles, on the other hand, show the kind of geometrical detail that was to become standard Islamic, after figurative decorations were forbidden to Muslims in the eighth century (as they already were to Jews under the prohibition against the making of graven images).

All three of these mosques are impressive buildings by any standards. But what was it that inspired men in the East to build this kind

Interior of El Aksa Mosque, Jerusalem

of building, a full century and a half before Charlemagne was crowned Emperor in Rome, at a time when in the West the basilican form of Early Christian architecture was still unchallenged? It was the prophet Mahomet, born in about 570 in Mecca, a city on the camel-routes, who was the inspiration. His revelations, couched in rhyming prose, were arranged according to length to form the *Qur'an* (Koran), which Muslims learn by heart and recite daily. This, with the later addition of two other holy books (the *Hadith*, comprising Mahomet's sayings and the *Law*, drawn from the first two), formed the basis on which scattered Bedouin tribes united to surge forth from the Arabian desert and along the Mediterranean as far as France in a tide of holy war.

It was not until 732, at Moussais-le-Bataille, near Poitiers, that Charles Martel managed to stop the invasion of Bedouin tribes into Europe. A measure of their achievement is that they had started to build the Great Mosque at Kairouan, Tunisia, some two thousand miles from Mecca, before Mahomet had been dead forty years.

Islam presents a life so simple, practical and complete that it has never lost its appeal across the centuries. There is only one basic dogma: that there is one God, Allah, and Mahomet is his prophet, and one basic requirement: submission to the omnipotent will of Allah. *Islam* means surrender, and a *muslim* is one who submits. This practical requirement is expressed in a daily way of life, which includes ritual prayer five times daily, fasting, paying taxes to support the poor and making a pilgrimage (*hajj*) to Mecca once in a lifetime.

The buildings of Islam enshrine this pattern of everyday life. The importance of leadership was readily accepted by the Bedouin faithful, who knew from experience that a leader was needed to protect them from the threat of one shepherd doubling his fortune by killing his neighbour and seizing his flock. Such a leader under Allah was the caliph who occupied Mahomet's place. Such are the three officials in the mosque: the *muezzin*, who calls the faithful to pray, the *khatib*, who preaches and leads prayers from a pulpit called the *minbar*— often the only furniture in the mosque—and the *imam*, the paid official who represents the caliph. They are not priests: there is no sacrificial ritual and therefore no sanctuary as such in a mosque. All worshippers have equal rights to prayer.

Al Ahzar Mosque, Cairo

Islamic architecture inevitably developed regional differences, which were mingled with the flavour of Syria, Persia and Samarkand as well as of Mecca and Medina. But none of them explains the character of Islamic architecture. The key fact is that Islam was a highly sophisticated society which had absolutely no tradition of 'great' building. And so what became Islamic architecture developed, like her rituals, directly from the everyday life of the believers; it is an architecture of the oasis. This applies to the characteristic features not only of mosques—in particular the Ulu Jami (Friday) congregational mosques that developed from the seventh to the eleventh century—and the theological colleges dating from the tenth century onwards, but also of the palaces, luxury houses and the dervish hostels on trade or pilgrim routes. They all consist of a high-walled compound for protection against enemies, thieves and the sun, with shady arcades and halls around it, and a water-source, a fountain, pool or well or, in some cases today, a large tank, often in the centre of the courtyard.

The main concern of the dwellers in these parched lands was water, and it was soon built into Muslim daily life with the ritual ablutions that preceded prayers. Under nomadic tents, no distinction is made between *inside* and *outside*, and an expression of this can be observed in mosques and in places with buildings and gardens mirroring each other—the symmetrical layout of rugs inside, or streams and flower-beds outside, repeating each other. We can see this in Middle Eastern carpets, in which 'rivers of life' flow between arbours of blossoms, flower-beds and pools, such as one woven to order for Caliph Shah Abbas (1587–1629). A similar arrangement can be seen in the axiality and symmetry of the Shalimar Garden, Lahore, Pakistan (1633–43), which is on three levels linked by cascades with, as its focal point, a throne-room on an island of marble approached by four bridges on the compass points.

The early palaces, whose high enclosing walls often make them appear fortresses from outside, reveal themselves structurally from within as a series of simple pavilions set in parks or gardens. Their furnishings may be rich and sumptuous, with silk hangings and gold and silver work, but in architectural terms they are little more sophisticated than the Bedouin tents. It is easy to be so dazed by the fairy-cavern impression of the fourteenth-century Palace of Alhambra (Qalat al-Hamra) at Granada, Spain, with its tessellated filagree of fretting and stalactites, that we fail to grasp that its plan is simply made up of a series of pavilion units linked by elaborate courts. Even in more complex buildings we find (as in China and Japan) that rooms and areas are rarely designated for particular functions such as eating or sleeping, but are more likely to be seasonal—winter and summer areas.

The major buildings are in cities. Mosques and palaces were isolated behind walls in the heart of cities for protection and to signify withdrawal from worldly concerns. Likewise, inside the mosque, the prayer-hall was placed farthest from the entrance.

Nowhere was the principle of defensive planning carried so far as in the magical city of Baghdad on the river Tigris, city of Haroun al

Alhambra Palace, Granada:
1 Court of Lions, 2 Baths,
3 Fish Pond, 4 Palace of
Charles V

Raschid and the Arabian Nights, not far from the ruins of Babylon and Ctesiphon, those magnificent capitals of past empires.

Caliph Mansur in the eighth century so planned the city that his palace and administrative buildings were in the middle of a great open space, encircled by three concentric rings of walls with an outer four-mile circumference. The city itself lay between the inner and the middle walls and was divided into four quarters by two intersecting roads. The four gates on the compass points were named after the provinces to which they gave access, and had bent entries—a device copied from the Crusaders. Military barracks lined the roads by the gates, and the circle between middle and outer walls remained open so that the caliph was in a position to mobilize troops in order to defend himself from external aggression, as well as from rebellion from within the ranks of his own people.

Isfahan, royal city of Shah Abbas, a contemporary of Queen Elizabeth I in England, shows similar protective planning, culminating in a great open space, the *maidan*, which was the royal polo-ground, flanked by two mosques, the palace, and royal caravanserais. The entry to the Masjid-i-Shah closes the maidan with a great *iwan*, or vaulted gateway, backed by a half-dome that is cut into the extraordinary flat façade, with twin-portal minarets 110 feet high on its corners. The iwan leads into an inner court, off which the corresponding iwan leading to the mosque had to be set at an angle of 45 degrees in order to orientate the mosque correctly. Over the internal courts rises the mosque's great dome, set on a pierced drum and subtly bulbous, adazzle in peacock, kingfisher and jade faience speckled in white like the glory of the southern heavens at night.

Masjid-i-Shah was a royal mosque. All mosques had certain essential features. They had either flat roofs supported on beams and wooden columns, or gently pitched roofs that rested on arcades running around three sides of the courtyard. They stabled camels as well as supplying shade and sleeping-shelters, for mosques had many

Masjid-i-Shah complex, Isafahan, built under Shah Abbas

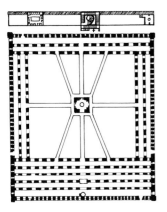

Ibn Tulun Mosque, Cairo

functions that were not strictly religious. Since community administration and community law were part of the Muslim tradition, clerks were permanently attached to the mosque, and the law was dealt with there. Treasures, too, were stored there. Their concern for ventilation dictated the open arcades; and even after these arcades were enclosed in prayer-halls running the length of the inner *qibla* or Mecca-facing wall of the courtyard, they still kept lofty arches as a feature to encourage coolness.

The classic mosque form, which developed from the most straightforward practical considerations, is well illustrated in the plan of the Great Mosque at Samarra, Iraq, of 847, of burnt brick buttressed with round towers, the largest ever built, having an outer enclosure (a *ziyada*) that measures more than a fifth of a mile square; and in that of the Ibn Tulun Mosque, Cairo, of 876-9. The courtyard of any mosque must have a water-supply, usually a fountain in the centre, for drinking and for the ablutions which became obligatory before prayers. There were arcades, probably two deep, along the entrance wall of the courtyard, pierced by the great *iwan* portal, under the minaret tower and also along both sides of the two adjacent walls. At the Ibn Tulun Mosque, date palms make up the roof of the arcades, a technique much used in ancient Mesopotamia. But along the opposite qibla wall, which was the sacred prayer area, there could be four, five or even six rows of arcades.

The court, the minaret, the fountain or ablutions pool, the arcades and the qibla wall together with the *mihrab* (a recessed niche in the centre of the qibla wall) make up the essential features of the mosque. The function of the mihrab was to indicate the direction of Mecca, so that believers knew which way to face in prayer. Originally a spear stuck in the sand had been used for this purpose. However, the alcove early became a distinctive feature and one on which the most beautiful decoration was lavished. Among the Egyptian labourers used in the renovation of the Prophet's House Mosque at Medina in 707 there were Coptic Christians who, perhaps, accustomed to building apses on the side walls, decided to incorporate one here. From here the imam could lead prayers while visible to the worshippers, and could himself survey his congregation wherever they knelt on the floor. The conversion of Christian churches with their long east/west axis into early mosques in Syria, where Mecca lay to the south, established a pattern for the qibla to be one long side-wall facing which the believers prostrated themselves in prayer. This established a pattern, so that when Islam spread across the world there were many examples—in the Great Mosque at Kairouan, Tunisia, for instance—of a southwards orientation quite incorrect in that part of the world. The mihrab in the south wall signified that the mosque, if it was enclosed, had to be entered from the middle of the long northern wall. This made it necessary to emphasize the mihrab. It was commonly done by introducing another set of arcades in the prayer area opposite the mihrab, which ran at right angles to the qibla, so that in an east/west orientated building they would run from side to side across the width of the mosque. The central arcade might be taller than its fellows and might stop short with a dome opposite the mihrab to give further emphasis—internal as well as external, for it can be identified by the raised roof on the outside. Such a dome appears in the Aghlabid Mosque of 836 at Kairouan, and in the many-domed Seljuk mosques. Rugs on the floor, a pulpit called a *minbar* to the right of the mihrab, and sometimes a railed enclosure for special worshippers such as the caliph, or women, normally complete the sparse furniture of the mosque.

Presumably Mahomet, in his garden at Medina, asked one of his followers to climb on the wall and call to the others when it was time to pray. However, as with the mihrab, the adaptation of the towers of the Christian church at Damascus gave birth to another Islamic component, the minaret. The first purpose-built minaret of which there is a record dates from 670 and is to be found in the sixteen aisle, open-court mosque at Kairouan, Tunisia, where, incidentally, we also find the first use of the sumptuous, glazed tiles which were to become the hallmark of Islamic architecture. Mosques in Mesopotamia and North Africa usually have a single minaret, placed at the entrance to the courtyard; coupled minarets are typical of Seljuk and post-Seljuk Persia, while in Turkey a single minaret off-centre between courtyard and prayer-hall is common. Some caliphs gave expression to their grand concepts by building four or even six minarets around the prayer-hall. The Ka'aba mosque at Mecca is unusual in that it has seven.

Minarets may be square, round, or like a factory chimney except that some are covered in incredible patterning in basket-weave and geometrical and calligraphic forms. Some minarets are fretted, some tiered and stepped like a lighthouse tower, ending perhaps, in a mode

Selimiye Mosque, Edirne, by Sinan

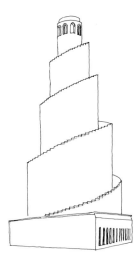

Spiral minaret: al-Malwiya Mosque, Samarra

peculiar to Cairo, in an open pavilion. Some are free-standing and show the idiosyncrasies of their origin. At Samarra, one-time capital on the Tigris, the minaret at the north end of the al-Malwiya mosque is a spiral ramp, reminiscent of early Assyrian ziggurats not far away, so wide that the caliph could ride up it to a pavilion 150 feet above ground. Four slim needles rising at the four extreme corners of a square complex are the hallmark of Sinan and the Ottoman buildings in Turkey and Byzantium. Some rise like horns from both sides of the iwan façade of mosque or medresa.

The medresa is the last of the courtyard forms we ought to look at. It is a theological or teaching college that developed in the tenth century, particularly in Seljuk Turkey in Anatolia, for the Turks were devout propagandists. Attached to mosque or palace, and part of an extended complex, it normally took the form of a series of cells round a courtyard. What is probably the world's first university was attached to the El-Ashair mosque in Cairo in 971. Some of the best examples were built under the Bahri Mamelukes in Egypt during the thirteenth and fourteenth centuries. Often, they were built from brick that had already been used, but in Anatolia they show how Turkey had learnt from the superb Syrian traditions of ashlar stonework. Sometimes they housed the tomb of their founder, as in the Medresa of Sultan Hassan (1356–62).

Entry to the medresa courtyard was through four vaulted chambers, the iwans, their enormous portals, much-sculpted in a series of receding and diminishing arches and sometimes vaulted with a semi-dome. In the twelfth century, emphasis on the main gateway made it bigger and let into it an upright rectangular panel (known as a *pishtaq*), which made a superb base for the fashionable mosaic of tiles in blues and greens and golds, which derived from Persian and Mesopotamian sources. The best example is probably the Jami Mosque at Yezd, Iran, a city set in the desert, but possessing its own water supply, making possible the creation of a city and even the growth of mulberry trees for the silk trade by Tamburlaine (Timur the Lame), the Turkish conqueror who, with his son, resurrected this area after the devastation caused by the invasions of Monguls and Turkish tribesmen during the thirteenth and fourteenth centuries.

What is fascinating about Islamic architecture is how its extreme simplicity of arrangement and structure could give rise to so many diverse shapes and decorations, many of which carry the seeds of future structural developments. The arcades of the mosques, for instance, started as mere supports for light, awning-type roofs, and this left their creators free to invent a multiplicity of arched forms: pointed, stepped and round, horseshoe, trefoil and scalloped, ogee or shaped like inverted ship's keels, or double-tiered as in the arches with variegated *voussoirs* at Cordoba. Whereas a round arch is one-centred (since in a semicircle, both height and width are radii from the centre point) these arches of complex design may be two- or even three-centred.

The fact that figurative representation was forbidden perhaps gave impetus to the exploration of shapes, resulting in a rich spectrum from

Jami Mosque, Yezd, Iran

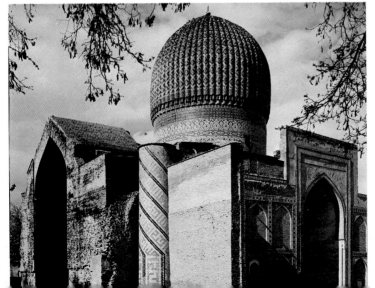

Tomb of Tamburlaine (Gur-i-mir), Samarkand

robust battlementing of Crusader origins to intricate but delicate interlaced arabesques developed from calligraphy. Part of the magic springs from the freedom with which shapes and patterns can be swapped from one use or medium to another: where else has ink brushwork or cursive writing been translated into brick? When later, Islamic faith extended into colder regions like Anatolia, where the Seljuks had to abandon open-court mosques for enclosed buildings, experimentation with the arcades continued, aided by the pavilion form, in which they were not required to support an upper storey.

The countries that adopted Islam were in no way backward in structural evolution. We saw how the Persians were originally far in advance of Byzantium in working out the squinch, forerunner of the pendentive, to carry a brick-domed roof. The squinch was originally used at the corners, but after the eleventh century its use was extended so that it covered the entire alcove, recessed portal or hall-pavilion. No longer used as a method of supporting a dome or vault, vast numbers of tiny squinches were often used in Islamic architecture as a decorative conceit; they were built up in overlapping layers, like the scales of a pineapple or a fir-cone, until they created a magical cave of little stalactites (called *muqurnas*). We can see how in the Hall of Lions and the Hall of Judgment in the Alhambra Palace, Granada, the muqurnas in lath, plaster and stucco have been transformed into filigree representing frost-flowers on a window pane. We see these Islamic patterns persisting right through the Mediaeval period in Sicily, in Cefalù and in the Royal Palace at Palermo.

Structures and flowing decoration come together in the roof silhouette. The tomb, which made an important contribution to Islamic architecture, made possible small-scale invention in dome shapes, again often betraying local origins. Domes were placed at important points, such as over the entrance or over the bays before the mihrab. Sometimes in Persia and in Mesopotamia, each bay of mosque, medresa or palace had its own dome. The Ottoman struggle to make all subordinate to the central dome can be seen in the Selimiye Mosque, Edirne, Turkey, and the Blue Mosque, Istanbul. Domes on Indian tomb-complexes display a calm, disembodied beauty, although they tend to be more bulbous in silhouette. The best example is the Taj Mahal at Agra, the beautiful marble palace which Shah Jehan built in memory of his wife. He set it in the midst of gardens by the river

Taj Mahal, Agra, by Shah Jehan

between four sentinel minarets. There is a still, breathless perfection about its massing, with four octagonal towers carrying the central pavilion. On the façade, a great open iwan rises two storeys to the drum and floating dome based on the earlier Tomb of Humayan at Delhi (1565–6).

Iran, however, sometimes built odd tall tomb-towers with conical caps resembling rather superior farm silos, like that of the Gunbad-i-Qabus dating from 1006–7. In Samarkand, now in Uzbekistan, USSR, a city on the silk route and once an Abbasid capital, Tamburlaine has left us an exotic legacy. This includes a tomb-city, and the lovely Gur-i-mir (The Grave of the Sovereign), his mausoleum, whose turquoise dome, shaped like a fig and with distinctive gadrooned ribbing, rises amid a flight of pigeons up to a lilac evening sky. Much of the calming influence that the tyrant's tomb has on the onlooker is due to the builder's proportioning of substructure, drum and dome according to strict aesthetic rules, so that they are in a perfect relationship of 3:2:2.

There is no doubt that Islamic architecture was inspired by the effect strong sunshine has on shapes and carvings and stucco mouldings in relief, emphasizing hollows, shadows, knife edges and raised areas and making them appear even more stunningly extravagant.

12

The Metaphysics of Light

Occasionally in the story of architecture there occurs a particular person, place or building that we can point to as a milestone, saying *here* started such a style. In the transition from the first to the second half of the Middle Ages, that is from Romanesque to Gothic, we have such a milestone. The man is a Benedictine abbot called Suger, the place the Abbey Church of St-Denis on the edge of Paris, the year 1144 and the occasion magnificent—the consecration of the new abbey choir, rebuilt after one of those disastrous fires so common when wooden roofs were vulnerable to lightning from without and to flares and tapers from within.

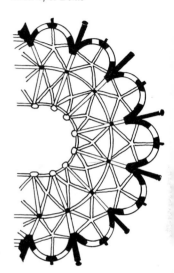

Choir of St-Denis

Abbot Suger belonged to the religious order that had for so long controlled Romanesque church building from Cluny. He was an important man in both Church and state, an adviser to kings and popes, a well-known theologian and a superb administrator. Before embarking on the rebuilding of St-Denis, he meticulously sorted out all the Abbey lands to ensure a stable income during the building period. And he set down on paper his thinking and aims in rebuilding St-Denis.

Suger's writings—a pamphlet on the *Consecration of the Church of St-Denis* and a *Report on the Administration*—present us with a rare description of the sources of Gothic architecture. His thesis was that 'the dull mind rises to truth through that which is material'; and his genius grasped how he could appeal at several levels to the dull mind by using the rib vault. He could create soaring arches which would draw the spirit of man up to heaven; he could transform walls into screens of glass which would teach the worshipper the doctrine and origins of his faith in picture stories while submerging him in celestial light. Anybody who has walked along the triforium gallery at Chartres Cathedral, bathed in the liquid fire of ruby and sea-green that flickers from the robes of the prophets, will know how successfully Suger's followers gave flesh to his vision. In church one was to have an experience of heaven on earth.

'This is the House of God and the Gate of Heaven' says the psalmist in the liturgy for the consecration of a church, a liturgy systematized at this period (the Gothic mind was full of systems).

Suger caught the temper of the times, which were swinging away from the obsession of the early Middle Ages with life's grimmer aspects, sin, guilt and death, to a triumphant Church which had put down the Albigensian heretics and achieved romantic success in the Crusades. The view of God's world was now one of beauty and comparative safety, in which the ordinary man could rejoice. Nature was let loose on choir stalls, portals, canopies and chapter houses, in an exuberance of tendrils and leaves, birds, animals and flowers. St

(opposite, top) *Interior of Chartres Cathedral*

(opposite, bottom) *The Five Lancets under the South Rose, Chartres Cathedral*

Aerial view of Chartres Cathedral

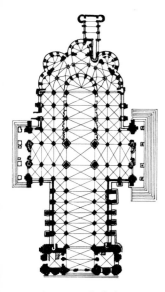

Chartres Cathedral

Francis, founder of one of the new orders of friars, went around exhorting his brothers and sisters—men, women, animals, birds—to praise and exalt the Lord above all things for ever.

The French called this new translation of beauty into stone 'le style ogival', recognizing the debt its shapes owed to the East. But the name by which it has come to be known was the scornful soubriquet of 'Gothic', or barbaric, with which it was dubbed by the sixteenth-century art-historian Giorgio Vasari. The prestigious congregation at the consecration of St-Denis, which included Louis VII of France and his Queen, seventeen archbishops and bishops from all over France and from as far away as Canterbury, did not see the style as barbaric. The soaring thin-ribbed vaults and walls incandescent with the 'un-created light of the Godhead', clearly impressed them. It appears that, on returning home, they all took the first opportunity proffered them by fire or by disrepair to build in Gothic. Within twenty-five years of the consecration, every diocese represented at the ceremony had raised a Gothic cathedral to the heavens.

What the new style offered in practical terms was the following. Liturgically, it preserved the basic cruciform plan with space for processions in the nave and with side-chapels for celebrating private Mass. Structurally, it did away with the need for massive masonry, yet made possible higher and more varied vaults. Wall space thus freed could be used as a means of instructing the simple worshipper through sculpture, painting and glass. In this way, an architectural synthesis was created, coherent in structure and detail, and capable of inspiring a vision of ultimate truth and reality.

Yet not one of the features by which we distinguish Gothic archi-tecture was new—not the pointed arch or window, nor cross-vaulting, flying buttresses or twin towers on the façade. What then was essen-tially Gothic in the way that these components were structurally combined in those cathedrals that followed St-Denis? One of the first things to be exploited was the freedom given by the pointed arch. In the semicircular Romanesque arch, height and width from a central point had, of course, to be equal, being the radii of the same circle.

However, the pointed arch, having several different curvatures, could be varied in width and still retain its original height, thus making possible an arcade with some columns closer than others, yet all having the top of their arches at the same level. Furthermore, they could be varied in both height and width and joined at right angles to vaults which could also vary in height and width. Thus a low side-aisle could give onto a higher transept, and the transept onto a higher and wider nave. The architects recognized a further possibility opened up by the pointed arch. They realized that by thinking of the main structural elements as cutting across the cathedral as well as running the length of it, they could send the main forces from the roof down to the aisles and then by way of flying buttresses to the ground. This made it possible to treat the outside walls no longer as structures holding things up but as panels which could be almost entirely glazed. The cathedral could now be a lantern of glass.

The pointed arch and all that it implied could coexist with the cruciform plan. In France a chevet could be punctuated by side-chapels running round the east end behind the choir. The plan remained open-ended; nave and transepts could be added onto as needs dictated, and monks' choir, behind the altar from which the daily office was sung, and chevet or side-chapels, where each priest offered his private daily Mass, could be extended.

The basis of the whole design had radically changed from the Romanesque for this reason: builders no longer had to assemble the structure over a series of cube-shaped units of space. The space they were enclosing could now be widened or narrowed, and, above all, it could extend upwards. Vaulted roofs no longer planted their weight, heavy footed, on the massive shoulders of the side-walls; the weight swung down through simple arches built transversely and diagonally across each bay, like the ribs of an umbrella. Until recently it was thought that the ribs were carrying all the weight and transferring it through the buttresses to the ground. However, instances in World War II, where the ribs were destroyed and the infill sections (like the webbing between a duck's toes) remained standing, have shown that the structure depends on a delicate balance and disposition of loads and thrusts throughout the whole building. De Honnecourt's thirty-three-page parchment sketchbook (probably commissioned as a source-book for his masons' lodge), made in the thirteenth century, is a rich source of information about mediaeval building methods. His sectional drawing of the stately royal cathedral of Rheims (1211–1481), the site where the kings of France had been crowned since the fifth century, gives us some idea of the intricate problem of weight distribution, often adjusted as building progressed. Further clues to building methods are given by work guidelines that have been left on some sites. At York and Wells we have found the re-usable plaster tracing-floor on which master-masons drew out plans and diagrams for apprentices. Renovation work on Westminster Abbey uncovered level boss stones at the point where the ribs of the vault meet, scored to show where the lines of the ribs were to come in.

It is surprising how often what we take to be mere ornamentation

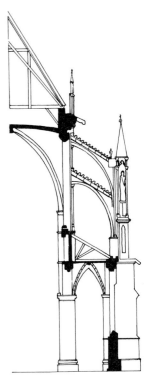

Rheims Cathedral. Cross-section

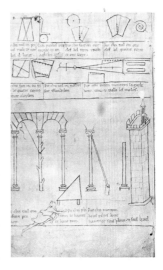

Page from Villard de Honnecourt's sketchbook. London, British Library

shows itself on further examination to be an integral part of this delicate balance of weights. The pinnacles on the top of the outer buttresses, for instance, are not just spiky decoration, but, as we can see in section, are built up to counter the thrust of the nave walls.

Nor did the double Gothic roof—wood outside and stone vault beneath—arise from mere whimsy. Tall buildings were a prey to lightning, until Benjamin Franklin invented the lightning conductor in the eighteenth century. While the outer roof might be struck and would burn, the inner stone vault protected the church. In rainy weather, however, the roles were reversed; the wooden roof protected the shallower vault below. The roof also provided space for the hoisting-gear needed to heave the stones of the vault into position. That is why, as the vaulting became more complicated in the late Gothic English, German and Austrian churches, the roofs became steeper, like St Stephen's Cathedral in Vienna. There are mediaeval cathedrals which still shelter their hoisting gear between the two roofs.

Bit by bit, the Gothic builders learnt how much they could cut away from wall, arch or buttress without impairing the functioning of the structure. The beautiful but simple late twelfth-century spokes of the early buttresses at Chartres, had, by 1500, become a fretwork of traceried gables and buttresses similar to those of La Trinité, Vendôme, and St-Maclou, Rouen. The more solid expanse of wall, exemplified in the early cathedral of Sens (1145), becomes increasingly aerated as greater confidence in the structure develops. In Chartres, a triforium passage is cut into the thickness of the wall; Bourges, with its unique pyramid shape of nave flanked on each side by two aisles of decreasing height, is perforated right through to the outside from aisle to aisle; and in the Chapel of the Holy Thorn, built by St Louis in Paris, usually known as La Sainte-Chapelle, the translation from solid wall to glass screens is complete. Here the stone mullions that hold the glass together are so slim that one can hardly perceive them for the dazzle of the stained glass. What the architect of 1243 had in effect achieved was to take Suger's example to its logical conclusion. He extended the upper, glassed-in area of Suger's apse on the end of the

Wells Cathedral

choir at St-Denis and made this the whole chapel, glass right down to the ground, so that the building glows like a reliquary casket cut from a faceted jewel.

The paring down of solid walls meant that glass increasingly took over. Early Gothic windows were simple lancets, as at Coutances, and plate tracery, as at Chartres and the Basilica of St Francis at Assisi, where a geometric pattern was, as it were, simply punched out of the wall surface. In 1201, bar tracery was invented: instead of the stone face of the wall being punched out into shaped holes, the glass was slotted into linear frameworks—stone mullions and window bars, carved into slim patterns as pieces of sculpture in their own right. These traceries are not fully appreciated from the inside, where the glory of the stained glass against the light claims all attention. But on the outside they take their place in an overall intricate pattern of lines and figures, which may cover the entire front of a Gothic cathedral, in the French manner at Rheims or Strasbourg, or make a screen as if of carved wood in characteristic English fashion at Wells, Somerset. Here the frontage 150 feet wide obscures all indications of the component units and is covered with four hundred statues—a brave sight, no doubt, in the Middle Ages when all were painted and gilded, but today providing a major headache for the cathedral architects who are attempting to preserve them.

The basic early window-shape of two lancet lights, a circle poised between their tips and all enclosed in a pointed window frame, later became freed from the circumscribing shape like a plant growing and putting out tendrils. The circles shot out petals or rays in the energetic manner that was to give this phase of French Gothic the name of Rayonnant. In England patterns of trefoils and leaves developed to

Bourges Cathedral

Interior of La Sainte Chapelle, Paris, by Pierre de Montreuil

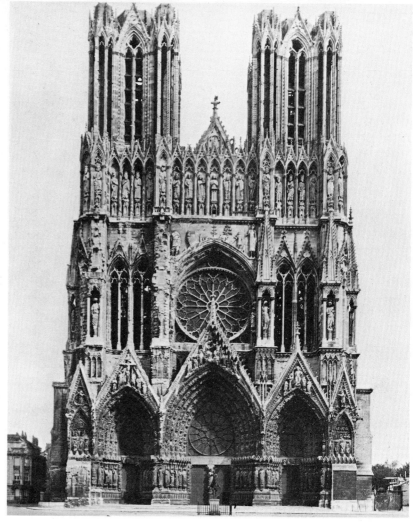

Rheims Cathedral by Bernard de Soissons

Gothic windows (English) (top to bottom): Lancet, Geometric, Curvilinear, Perpendicular

give the term Decorated to the corresponding phase there. From the end of the thirteenth century the leading ideas were to be found in England, whose Gothic period was to culminate in the staid upright dignity of the Perpendicular of the east end of Gloucester Cathedral. But before this example of typically English aloof reticence, the Decorated phase became more extravagant in the Curvilinear style, which undoubtedly owes much to England's contacts with the East, through trade and the Crusades, giving us excitingly mobile forms that reach their peak in the ogee traceries and carved hoods of the seats in the Lady Chapel at Ely, a building set apart from the main cathedral in the manner of a chapter house. Even in the purity of the Perpendicular, where all the lines of the traceries are pulled upwards, straight and smooth within a vertical rectangular panel, there is more than an echo of the pishtaqs of Isfahan.

The fashions in Gothic were carried through Europe from Norway to Spain by the master-masons, who travelled widely from job to job, so that by the fourteenth century they were referring to themselves as 'free' masons. Charles VII of Bohemia snatched the opportunity of Prague's lucky escape from the plague to employ Matthew of Arras from Avignon and one of a famous family of masons, Peter Parler from Gmünd, on his new cathedral. William of Sens built Canterbury

Cathedral; Etienne of Bonneul went from Paris to work at Upsala, Sweden; and a bevy of foreign experts from Paris and Germany worked on Milan Cathedral.

It was by such interchanges that the flowing English curvilinear form of decoration came to the Continent, there to be translated into particular national versions from the fourteenth to the sixteenth century. In Spain it manifested itself in the ornate Manueline style of, for example, Burgos Cathedral. The Portuguese version, known as Plateresque, from the much-chased silverwork of the time, often has a nautical flavour with knotted ropes and encrusted sea symbols, for, like England, the seafaring Portuguese were embarking on world exploration. In Germany, English influence was far reaching, as we shall see when we compare vaulting forms. And in France in her late blossoming—the Flamboyant of the churches of Rouen, for instance—it inspired traceries that whirl and lick across the windows like leaves tossed by an autumn gale or the flames of the bonfires that consume them. In the rose windows, one of the most glorious architectural forms in Gothic architecture, patterns change from wheels to roses, from roses to flames.

Chapter House, Tomar

Clearly, trial and error played their part in the development of the vault. The early vaults were divided into four parts by the two hooped diagonal ribs that intersected at the boss stone. In the twelfth century, in Sens Cathedral, the rib number was increased to three hoops, so that the division of the vault became six. Closely linked with the development of the vault was the question of height, an important factor in producing the verticality so characteristic of French Gothic. It is thought that individual lodges each had their own rule-of-thumb as to the relation of height to width, but little more than that broad proportion was specified. If we compare the section of Rheims showing weights, buttresses and roof positions with the interior of Chartres, we have some insight into the factors controlling the building of vaults.

Chartres is the classic example of early French Gothic. Its basic shape was built in twenty-seven years, between 1194 and 1221; that is, all but its towers, which were built centuries apart, the simple octagonal south tower in the early thirteenth century, and the more elaborate north spire in about 1507; they were built, it should be noted, without any attempt to match the later to the earlier. However, it is not only in the matter of towers that Chartres is classic. Unlike the typical Romanesque church, built and financed by a great abbey, Gothic cathedrals belonged to the town. They were built not only in competition with neighbouring towns to the Glory of God, but also out of civic pride. As at St-Denis, much of the physical work was done by the parishioners themselves, lords and commoners together, peasants dragging the carts with stone from the quarries, tradesmen and craftsmen laying down their tools and deserting other jobs to meet the wagons at the town gate and pull them to the cathedral site.

Structurally, Chartres provides the classic three-storey model: an *arcade*, or row of arches, down either side of the nave, supported on piers; a middle row of arches, often quite low and frequently with a

*Nave of Amiens Cathedral
by Robert de Luzarches*

walkway, running round the *inside* of the church, called the *triforium*; and an upper row, or *clerestory*, that is heavily glassed. The section shows the two great sources of light: first, from the side-aisles, filtering through the nave arcades, and secondly, from the clerestory. The triforium runs inside the roof-space of the aisles and has no outlets to the exterior. There are examples where the triforium is pierced through to give light, and some where even a fourth level, a gallery, was introduced, but that was a relatively short-lived fashion.

Between the windows are the flying buttresses, connecting with the piers of the vault. These piers are always slimmer than the smooth expansive boles characteristic of Romanesque columns, but in some of the earlier cathedrals like Laon and Notre-Dame, Paris, the arcade is still made of single round columns, at least as far up as the capitals and the springing of the arches; it is only above that that we find the characteristic Gothic clustered shafts resembling bundles of wands. However, from the building of Bourges onwards, such clustered pillars became typical. In Chartres, Rouen, Soissons, Rheims, Amiens,

Tours, Strasbourg, Auxerre, Cologne, Toledo and Barcelona and in many English cathedrals, the upward movement of the clustered piers, like a fountain, starts from the floor and spurts, unfettered, into the roof vaults. The style reaches its pinnacle in the choir of Bristol Cathedral of 1300–10, where not so much as a capital causes a break in the upward surge.

Just how high they could shoot upwards without overreaching themselves had to be learnt from experience. Beauvais Cathedral, whose bishop is said to have suffered from the sin of pride, courted disaster: the double-aisled choir, probably built by Eudes de Montreiul, a master-mason who accompanied St Louis on his Crusade, speaks volubly of ambition, as does the soaring vault. And sure enough first the nave roof, and later the tower, fell. Nevertheless, at nearly 158 feet, it remains the highest Gothic vault.

But regal Rheims Cathedral drew herself up to 125 feet without incurring heavenly displeasure. Inside, the sensation of height is cleverly exaggerated by making the bases of the pillars shoulder-high, so that, standing in the aisle, one is dwarfed by the pillars before they even commence their upward climb. The unusual pyramid-shape of Bourges, with its double side-aisles of decreasing size, masks its height; it is only when you go into the inner aisle and look upwards and note that it has its own arcade, triforium and clerestory as if it were a nave, that you realize the very aisles swoop up to a vault as high as that of many a cathedral nave.

All things, says St Thomas Aquinas, should be ordered towards God, and so the clustered shafts draw the eye in two directions. Firstly they quicken and flicker towards God-made-man in the sacrament of the altar at the east end of the church; secondly, they carry the eye upwards to God-in-heaven, as in a copse of slim birch trees, one naturally looks up to where the sunlight is filtering through the leaves. In contrast to the austere development of barnlike preaching-churches of the friars, particularly in Germany and Italy, the aping of nature is carried to extremes when the copse becomes tropical forest in the extravagant spiral shafts bursting into painted foliage or palm-leaf vaulting above star-shaped serrated capitals in the late-German Gothic of Brunswick Cathedral (1469).

Some countries emphasized verticality on the exterior. Germany and Bohemia, particularly, liked towers; the soaring spire of Ulm Minster, designed by Ulrich Ensinger, was the highest of all.

But impetus in the development of pillars and vaulting came from England. In France, the classic period ends in about 1300, and there is a gap before the flourishing of the Flamboyant. The first half of the fourteenth century (before the Black Death killed a quarter of the population in 1348-9), was a particularly rich period in England. During this time there emerged window, vaulting and roofing styles which were to be highly influential in Europe.

In England Gothic had started quite humbly when the Cistercian orders settled there, establishing sheep farming and the woollen industry that were to provide the source of much of her wealth during the Middle Ages, as well as international contacts through her membership of the Wool Staple. Durham had early experimented with Gothic arches along with the round-headed Romanesque. But the classic French cathedral pattern, apparent in Canterbury, Lincoln, Chichester and the Henry VII Chapel at Westminster (built later, but consciously modelled on the French), was introduced when a French architect was recruited by the Chapter of Canterbury Cathedral. William, a native of Sens, a city then engaged in building a cathedral, persuaded the Chapter that the Norman remains, unsafe from a fire in 1174, should be scrapped and the project started afresh; and so, up until the time that he was injured falling off a scaffold and had to pass the work to another architect, he built at Canterbury a cathedral similar to the one at Sens.

But the native tradition, which can be traced back through the Norman Romanesque to the Anglo-Saxon church of St Lawrence, Bradford-on-Avon, doggedly persisted, however fashionable French ways were. It was this more rugged tradition which gave English Gothic its original characteristics—square-ended choirs without chevets (a direct continuation of the Saxon plan), exaggeratedly long naves, as at Lincoln, and sometimes double transepts. Most characteristic of all, in contrast to the astringency of French plans, where everything is economically drawn together within one over-all outline, English cathedrals have no concentration of space, but scatter their component units around in irregular patterns. If you look at all those differently shaped structures on the plan of Salisbury, for example, and remember that they all have to be roofed, it is not difficult to understand that experimentation in roofing and vaulting emanated from England.

There was another factor that encouraged English builders to experiment in roofing. Britain had always been to the fore as a seafaring nation, and was given to making full use of wood from forests which still covered much of the land—land often owned by the Church. It takes no feat of the imagination to see the similarities between the upturned keel of a boat and the vaulting of a church. All over England at this time, village churches sprang up, many built to the highest standard. Between the Conquest and the Gothic Revival of the nineteenth century, at least 1001 parish churches were built.

Apart from the use of a rich variety of local materials—different stones, brick, flints and tiles—their roofs and silhouettes are an interesting feature. There is an enormous variety of towers and spires, which are often bell-towers, particularly in the coastal areas, where the bells could be used to give warning of invaders; and inside there is a marvellous use of wood, both in the rood screens on which the *rood*, or cross, was carved or painted, and above all in the roofs.

The wooden structures, which bear names like trussed-rafter roofs, tie-beam roofs, collar-braced roofs and hammer-beam roofs, were to provide important ceilings in many of the grand secular buildings of the late Gothic period, demonstrating a continuing link between structure and beauty at a time when stonework decoration had ceased to have functional significance. In villages like March in Cambridgeshire, one can chance on a hammer-beam angel-roof, in which the

Salisbury Cathedral

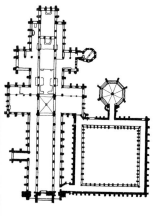

hammer-beam construction sends the weight of the roof-beams through the struts onto cantilevered-out hammer-beams, and we marvel at the sheer beauty of the flight of angels.

When those wooden techniques were translated into stone, the ribs on the vaulting were multiplied, far beyond structural necessity, so as to create a decorative web of carving comparable to the intricate work that was being developed in the window traceries. These extra struts have lovely names: *tiercerons* are the ribs that fan out from the wall shafts to meet the ridge, forming palm-tree shapes, as at Exeter Cathedral (1235–40), while the small decorative struts between the ribs, visible in the roof of Ely Presbytery (1335) are called *liernes*. After that, ribs proliferated in English cathedrals, and were rapidly adopted and further exploited on the Continent, notably in Germany, Bohemia and Spain, where the wide hall-churches (the Hallenkirchen of Germany) were popular with the friars because of their potential for preaching to large congregations. There was the skeleton vault, where the ordinary structural ribs are themselves supported by a separate series of detached vaults, seen in miniature in the Easter Sepulchre Chapel, in Lincoln. Perhaps the most thrilling examples of star vaults are in Germany. German masons brought the complex vaults to Spain, where they culminated in the star lantern of Burgos Cathedral. Net vaults, where the structural hooped ribs are interrupted to make lozenge and triangle patterns, provide another development. In England there appeared the beautiful fan-vault, the chief beauty of King's College Chapel, Cambridge, and of Henry VII Chapel, Westminster. A fashion peculiar to England, it was to retain popularity and develop well into the Jacobean period with extended pendant central bosses.

Gothic architecture was by no means without effect on secular buildings. Its influence was felt towards the end of the fourteenth century, about a century later than with the cathedrals. In the first half of that century, life was too hard for attention to focus on aesthetic matters. Famine resulting from a series of bad harvests in the early part of the century had left a population without resistance to the regular epidemics of disease (1400 people are said to have died

Star lantern, Burgos Cathedral

in three days in Avignon at one point) that led to the Black Death of 1348–50. A papal inquiry estimated that it killed about 40 million, a quarter of the population of Europe. But from then onwards, whether because the weather improved or because there were fewer mouths to feed, standards of comfort began to pick up. An interest in intellectual matters emerged, which was later to blossom in the individuality, learning, and commerce of the Renaissance.

The castle was the major example of Gothic in secular building. Its story is typical of the changes of the time. As the feudal wars tailed off, and particularly after gunpowder (invented between 1327 and 1340) became effective, it underwent several stages of evolution. The superb defensive fortifications based on the expertise of the Crusaders gave place to castles which still retained the trappings of a fortress, but whose defences were never put to the test; then came castles which retained their defences largely for stylistic reasons; and eventually there developed the fortified and moated manor-houses of England and ultimately the Renaissance palaces.

Towns also developed as trade increased. We have seen that the great Gothic cathedral belonged to a town or city, just as the great Romanesque abbey belonged to the country. Now there was another important development: the parish church. In the new atmosphere of peace and prosperity, towns, rarely with more than 5,000 to 10,000 inhabitants, were granted charters to run markets, and market-spaces appeared, usually under the shadow of a cathedral or parish church. English towns had market crosses, from where the town-crier proclaimed the news. Many still survive, like the fine octagonal Poultry Cross in Salisbury, with its ogee ribs and crown on top.

With increasing trade, other buildings appeared round the market area—town halls, craft and merchant halls and trade exchanges, some of whose high towers indicated that the secular world was competing with the Church in daily life. The silk market at Valencia had a high vault and twisted pillars. The magnificent Cloth Hall at Ypres, with its 440 feet-long façade, took one hundred years to complete. Although destroyed in 1915, it was so much loved that it was rebuilt.

Royal Castle of Saumur, from Très riches heures *of Duc de Berry, c. 1416. Musée Condé, Chantilly*

The half-timbered Guildhall at Lavenham, Suffolk, was built in 1529 during a boom in the wool trade. Few such structures were more elaborate than the beautiful Merchant Adventurers' Hall in York with its lovely timbering. Prosperous ports of the Hanseatic League of wool importers, like Hamburg, required harbours, wharves, customs houses and warehouses. Rich merchants built themselves beautiful houses; taverns appeared, so did theatres like the famous Globe Theatre in London, where some of Shakespeare's plays were enacted.

Some buildings developed from religious organizations and were associated with charity, like almshouses and hospitals, or with education, like the cathedral schools. But the new universities were symptomatic of a growing tendency towards independence from the Church. Neither the law school at Bologna, the second oldest university after Paris, nor the medical school at Salerno were associated with cathedrals. Oxford originated from a Church/State quarrel, when Henry II, furious that archbishop Becket took refuge from him in France, decided that English students should be barred from attending the university in Paris. Architecturally, the university derived from monastic buildings, its quadrangle for walking and reading mirroring the cloisters around which the monks walked and prayed. The chapel, the great hall which functioned as a refectory, and of course, the library were also monastic in origin. Stairs leading to the fellows' study-bedrooms were built into the corners of the courtyards. Ablutions in these venerable and civilized surroundings may today still be some distance away in a back alley as they were in the fourteenth century.

Carcassonne, Aude

Beaumaris Castle, Wales, by James of St George

Some great houses which were to become the homes of the rich started out under the aegis of the Church as the homes of bishops, the princes of the Church. They could be very grand, like the papal palace at Avignon, where the popes lived during the Great Schism. With a defensive fourteenth-century city clustering around it the papal palace shared with many other castles the feature of being not so much one building so much as a fortified town. This is also true of Aigues-Mortes, of 1240, a grid-plan town with about one hundred and fifty towers around its massive walls, and of the Emperor Frederick II's Castel del Monte, Naples.

Carcassonne is a walled town which shows the increasing pride in symmetrical defences. Frederick II, who was brought up among Roman remains in Sicily, set the fashion for symmetrically arranged fortifications which seem to have derived from ancient Roman forts. His castle at Prato, and the original Louvre palace, built by Philip II in the thirteenth century, moated, with a round central keep with pointed turret, were designed symmetrically, as were other châteaux in France and above the Rhine in Germany. Characteristically these castles were protected by water—sea, river or moat—above which the walls rose sheer and usually sloping inwards, with rounded corners so as to foil any besiegers' attempts to tunnel under and blow a breach across the corner angle with gunpowder.

Probably the best preserved remains from this period are in England. They include the 'perfected' castles built by Edward I in the thirteenth century to subdue Celtic revolts in Wales—Conway, Caernarvon, Pembroke, Harlech. Beaumaris, with its double curtain walls and outer moat, and two massive gateways each with four towers, two large and two small, one facing inland and the other out to sea, is as symmetrical and as comprehensively organized for defence as any. It was the last castle Edward I built, and was supervised by James of St George, Master of the King's Works in Wales. The Tower of London has a similar unity and coherence, although it has been changed and rebuilt in parts at later periods.

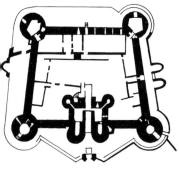

Harlech Castle, Merionethshire

Domestic arrangements were complex at this time, with provision
in different wings or towers for the private life of families whose
business made them live in the castle. Fireplaces still in the walls and
the relationships of suites of rooms within a great castle like Castle
Bolton in Wensleydale, Yorkshire, where Mary, Queen of Scots spent
part of her imprisonment, bear testimony to the tenement aspect of
castles of this time.

Where a single family owned the castle, the standard arrangement
was a central hall, used as a living-space by both family and servants,
going up through two storeys, with, grouped round it on one or two
floors, bedrooms, garderobes or lavatories in the corners, kitchen
quarters, a chapel, and sometimes a solar or private room. This
arrangement, sufficient but simple, can be seen in the lovely moated
manor house, Stokesay Castle in Shropshire. It was built in the late
thirteenth century and today, drowsing among ducks, wallflowers
and gilly flowers, looks far from warlike. The great hall has been
preserved for posterity by having been used as a barn.

In England, the progression from castle to manor house was
through the L-shaped plan of great hall and tower, to the T-plan,
where two-storey dwelling-quarters were set at right angles to the
hall, and finally to the arrangement whereby a second wing was added
on the other side to form an H-shape, so that the lord's family could
inhabit one wing and the servants the other, with access to each other
only through the hall. The staggered entry, a defensive feature, persisted for a long time.

In country and in town, the rich were buying themselves a civilized
life and creating houses decorated with great beauty and refinement
in a Gothic style which might betray their national origins. We see
this in the very French Gothic house of a merchant, Jacques Coeur, at
Bourges (1442–53)—with its decorated façade, fretwork balconies,
fireplaces carved like little windows, statues of ladies and gentlemen
leaning out to chat to their neighbours across the way, knobbly
pinnacles and canopies of the sort that characteristically appear in the

Jacques Coeur's house,
Bourges

William Grevel's house,
Chipping Campden,
Gloucestershire

background of fifteenth- and sixteenth-century stained-glass windows. Equivalent forms of all these details could be found on the façade or the furniture of late-Gothic cathedrals. That kind of Gothic detail was to persist in France for some time, amalgamating with Renaissance detail and arrangements in the rich houses and châteaux in France, the country most loath to relinquish the Gothic style, which had provided her period of greatest architectural glory.

An English translation of national Gothic detail from religious to secular use can be seen on a house of social standing similar to that of Bourges—the house of the wool merchant William Grevel in Chipping Campden, Gloucestershire. On the bow window on the street façade, slim stone mullions connect ground and first floor ranges of windows in a distinctly Perpendicular-style panel. The country-house of the abbot of Forde, Dorset, of 1521 is an elaboration of this style.

But the most splendid of the merchants' houses are those in Venice, the palazzi on the Grand Canal, and above all, that of the Doges, or heads of the Republic. Here the simple massing is complemented by the delicacy of the double row of arcades and discretely patterned rose and white marble on the upper storey, reminding one that Venice was a great trading centre that looked eastwards.

Distinctively national forms of Gothic manifest themselves not surprisingly in the town halls, the first secular expression of local civic pride. Germany and the Low Countries were well to the forefront and expressed their commercial dignity in characteristically steep-pitched roofs, often cut into with dormer windows, and combined with narrow decorative towers. Jan van Pede's Town Hall at Oudenarde, Brabant, of 1525–30, displays the integrity of a great work of art: its bottom arcade, two rows of Gothic windows, lacework parapets, steep roof and central crowning belfry have a total harmony of proportion and decoration. Less successful was the fourteenth-century top-heavy belfry that sticks up—not merely like a sore thumb but like

*Doge's Palace, Venice, by
Giovanni and Battista Buon*

Town Hall, Oudenarde, by Jan van Pede

Palazzo Publico, Siena

a sore thumb swathed in successive layers of bandaging—over the town hall of Bourges. There is a similar contrast between the unusual curved façade in stone and brick and slim bell-tower of the Palazzo Publico of Siena (1298) and the Palazzo Vecchio in Florence, which was started only one year later, an ungainly prison-like block with a clumsy torch-like belfry stuck on top, perhaps in the vain hope of emulating the beautiful striped campanile of the Cathedral.

And so we find ourselves at the transition from Gothic to Renaissance appropriately in Florence, where Renaissance architecture began. It is there that we start the next chapter of our story.

13

The Scale of Human Perfection

Architectural periods are never neatly bounded. So much do movements overlap that a mason working on Milan Cathedral (the greatest and according to some the only really Gothic cathedral in Italy) in the 1440s could have travelled to Florence one hundred and fifty miles away and found work there on a cathedral that represented a quite different attitude towards design. The work in question was the dome of Florence Cathedral, and its architect Filippo Brunelleschi (1377–1446), who trained as a goldsmith, was revolutionizing design and taste.

There had, of course, been domes before, like the Pantheon in ancient Rome and the Byzantine domes of the Ottoman empire. This one was different. Brunelleschi fitted a dome on top of an octagonal drum, and made no attempt to use pendentives. He invented a com-

View from Belvedere showing the dome of Florence Cathedral by Filippo Brunelleschi

plicated wooden form, around which his eight-panelled dome could be built in two layers, an inner and an outer masonry shell. Also different was the fact that the masonry ribs were tied together in a series of reinforcing 'chains' at strategic points in the form of bands of timber clamped with iron or of stone and iron. The cupola on the top was a temple of masonry acting as a weight holding the rather pointed dome together and preventing it from spreading apart.

That dome was by no means Brunelleschi's only or his most revolutionary contribution to the new movement. His Foundling Hospital of 1421, simple and serene, with graceful arcades of round-headed arches above slim Corinthian columns, plain rectangular windows directly above the centre of each arch and simple triangular pediment, was another inaugural building of the Renaissance. As for the chapel he created for the Pazzi family in the cloisters of the Franciscan friary of Santa Croce, it was not only perfect, but it was also a copy-book for Renaissance buildings.

In the first place, the Pazzi Chapel, entered through a tall arch in the loggia, was a revolutionary shape—no longer a nave and aisles, but a square covered by a dome, this time using pendentives. The centre of the chapel was the centre of the circle below the dome; the building seemed complete from every direction. Furthermore, the dimensions were all exact: the square of the chancel below the dome was half the total width. And the atmosphere was created by a very precise treatment of the wall surfaces, with decorative bands on the walls, arches and floor in a darker tone, indicating the proportions. Brunelleschi's two great churches, San Lorenzo and Santo Spirito, had basilican plans, but the same exactitude was there and domes were used at the crossings.

This kind of architecture came to dominate first Europe, then much of the world, for many centuries, and it is still to be found today. What had caused the transition from Gothic to Renaissance? On the one hand Gothic seemed played out. Every architectural style is bound at some time or another to reach a stage when it can no longer yield anything new. On the other hand, important changes had been taking place in society, especially in that section of society that commissioned buildings and employed architects.

Gunpowder changed the nature of warfare and therefore relations among nations. The invention of the compass and the development of new techniques in shipbuilding made it possible to expand the limits of the known world into China, the East Indies, India and America. Banking, no longer frowned upon by the Church, began to play a central role in society. Trade and banking made Florence rich. The hereditary nobles of feudal times were ousted by a new class of merchant princes—such as the Medici, the Strozzi, the Rucellai, the Pitti—whose commercial empires spread throughout Europe.

Merchant princes and the artists to whom they extended financial patronage became the new universal men of the Renaissance. Piero della Francesca's famous profile of Federigo da Montefeltro, Duke of Urbino, with its basilisk eye and hooked nose, does no justice to this renowned art-patron. Ruler of a little mountainous northern Italian kingdom, the Duke was a man of principle, gentleness and humanity. He was a distinguished soldier, but the Palace of Urbino, built for him by Luciano Laurana, a contemporary of Alberti, accurately represents the artistic side of his nature. The castle dominates the pantiled hill-top village. In the staterooms and courtyards (one lined with a loggia based on the Foundling Hospital, another sheltering a secret garden with access from the Duke and Duchess' apartments) scholars, philosophers, musicians and artists gathered, discussed and created. The Duke was himself accomplished in all these areas. He collected one of the finest libraries in Italy, now part of the Vatican Library, employing, it is said, thirty or forty scribes for fourteen years to copy the great classical and modern texts.

The key to a new vision of human life and therefore of architecture came from the scholars' access to these classical texts. International trading exchanges had helped to disseminate ideas, and a group of teachers of the humanities (grammar, rhetoric, history and philosophy), who acquired the name of Humanists, played a crucial part in their propagation. These texts were spread through developments in printing. Printing was invented long before in China, but in Europe a tremendous impetus was given to the spread of ideas by Gutenberg's invention of movable type in 1450. The first printed Bible was in 1456. And architectural texts followed shortly afterwards.

In 1415, G.F. Poggio, a papal secretary, had produced a definitive version of a manuscript by Vitruvius, the first-century architectural historian, which he had discovered in the library of St Gall in Switzerland. Now, in 1487, Vitruvius was one of the first writers to appear in print. The impact was tremendous. The architects of the revived antique style made great use of the new means of communication: Alberti, Serlio, Francesco di Giorgio, Palladio, Vignola, Giulio Romano wrote treatises that owed something to Vitruvius. These men were no longer master-masons, however brilliant; they were scholars. Architecture was no longer the continuation of a practical tradition, handed on through masons' lodges; it was a literary idea. The architect was not just putting up a building; he was following a theory.

The architect had at his disposal some exciting new discoveries. A new concept of spatial relationships had been made possible by the discovery of perspective by the Florentine painters in about 1425, or possibly by Brunelleschi himself. On top of that came one of those revelations that give a sudden unity to experience and open up a whole realm of meaning. That was the discovery that musical intervals in harmony were exactly proportional to numbers in physical dimensions. This was something that totally captured the imagination of the Renaissance. If harmonic ratios could be the same as physical ratios, not only was there a rule on which to base proportions but also music and architecture were mathematically related, and nature was displaying a wonderful unity. Thus it followed that a building could reflect in its dimensions the fundamental laws of nature and of God. A perfectly proportioned building would thus be a revelation of Godhead, a reflection of God in man.

The architect who brought such theories together in practice was

Leon Battista Alberti (1404–72). He was himself the ideal Renaissance man. An accomplished horseman and athlete, of whom it was said he could jump a man's height with both feet together, he painted, wrote plays and music and had written a treatise on painting before he produced what was to become one of the essential books of the Renaissance, *De re aedificatoria*. It was the first architectural book to be published, in 1485, in moveable type. He explained the theory of beauty based on the harmony of numbers and used Euclidean geometry to lend authority to the use of basic shapes—the square, the cube, the circle and the sphere—working out ideal proportions from these figures by doubling and halving. And he produced one of the crucial architectural statements of the Renaissance in defining beauty in a building as the rational integration of the proportion of all the parts, where nothing could be added or taken away without destroying the harmony of the whole.

One further aspect of Alberti was crucial to architecture and characteristic of the Renaissance—an interest in the powers and talents of the individual man. Man was, of course, as the mediaeval Church had stated, 'created in God's image and likeness'; but now the emphasis shifted: man assumed a new dignity in himself. Knowledge of the classics, geometry, astronomy, physics, anatomy and geography suggested that man had godlike capabilities. The humanists resurrected the adage of the ancient Greek philosopher, Protagoras, that 'man is the measure of all things'. Alberti, in creating a perfect church by combining ideal forms, believed himself to be creating an image of the Godhead. And this ideal form had a human face. Vitruvius, in Book III of *De architectura* had suggested that a building should reflect the proportions of the human figure. Leonardo da Vinci's famous drawing related human proportions to the ideal shape—the square and the circle; Francesco di Giorgio's diagram related them explicitly to the architecture of the time—a centralized Greek-cross plan with extended nave superimposed on a man's body.

Alberti's buildings are some of the landmarks of the Renaissance. To the church of S. Maria Novella in Florence he added a façade, strictly proportioned, which is one of the most memorable of all elevations. To link the nave and the lower aisles without sacrificing the horizontal layout characteristic of the new style, he designed huge scrolls which were to become part of the vocabulary of later architects. He created most of the façade of Sant' Andrea, Mantua, out of a triumphal arch. Here emerges the ancient Roman ABA motif, which was to appear in a hundred guises on Renaissance buildings—low

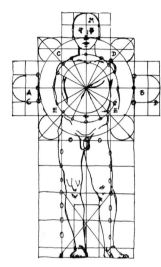

Francesco di Giorgio's human figure superimposed on centralized cruciform church plan

Palazzo Rucellai, Florence, by Leon Battista Alberti

arch, high arch, low arch; pilaster, window, pilaster; turret, dome, turret. In the Palazzo Rucellai, he used different orders for different floors—Doric, Ionic and Corinthian—as the Romans had done on the Colosseum. They were all very carefully proportioned.

The Palazzo Rucellai was only one of the many Florentine palaces that became a new building type. They usually presented tough un-inviting façades to the street, using rough masonry on the lower floors, known as 'rusticated' masonry, a word meaning 'countrified', for the stones were not smoothed off, but deliberately left rough-hewn as if they had come from the quarry. At the top, Alberti introduced a huge, jutting cornice which virtually hides the roof. Again this tended to become typical Renaissance, giving a concentrated boxy outline to a palace. The largest of all the Florentine palaces, the Palazzo Pitti, whose author is not known, makes a feature of the ground-floor windows by having a whole unit within an arch of rusticated masonry. Once inside the courtyard all was different; the prison-like exterior gave way to a scenario for gracious, hospitable and elegant living for very rich people.

Florence was the first of the three great Italian cities to foster the new style. The second was Rome and the third Venice. The phase which reached its climax, encouraged by papal patronage, is known as the High Renaissance. The architectural events in Rome were at first not unlike what had happened in Florence. Of the Renaissance palaces, the Cancelleria, built from 1486 to 1498 for Cardinal Riario, nephew of Pope Sixtus IV, marks the move of the hub of architectural enterprise from Florence to Rome. The elements are still apparent as the guidelines for the beautifully proportioned Palazzo Farnese com-menced by Antonio da Sangallo the Younger in 1541 and finished off by Michelangelo. A tunnel-vaulted passage plunges through the cen-tral doorway into the courtyard, and on either side are similar ranks of windows with straight cornices on the ground floor, while on the first floor the pediments above the windows alternate between tri-angular and round-headed segments.

The architect who dominated the early Renaissance in Rome was Donato Bramante (1444–1514). He grew up near Urbino, became a painter, spent some time in Milan, where he certainly knew Leonardo da Vinci, and came to Rome after Milan fell to the French king, Louis XI, in 1499. He had already shown the influence of Alberti in his work in Milan, but it was the work of the last twelve years of his life, in which he seems to have become imbued with the spirit of the ancients, that give him his place in history.

The building which came closest to representing the pure classicism of the Renaissance was the little temple he built on what was then thought to be the site of St Peter's martyrdom, the cloister of San Pietro in Montorio, on the Janiculum Hill. The Tempietto, con-sciously modelled on the ancient Roman temple of Vesta, fulfils all Alberti's prescriptions. Freestanding within its courtyard, with steps rising to a circular plinth, its form is a drum encircled by a Doric colonnade, trimmed with a low balustrade, through which the drum reaches up and is crowned with a dome—possibly architecture's finest gem. Its internal arrangements obey the rules, with high-placed windows showing blue skies, but are otherwise of little account. It is designed from the outside, and has that peculiarly dense quality of High Renaissance architecture, lacking the modelling of the interior in terms of space and light which we associate with the styles which were to follow. Yet it is not heavy, nor proud and intimidating like the palazzi. The wide-spaced colonnade on its raised plinth and the cut-out balustrade around the upper storey have all the charm, elegance and delicacy that you could ask of an ideal building.

Bramante's remarkable achievement was that, while the proportions of this building were in such harmony that it seemed that nothing could be added or subtracted without ruining the whole, its original conception has proved immensely flexible, for it has been successfully copied throughout the world. It was the inspiration for Gibbs' Radcliffe Camera in Oxford (1739-49), Hawksmoor's Mausoleum at Castle Howard, Yorkshire (1729), the dome on St Peter's, Rome (1585-90), on Wren's St Paul's Cathedral, London (1696-1708), the church of St-Geneviève (le Panthéon), Paris (1755-92), and even the Capitol, Washington (1851-67).

The building which symbolizes all the spiritual pomp and worldly power of Renaissance Rome is, appropriately, St Peter's. The old

Tempietto San Pietro in Montorio, Rome, by Donato Bramante

basilica dated from AD 330 and was built on what had been the Circus of Nero, where St Peter's martyrdom took place, beside an obelisk from the upper Nile which had been erected on the site in AD 41, before Nero built his circus. This obelisk, 84¼ feet high, had in due course to be moved—a feat of engineering which took six months and was conducted by Domenico Fontana (1543-1607) with the help of 907 men, all freshly shriven, 140 horses, 40 windlasses and two masses said at dawn on the first day.

Nor was the building of the cathedral easily accomplished. It involved many plans and major disputes on structural theory. The foundation stone was laid in 1506, but the building was not completed until over a century later, in 1626. The builders sound like a roll-call of the High Renaissance: Bramante (who was sixty when the work started), Raphael, Peruzzi, Sangallo the Younger, Michelangelo, Vignola, della Porta, Fontana and Maderna.

Bramante's original plan, which he and Leonardo da Vinci may well have discussed (Leonardo's sketchbook shows a design for a cathedral on a Greek cross-plan with five domes), was a Greek cross superimposed on a square with a central hemispherical dome supported on four massive piers. Each symmetrical arm of the cross protrudes in an apse beyond the square, allowing for four small Greek-cross side chapels, each roofed with a little dome, to be tucked into the angle of the arms of the big cross, with a tower on each of the four corners of the square. Bramante experimented with Roman concrete for the enormous piers and the great arches—far larger than any other used in this period. Raphael took over from him, but contributed nothing of great import. It was Giuliano da Sangallo (1445-1516) who brought the work on a step further, by strengthening the pillars and building the nave vault and pendentives to support the dome. He changed the designs for the dome from the classical hemisphere to a segmental one with ribs, some thirty feet higher than Bramante had intended.

But the dome, eventually completed by Giacomo della Porta (about 1537-1602) and Domenico Fontana, was in fact designed by the seventy-two-year-old Michelangelo, painter, sculptor and military

Interior of Medici Chapel, Florence, by Michelangelo

Staircase of Laurentian Library, Florence, by Michelangelo

engineer, who had turned architect in his old age. He returned to Florence for his inspiration, and to Brunelleschi's dome. The structure he designed has strong similarities to the Florence dome: it is made in two shells, it is mostly brick internally and its shape is of orange-peel segments supported by ribs held together with three iron chains.

What was Michelangelo's contribution? With a sculptor's eye for the three-dimensional, he bypassed the contemporary preoccupation with proportion to open up new concepts of scale and space—two areas in which the Baroque was later to experiment. It was, after all, through sculpture that he had come to architecture. He provided the setting for his sculptures of figures representing Night and Day, Evening and Dawn, around the chapel built onto Brunelleschi's San Lorenzo in Florence to house the tombs of the Medicis. But his stature and originality became apparent only a few years later in his designs for the Laurentian Library adjoining San Lorenzo (which was eventually to be completed with some modifications by other architects). The task here was to design a library in a long wing, where access was from a vestibule on the lower level. He made no attempt to recreate the balanced proportions of the Renaissance. On the contrary, he exaggerated the disparity of the two elements, by running a long low room off the upper part of a high, narrow block. A popular late Renaissance Mannerist trick, as we shall see, was to emphasize perspective by lines in moulding and decoration so as to create a room, a court or a street like a tunnel. Vasari uses it cleverly in his courtyard to the Uffizi, Florence, which sucks the visitors along and through the ABA gateway to the Arno beyond. Michelangelo managed somehow at the same time to provide a light-filled calm and dispassionate atmosphere essential to the reading-room that has become the model for a host of university libraries since. The anteroom, with its triple staircase and pillars halfway up the wall supporting nothing, but indicating the upper storey, is quite original.

Another Michelangelo hallmark, to be widely adopted by Palladio and others, was the creation of giant orders, that is to say, columns running up through two or more storeys, sometimes the entire height of a façade. They are best seen on the palaces that surround the Capitol in Rome. It was the sorting out of a cluster of very down-at-heel palaces here that gave Rome one of her most exciting vistas. On the spot where Romulus and Remus are said to have been discovered, and where Romulus founded the city, Michelangelo created a wide, shallow-stepped ramp rising to pass between antique statues of Castor and Pollux, protectors of Rome, to a trapezium-shaped piazza. A star in white stone spreads cosmic rays out across the paving in an oval pool of ripples—the first use of this shape in Renaissance architecture. On the Palace of the Senators, which closes the top of the square, and the two matching palaces to left and right, giant orders and pilasters link several storeys together.

Michelangelo's original use of classical motifs introduces a new phase in the Renaissance, Mannerism. This late sixteenth-century style deliberately flouts classical prescriptions. Jacopo Sansovino (1486–1570), Baldassare Peruzzi (1481–1536) and Sebastiano Serlio

Courtyard to Uffizi Gallery, Florence, by Giorgio Vasari

Campidoglio, Rome, reconstructed by Michelangelo

Cortile della Cavallerizza, Palazzo Ducale, Mantua, by Giulio Romano

(1475–1554) were among its exponents. The greatest Mannerist figure, Giulio Romano (1492–1546), a pupil of Raphael's and the first Renaissance artist to be born and raised in Rome, could play the classical game with as much ease as anybody. In fact, he expended as much intellectual exertion on breaking the rules as he did on keeping them in, for example, the Cathedral at Mantua. What the Mannerists did with classical detail was really a sort of in-joke. When Romano dropped a few wedge-shaped stones below the architrave in the courtyard of the Palazzo del Tè at Mantua, built for Duke Frederico Gonzaga II, he knew perfectly well that he was not actually making the structure unsafe, but he hoped it might make the uninitiated gasp with shock. The ruses reached fever-pitch in his Cortile della Cavallerizza of the Palazzo Ducale at Mantua, with its pock-marked rusticated arcades and giddy columns, like mummies attempting to struggle out of their wrappings.

A more serious Mannerist building is the Palazzo Massimo alle Colonne in Rome which Peruzzi started to build in 1532. It has a revolutionary façade, for it is curved. It is broken in the middle by an irregular portico, formed by a pair of columns, a space and a single column, on either side of the entry to a recessed front door. The first-floor row of windows in the upper wall is unexceptional, but the two rows above are quite odd, horizontally rectangular holes cut out of the façade, framed, as it were, in stone picture-frames, of which the lower row have scrolled curves like a sheet of parchment. The interior of the courtyard is much more impressive, while still maintaining an oddly modern appearance. At one end, an open loggia composed of two large single Tuscan columns, well spaced, shows an open hall with the passage of the front entrance leading away behind, and stairs going up on the left. The loggia is repeated by the balcony on the floor above, through whose pillars a coffered ceiling and a doorway beyond can be glimpsed. The total façade is much bolder and less regular than one would expect, extending beyond the private jokes of Mannerism and suggesting an impetus towards a new, broader canvas similar to that shown in Michelangelo's work.

The other great Mannerist architect was Giacomo da Vignola

*Palace of Urbino, Florence,
by Luciano Laurana*

*Pazzi Chapel, Florence, by
Filippo Brunelleschi*

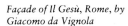

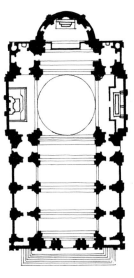

Il Gesù, Rome

(1507–73), whose church for the Jesuit order Il Gesù (1568–84), became the type for many later churches. But it was his pentagonal Palazzo Farnese at Caprarola (1547–9), incorporating many original features, like the circular open staircase off the circular cortile at its heart, terraces and oval paired steps, gardens and moat, that marked his work as some of the most imaginative and spectacular of the period.

The third centre of Renaissance architecture was Venice and its surrounding region. There the commanding figure is Andrea Palladio (1508–80). He was a precise and exact classicist. In his Villa Capra (Rotonda) near Vicenza (1550), a symmetrical building, he created an ideal place for a secular purpose, closely following Alberti's rules and spirit. He controlled the classical rules—not they him. It was as if he distilled the essence of classicism from the Vitruvian rules and the ancient models, and held the pure and colourless liquor up to the light. His buildings have the hallmark of elegance: the same ability that a diamond has—to be cool, and, simultaneously, to sparkle. Except for two churches in Venice, his buildings are around Vicenza. They are secular, reflecting the new importance of secular rather than religious buildings that makes the architectural character of the six-teenth century onwards different from what had gone before. Un-doubtedly aided by the dissemination of his architectural treatise, *I Quattro Libri dell'Architettura* of 1570, his work had an enormous influence in other countries, notably on the Georgian architects in eighteenth-century England, Thomas Jefferson and other architects in America, and in Russia. It is tempting to describe him as a symbol of the classical style, since he achieved, in a seemingly effortless manner the two most prized qualities of Renaissance architecture: exactitude and centralized plans. It is these qualities that give his buildings the humanity sometimes lacking in strict, formal classical buildings.

The plan of the Villa Rotonda, with its circular room covered by a

Palazzo Farnese, Caprarola, near Rome

dome set within a raised square, approached on all four sides by even flights of steps, shows that it was not particularly comfortable to live in. We shall see how Jefferson dealt with this problem in his version at Monticello. Its symmetry may undermine its comfort, but there is no questioning the beauty and dignity of its exterior and the views of the countryside it commanded.

With the Basilica (Palazzo della Ragione) in Vicenza, Palladio gave Europe one of its most popular architectural motifs, the Palladian motif, a central arched window or opening flanked by a flat-topped window on each side. It became one of the most widely used and effective features of great houses for several centuries. In his many other villas it was his extension of a regular plan to embrace outbuildings and the landscape that gave a lead to the landscaping movements of the eighteenth century. Rarely has an architect whose work was concentrated in such a relatively small area had such a world-wide influence upon buildings and their surroundings.

(below left) *Palazzo Massimo alle Colonne, Rome, by Baldassare Peruzzi*

(below right) *Villa Rotonda, Vicenza, by Andrea Palladio*

(bottom) *Villa Barbaro, Maser, by Andrea Palladio*

14

Urbanity crosses the Alps

Italian Renaissance forms were slow in crossing over the Alps. When it happened, the sixteenth-century Mannerist challenge and seventeenth-century Baroque theatricality were already opening up new fields of interest in Italy. Throughout most of this period the rest of Europe was still preoccupied in working through the national forms of Gothic they had evolved. Nationalism was emerging. In 1519, three monarchs, Henry VIII of England, the Habsburg Charles V of Spain, whose possessions included much of Italy and the German principalities, and Francis I of France all laid claim to the title of Holy Roman Emperor. Henry VIII's daughter Elizabeth established England as a power of consequence in Europe and beyond when she sent her pirate knights across the Atlantic to explore the New World. Spain and Portugal, briefly united under Philip II, were also intent on extending their realm of gold in the Americas. As for France, successive ministers—Richelieu, Mazarin and Colbert—built up the absolutism of their monarch until Louis XIV (1643–1715) could style himself Le Roi Soleil and say grandly: 'L'état c'est moi'.

All of this affected the changes in architecture. Before Louis XIV's time, Francis I had transferred his capital from the hunting lodges and

Château de Chambord, Loire, by Domenico da Cortona, modified by French masons

Château de Chambord, Loire

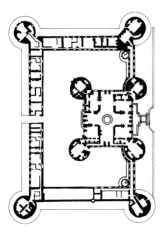

the easy aristocratic life of the Loire Valley to hard-centred and politically conscious Paris. The king's court became the administrative centre of French life—not just for law and commerce, but also for the arts and the basic services—roads and canals and even forestry. Architects were among those whose status was affected: Claude Perrault, who was working on a new wing of the Louvre Palace in the 1660s formally became a civil servant. England too made architectural status official; the king had long had his master mason, but in 1615 Inigo Jones received the title of Royal Surveyor.

Nationalism was not the only thing working against the import of Italian ways from the sixteenth to eighteenth century: there was also the question of religion. To the more austere northern countries that had embraced Protestantism, the Catholic temperament demonstrated in the later Italian Renaissance held no attractions; in some cases it actually repelled. Europe at this period was racked by religious conflicts and wars.

What happened to the architecture of those countries was simply this. Italian architects might enjoy themselves breaking the rules. Beyond the Alps this did not apply. For these people not only did not know the classical rules, but also did not know that there were any rules to break. Slowly, Renaissance details, patterns and structures filtered through, first into France and later throughout Europe. They were sometimes adapted, but often, they were simply copied and added on quite incongruously to buildings which were still fundamentally Gothic in style.

One of Francis I's châteaux on the Loire, Chambord, is a case in point. At first glance, the symmetry of its plan seems perfectly respectable from a Renaissance point of view. It shows a square within a square, although not concentrically placed. As with Italian palaces, the inner courtyard, surrounded on three sides by wings, is reached through a centre doorway on the front façade. But at Chambord, two thirds of the entry façade is just a screen, and it is only the central block, the *corps de logis*, which is the actual living quarters for the family. We now see that the plan is basically that of the English Gothic castle: the *corps de logis* is the keep, the courtyard the bailey, but so well integrated is this in Renaissance symmetry that we can only fully spot it from the air or in plan when we note that there are corner towers on the corners of the courtyard and on the four corners of the *corps de logis*.

Apart from the symmetry, what other Renaissance elements can we identify? There is an arcade along the ground floor, and horizontal rows of windows above. But while on an Italian palace each storey of windows may be different—perhaps with a different order, or one row with double or coupled columns on each side of the windows, the next with perhaps only an intermediate pilaster—here the windows are equal, and so placed that they create vertical stripes up the façade which are quite as assertive as the horizontal divisions. And what about the roof? Far from melting away behind a parapet, here are steep northern slopes, dotted with dormer windows. On the corner turrets and especially over the central *corps de logis*, there is a host of

Renaissance detail in the form of gables, chimneys, lanterns and crowns. But would any Italian skyline ever permit such a mixture of shapes to jostle so violently against each other? It is like a market-day crowd; one can almost hear the hubbub. That rooftop is very mediaeval and very French, no matter how its architect, Domenico da Cortona, tried to disguise it with sophisticated Italian trappings.

And what do we make of the little miracle of engineering, the unique double spiral staircase? It is a free-standing cage of stone

*Galerie François I,
Fontainebleau, decorated by
G.B. Rosso, Francesco
Primaticcio and others*

*Double staircase, Château de
Chambord, Loire*

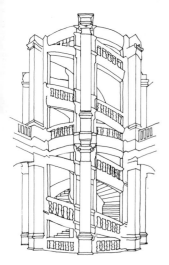

placed at the crossing of the Greek-cross hallways within the square *corps de logis*. It rises through the elliptical barrel-vaulted ceiling and up to the central lantern on the exterior. If the supporting piers have something in common with Gothic buttresses, its ingenious planning (so that people entering or making a getaway might not see each other as they pass on the same stairs) could only have been fathered by Renaissance intrigue. In fact, Leonardo da Vinci made a sketch for such a staircase.

Leonardo was only one of several Italian artists who made their living in France, having been recruited by Francis I to his court. He died twenty-five miles away from Chambord, in 1519, the year they started building the château. The wars in Italy between the Emperor Charles V and Francis I of France were one reason for his move. Francis I's patronage was an enormous draw, for it ranked second only to that offered by the papal court. Sebastiano Serlio, a Mannerist whose writings were to have an impact in Europe, came to Francis' courts in 1540 and stayed until his death twenty-five years later. He designed the château at Ancy-le-Franc in 1546 on a somewhat similar layout to Chambord, only really giving way to French taste in the matter of the high, steep roofs, and even here, he dispensed with the dormers. (Roofs were very important to the French, one kind of roof is even called after the architect who invented it—the *mansard* roof with a steep boxy side to it that allows the architect to stuff virtually a full-height row of rooms into it.)

In 1532 arrived the painter Francesco Primaticcio, a friend of Giulio Romano with whom he had worked on the Palazzo del Tè. He made the Galerie François I inside the Château of Fontainebleau sizzle with vitality. Here was the first use of strapwork—stucco shaped like curled leather—which was to prove one of the most popular and character-

*Château de Chenonceaux.
Bridge and gallery by
Philibert de L'Orme and
Jean Bullant*

istic motifs of the transalpine Renaissance, particularly in the Low Countries and in Spain.

Francis I was an important patron of the movement. He commissioned much of the Renaissance work on the palaces of the Loire, Chambord, Blois, Fontainebleau and, after the move to Paris, the Louvre. The Bohiers, a bourgeois family of financers, commissioned the Châteaux of Chenonceaux and Azay-le-Rideau. Chenonceaux consisted of a simple *corps de logis* descended from the Gothic keep, until Philibert de L'Orme, at the command of Henri II's mistress, Diane de Poitiers, added, in three years, a ravishing five-bay bridge in white stone, along which Jean Bullant later added a three-storey gallery to preen and admire itself in the ripples of the blue-green water. At Blois it is undoubtedly the wing, full of Renaissance motifs, that Francis added to the château Louis XII had begun in 1498 and later work by François Mansart (1598–1666) that excites the attention. It is emphatically horizontal with an elegant arcaded gallery along the garden front. Here again, built into an octagonal tower, is a sophisticated open spiral staircase, up whose balustrade creeps the King's salamander and the initial 'F' for Francis.

Interior of St-Etienne du Mont, Paris, by Philibert de L'Orme

But the coming and going of artists was not the only way in which Renaissance ideas filtered through to the rest of Europe. Some ideas were expressed on paper, in the pattern-books that were being produced in abundance in Italy. Since most transalpine architects had never seen the ancient ruins nor their Renaissance derivatives, they were very dependent on these books, and too often, with no true understanding of the classical revival, they used them as a bran tub, dipping in and picking out ideas and employing them at random. Sometimes, where an architect had individual flair, an extraordinarily effective marriage of disparate elements took place.

Philibert de L'Orme, on the basis of pattern-books and a few brief visits to Italy, was capable of such inventiveness. In the Church of St-Etienne du Mont, Paris, he built an incredible screen with a balcony across an unaltered Gothic nave. It could be reached from either side by a swelling, curving staircase. The breathtaking charm of the screen owes its sweeping concept to Renaissance freedom of approach, yet when we look at it closely we realize that the fretwork patterning is Gothic in origin.

But not all transalpine architects had de L'Orme's genius. Many misapplied the orders, transplanting them out of context, with no reference to structure, proportion or scale. So the Renaissance effect was often only skin-deep. Matters were not helped in the latter part of the period, when pattern-books of decoration only, separate from their architectural basis, started to go the rounds, mostly in the Low Countries and in Germany. Cornelius Floris (1514–75) and Vredeman de Vries (1527–1606) of Holland were two such authors; Wendel Dietterlin of Germany, said to be demented, was another. The writhing fantasy, verging on a Bosch-like phantasmagoria, that Dietterlin would project onto a flat wall surface gave the kind of effect to be seen on the Otto-Heinrichsbau in Heidelberg Castle. It is as clotted with writhing figures as a Hindu gopuram.

There is another basic drawback to the learning of styles from books, namely, that prints are two-dimensional. At this time, we must remember, many architects were still coming into this field of work from outside. Francesco Primatticio was a painter, Inigo Jones a designer of masques; Claude Perrault (1613–88), who built the later wing on the Louvre, was actually a doctor. Relationship of outside to inside, which makes for truly great architecture, is not easy to achieve; not all architects are capable of thinking in three dimensions. Some façades evolved from copy-book plates, however originally employed, retain a flat appearance, a steel-engraving quality of over-precision, which can render them very dead. The Louvre has a copy-plate flavour about it, even though Perrault made history by treating a tall ground floor as a podium on which to build a ground-floor loggia of giant coupled columns.

Luckily the story at this point is brightened by the odd original. Elias Holl (1573–1646), City Architect to Augsburg, came back from a visit to Venice in about 1600 with a taste for Mannerism. A contemporary of his, Jacob van Campen (1595–1657) built a Town Hall at Amsterdam that was sufficiently grave and classical to be transmuted into a royal Palace. But Holl in his Town Hall at Augsburg took the bold step of adopting, as Cornelius Floris (1514/20–75) did at Antwerp, a council room that ran right through the top floor; moreover Holl filled his with light from windows placed on both sides and by painting it white. Even more original was what he did with the Arsenal at Augsburg. In a masterly way, he retained the tall narrow height so characteristic of a German house, traditionally set gable-end onto the road. But the Arsenal looks you proudly in the eye, in spite of the extremely mannered way in which window frames are wrenched apart on either side of the window, and its gable end culminates in a broken pediment with an odd bulbous ornament in the middle.

Town Hall, Antwerp, by Cornelius Floris

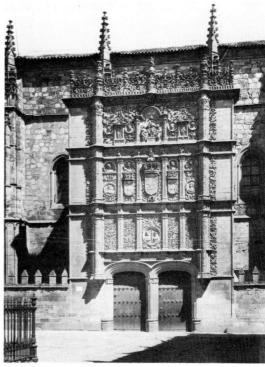

The same conflict between an undiscriminating adoption of motifs and a serious attempt to build in the classical idiom can be seen in other countries. In Spain, the Plateresque or silversmith's style of elaborate and close decoration in low relief on a flat wall surface was carried over from the Gothic of Queen Isabella with no pause—merely a further mixture of motifs. The incrustation of a seafaring scene, which we saw on the outside of the convent at Tomar, is reiterated, with the addition of strapwork and other devices, on the classical doorway of Salamanca, the university that had nurtured so many humanists.

Arsenal, Augsburg, by Elias Holl

Doorway to library, University of Salamanca

It was in Spain that there occurred the most bleak expression of religious feeling; it had its roots not in reformist puritanism but in Counter-Reformation Catholicism (as well, that is, as emotional desiccation on Philip's part). Pope Pius V was deeply ascetic and zealous in his clearing up of the libertine church of Renaissance Rome. The spirit of penitence spread to the Emperor, Charles V, who in 1555 abdicated to live out the rest of his live in a monastery. His son Philip II followed the architectural style of his father, shunning the elaborate forms being developed in Italy and built a palace that centred around a chapel and included a monastery and a college. There was no room here for private Mannerist jokes or any hint of relaxation or pleasure.

The Palace is called the Escorial since it is built on a slag-heap on the lonely rolling plains thirty miles from Madrid. It dominates the surrounding village as that other palace at Urbino did, but in a very different way. The gaunt cliff of its podium base, with rows of windows higher up, suggests at first that it could be a prison. Its high severe walls enclose a symmetrical complex of courtyards and buildings, in the centre of which a classical portico with a pediment identifies the position of the domed chapel which replaces the Holy of Holies in Solomon's Temple, on which the palace was modelled. That this bleak, bloodless appearance was intended we know from recorded instructions given by Philip to his architect, Juan de Herrera (about 1530–97), who took over from the original designer, Juan Bautista de Toledo (d. 1567). He demanded 'simplicity of form, severity in the whole, nobility without arrogance, majesty without ostentation.'

But in more bourgeois parts of Europe, where prosperous middle-class housing was springing up, a smaller palace design was demanded of the architects. This indicates the changing social and economic climate of the time. Whereas in the Middle Ages the bulk of building was ecclesiastical, now the stock of secular building started to increase. In the Catholic countries during the Renaissance, about half the buildings were used for religious purposes, the other half for secular. In the Protestant areas, with their emphasis on commerce, secular far outweighed religious. One reason for this was that since so many churches had been built in the Gothic period there was no need for more. England's inheritance of parish churches was so great that none were built for over a hundred years.

During this time in England, small manor houses mushroomed. They were built to house the rich merchants. The half-timbered wooden house at Weobley, Hereford, and the Cotswold-stone house at Chipping Campden, Gloucestershire, are good examples of merchants' houses. The E and H plans, to be found at Cothay in the Tudor and Jacobean periods, now widened. The middle section of the H was filled to create a distinctive house type that was less dependent on Gothic or Renaissance influences than on its own needs. The

Escorial Palace designed by J. B. de Toledo and completed by J. de Herrera

Elizabethan house at Longleat in Wiltshire, for which Robert Smythson was mason, set the tone for that distinctive English type of building, striped vertically down its wide frontage with slightly projecting bay windows, and emphasized horizontally with slim stringcourses separating the rows of hundreds of mullioned windows. In a country where it was important to let in as much light as possible, new techniques in glass-making were promptly incorporated into the new designs. Clear glass, known in the Roman Empire, was rediscovered by the Venetians in the fifteenth century and glass-blowers brought it to England in the sixteenth century. During the sixteenth and seventeenth centuries windows got larger and larger, until of another Smythson house it could be said 'Hardwick Hall, More glass than wall'. The same was true of Wollaton Hall.

Wollaton Hall, Nottinghamshire

Bay windows and the sharply jutting bays called oriel windows were popular. Perhaps England was more concerned with her womenfolk and their comfort than were other countries; there was great play with windows with built-in window seats, where the ladies might sit and sew, and, another English peculiarity, long galleries running the length of the house on the first floor, where the ladies might promenade when the weather proved inclement. Then in the seventeenth century sash windows with chequered window-bars came to England from Holland. Their name derives from Dutch *sas*, sluice, and French *chassis*, frame. They were universally adopted and arranged in double squares one above the other, to impart the characteristic verticality of the English Georgian terraced town-house.

Chimneys connecting with enormous hearths shaded by handsome chimney-pieces had always been important in England. Tudor houses also went in for marvellous skylines: twisted, chevroned, clustered and proudly single chimney stacks, turrets, crenellations and Dutch

Wollaton Hall, Nottinghamshire, by Robert Smythson

Escalera Dorada, Burgos Cathedral, by Diego de Siloe

gables abounded, and persisted in English taste for many years. It is such details, in a period of domestic growth, that determine not only the plan but also much of the character of a house.

Stairways, for example, were highly expressive of the architectural character of the age. The mediaeval stair had been little more than an enclosed ladder, or, in the case of castles, a stone spiral enclosed in a turret. Now in sixteenth-century Spain, experiments in the development of new stair types were taking place. There were three types: stairs that spiralled around a usually rectangular stair well; T-shaped stairs where the bottom flight split into two arms moving off to left and right (this form has almost unlimited variations according to stair shape, angles and balconies, for example the Palazzo Farnese at Caprarola and the Escalera Dorada of 1524 at Burgos Cathedral, by Diego de Siloe); and stairs set around a rectangular well, with each successive flight bending sharply back to run parallel to the lower flight. This type makes its first appearance in the Escorial. To these Palladio added a fourth type: a free-standing flight fixed to the wall at one end only and supported on an arch. This last pattern was made good use of in street scenery, perhaps most excitingly in stair-bridges over canals in Venice.

The adoption of the first type of stairs, starting immediately within a hall at the front door, spiralling around an open well and lit from above by a cupola or skylight, established the pattern for English town-houses built after the Great Fire of London of 1666 and up to the twentieth century. They were tall narrow houses, at first with only

(opposite) Double-Cube Room, Wilton House, Wiltshire, by Inigo Jones

a few rooms on each floor, often one to the front and one to the back. In the gracious version of Georgian Britain, notably in the three capitals, London, Edinburgh and Dublin, the family living-rooms were on the first floor. The dining-and sitting-rooms were often connected by folding doors, hence the term 'withdrawing' or 'drawing room'—the room to which one withdrew after dinner. Houses were entered from the street, usually up steps which curved over the basement area and servants' entrance. Behind the basement, there was a straight strip of garden between walls.

In France the town-house layout was much less uniform in regard to the number of floors and patterns of accommodation. A central gateway in the street façade, with a concierge on guard, very commonly gave access to a courtyard around which lay service wings, stables and later coachhouse wings. Behind the far side of the courtyard was a formal walled garden. The later development was to set the living quarters across the back of the service courtyard, with the salon and display rooms overlooking the garden behind. More modest were some early terraced planned schemes like that of Henri IV's Place de Vosges (until 1800 called the Place Royale) of 1605-12. It consisted of quiet, practical houses of brick, with stone window surrounds and quoins (corner edges) and dormers in the mansard roofs, laid out in a scheme alongside his new Pont Neuf, which joined islands in the Seine—the first Paris bridge to have no houses on it. In Brussels, a public square surrounded by guild houses was built after the siege of 1695. It was the last example of what was once standard in mediaeval Flemish towns. The Grand' Place has a typical Low Countries Renaissance collection of Gothic decorative detail mixed with porticoes supporting balustraded balconies, restrained pilasters, pedimented gable-ends, some with a clutter of urns and shells added at a later date.

In the seventeenth century, Holland was the place for the mature creation of Renaissance town-housing on a large scale. The houses along canals, such as the Prinsengracht in Amsterdam, are tall and narrow, built in a terrace with their gable-ends onto road or canal.

Prinsengracht, Amsterdam

But they are not uniform. The narrow frontage announces few rooms per floor. Unlike the English, the Dutch, constrained by the canals, retained into the twentieth century the steep narrow enclosed flights of stairs of the Middle Ages. The corollary was large windows, for furniture had to be hauled into upstairs rooms on ropes. The Prinsengracht was the fashionable street for gentlemen, but many humbler streets are equally charming, with their rising and dipping skylines of curved gables. The interiors of some of these houses, with patterned floors in black and white tiling and the distinctive contrasts of light sources with smudged shadow, have been preserved in the paintings of Vermeer and Pieter de Hooch. Similarly varied skylines were created elsewhere in Europe, for instance in the old Moravian town of Telc in Czechoslovakia.

Banqueting House, Whitehall, London, by Inigo Jones

Mauritshuis, The Hague, by Jacob van Campen

It was Holland that produced outstanding examples of another very northern translation of the Renaissance: small palaces, neat and comprehensive, yet retaining dignity and elegance. Such is the Mauritshuis in The Hague—a small-scale palace beside a lake, built in about 1633 by Jacob van Campen. Its rooms are set symmetrically about a central stairway, and the exterior is given an appearance of natural and quiet imperiousness by the use of giant pilasters. The inspiration for these buildings was, of course, Palladio. But the Dutch discovered a scale fitting for both dignity and domestic comfort.

The same qualities and the same influence are apparent in England in the work of Inigo Jones (1573-1652), who discovered Palladio on a journey through Europe at the age of forty, and became so enamoured that he covered the flyleaf of his copy of Palladio's *I Quattro Libri dell' Architettura* with attempts to make his signature like that of his hero. Before becoming interested in architecture, Jones had excelled in designing costumes and theatrical effects for the mythological masques beloved of James I and his court. Perhaps he had had enough of excesses by the time he came to architecture; at any rate he took his new art very seriously. After he was appointed Royal Surveyor, he returned to Italy for serious study. In the Queen's House at Greenwich, the Banqueting House in Whitehall, and Wilton House in Wiltshire, he conceived both plan and façade in a Palladian unity of proportion and design. In all three he used the cube.

The Queen's House, the first English villa in the Italian style, was originally built, by a whim of Queen Anne of Denmark, in two wings of three cubes each, connected by a bridge that straddled the main London to Dover road. After Jones' death his pupil, John Webb, added two further bridges in 1662 to make the total building a cube; later the road was re-routed and long, flat-roofed colonnades were built, where before the road had been, to connect the two wing pavilions. The rooms are beautifully proportioned, and the famed Tulip Staircase, whose wrought-iron balustrade is composed of swaying tulips, spirals upwards in a breathtaking Baroque curve, delicate as the whorl of a shell. The Banqueting House in Whitehall was built to replace the Old Banqueting Hall that was destroyed by fire. Rows of Ionic and Composite columns on the classical exterior suggest that it is two-storey, but inside there is one superb double-cube room, with a gallery at first-floor level, and a magnificent ceiling painted by Rubens.

Briefly imprisoned by the Parliamentarians in the Civil War, Inigo Jones was released to work with John Webb at Wilton House. Here there are two state rooms, a single and a double cube, the latter with white and gold decor to show off a collection of portraits by Van Dyck. To balance the excessive height demanded by the double-cube proportion, Inigo Jones used what is known as a coved ceiling, where a deeply curved section joins the walls to the ceiling. Here it is richly painted and delineated with gilt swags of fruit.

The wealth and diversity of inspiration in Renaissance architecture escalated into an even more richly spectacular movement in the seventeenth century—the Baroque.

Queen's House, Greenwich

15

Drama: Baroque and Rococo

The Renaissance return to classicism lasted for two hundred years. During the second half of this period, as we have seen, there was a growing dissatisfaction with the strict, rational ordering of the elements of building, which was the essence of the style; people had begun to find it mechanical, boring or constricting; the quest for the ideal and for perfect equilibrium no longer seemed significant.

Beginning where Michelangelo left off, a new generation of Roman architects abandoned the antique and threw themselves into an art that overspilled all established boundaries and conventions. Some people consider this effusiveness as bad taste and speak of Baroque architecture as decadent Renaissance. We can see what is meant by this if we look at the extreme form that developed in Spain, in the work of a family of stuccoists called Churriguera. The sacristy of La Cartuja (Charterhouse) at Granada, 1727–64, shows this incredible

Interior of the Cartuja, Granada

style at its most prolific, with an embarrassment of mouldings in white stucco, repeated three or four times like a series of little pleats or folds. Others respond to Baroque as the artists intended them to: they involve themselves in the drama and excitement that the artists sought to communicate, and are carried away by the infectious vitality of the art. For those who respond in this way, the Baroque period constitutes not a distasteful exhibition of excess, but the glorious fulfilment of the Renaissance.

Artistically, the Baroque was a very rich movement in painting, sculpture, interior decoration and music. The Renaissance proper had not concentrated especially on music; but now the Baroque countries led the field. It was from the curved walls of Italian churches that the Mass settings of Monteverdi and Vivaldi first reverberated, and from the palace salons of Germany and Austria, from gold-legged chairs between walls decorated with white and gold stucco and beneath ceilings crowded with tumbling figures trailing draperies in rich blues and reds, that the chamber music of Haydn, Bach and Handel were played. It was probably about this time, too, that the process of composing music to fit the room was reversed and a start was made on the science of acoustics in architecture. Rooms were built that had the reverberation time that music required. Theatre made a comeback at this period, and opera, which had originated in Italy at the end of the sixteenth century, came into its own and spread throughout Europe as a popular art form.

This exuberant architecture, starting in Rome, was confined within a territory which included Italy and Spain, Austria, Hungary and Catholic Germany. France really came into the story only at the end of the period, in the first decades of the eighteenth century, with the elegant form of interior decoration called Rococo. On the other hand, parts of the Holy Roman Empire—southern Germany, Austria and Hungary—were to produce much of the richest and most magnificent examples of Baroque, like the abbey church at Rohr near Regensburg, the abbey church of Ottobeuren, Bavaria, and the pilgrimage church of the fourteen saints, Vierzehnheiligen, in Franconia. Several German provinces and the Vorarlberg in Austria became nurseries of craftsmen-builders, sculptors and stuccoists, and there are lavishly decorated Baroque palaces in Russia and Scandinavia, like the Royal Palace in Stockholm by Nicodemus Tessin (1615–81). What the original Baroque countries had in common is that they remained Catholic after the Reformation.

The Jesuits, the spearhead of the Counter-Reformation, who planned their missionary forays with all the care of a military campaign, recruited some of the leading exponents of the Baroque movement. In *The Architecture of Humanism* Geoffrey Scott suggests that it was a piece of conscious (and brilliant) psychological insight on the part of the Jesuits to use the exciting forms of the Baroque to 'enlist in the service of religion the most theatrical instincts of mankind'.

And unquestionably Baroque was dramatic. The adjective applies to all the things by which we distinguish Baroque from Renaissance architecture. Brunelleschi, it is said, desired to please, Bramante to ennoble. But both were very concerned with whether their work was correct. Neither of the third or fourth Bs by which we can remember the founding fathers of the Renaissance's stylistic phases, Bernini and Borromini, had any such concern. The Baroque has no pedantic desire to teach, no moralistic desire to judge if the finished object is up to standard. It seeks only to carry us away with emotion.

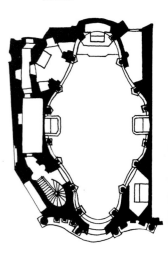

Baroque architects deserted symmetry and equilibrium to experiment with new and vigorous massing. We can see this in the Belvedere, Vienna, built in 1720-4 for Prince Eugene of Savoy by Lucas von Hildebrandt (1668-1745). The Belvedere has a wide, expansive window-patterned façade, low-domed turrets at the sides and dramatic stepping roof line, all pulled together by the great centrepiece with giant triple-arched doorway and giant curving pediment. It *is* symmetrical, but not with any pompous regularity. We can see similar banked-up massing, with detail converging to a central point on many other palaces. There is the Stupenigi at Turin by Filippo Juvarra (1678-1736), which although a mere hunting-lodge has a ballroom three storeys high; the Zwinger, Dresden, a pavilion by Matthaeus Pöppelmann (1662-1736), whose upper floor is an open gazebo topped by an ornate crown lantern and whose crazy festivity tells all the world of the flamboyant purpose for which it was built—as orangery, play-house, art gallery and background to the great open square in which Augustus the Strong of Saxony intended to devote himself and his court to games, jousting and feasting in the mediaeval manner.

That was the Baroque's first bid for freedom. The second was that it deserted the static form of the square and of the circle for shapes that swirl and move: S-curves, undulating façades and plans based on ovals. We can look at no better example than Borromini's first church, his tiny, exquisite San Carlo alle Quattro Fontane in Rome, on which he put the façade in 1665-7. Although he had to squash it into a very cramped site, both the plan and the rippling front set the pattern for future Baroque church experiments.

The third breakaway feature of the Baroque was an extreme form of theatricality, which involved the creating of illusion. The Baroque is fertile with examples of *trompe-l'oeil*; there are the carved curtain swags of blue painted wood around the curtains in Harewood House, Yorkshire, and a violin appears to hang from a ribbon on the back of the music-room door at Chatsworth, Derbyshire, amazingly realistic, with the door appearing to stand slightly ajar.

The sculptor Giovanni Lorenzo Bernini (1598–1680) makes it quite clear in the Ecstasy of St Theresa in the Cornaro Chapel of Santa Maria della Vittoria in Rome, that he is staging a little play, for although St Theresa's central figure is agonizingly realistic, he has carved theatre boxes near the tableau and set members of the Cornaro family in them, watching.

Let us look at some of these Baroque effects in actual use. The two founding figures of the Baroque were Bernini and Borromini. They set the style; but their genius was too incendiary for general export, and it was the rather milder forms of their innovations propagated by Carlo Fontana that spread throughout Europe as 'late international Baroque'. Architects came to Rome to study under Fontana. He taught two of the great Austrian architects, J.L. Hildebrandt, designer of the Belvedere, and his fellow church and palace builder Johann Bernhardt Fischer von Erlach (1656–1723), as well as Filippo Juvarra, whose work is largely round Turin, and the Scotsman, James Gibbs (1682–1754). Another fascinating figure was Juvarra's predecessor, Guarino Guarini (1624–83). Like Juvarra, he was a priest—indeed a professor of philosophy and mathematics—who turned to architecture and created the highly influential churches of San Lorenzo, Turin, and the

Ecstasy of St Theresa, Santa Maria della Vittoria, Rome, by Lorenzo Bernini

Dome of the Chapel of the Holy Shroud, Turin, by Guarino Guarini

Aerial view of St Peter's, Rome

Chapel of the Holy Shroud (Il Sindone) which houses the famous and disputed length of linen that is said to bear the marks of Christ's body.

Bernini opened the Baroque with a fanfare of trumpets from where Michelangelo had left off, first by building inside St Peter's an ornate canopy over the tomb of St Peter directly under the dome, secondly by creating an illusion of a burst of heavenly glory round the ancient wooden throne reputed to be St Peter's, and finally by erecting the double colonnade which clasps the vast piazza before the Cathedral.

Giovanni Lorenzo Bernini had more things in common with Michelangelo than his association with St Peter's. His first medium was sculpture. He was an infant prodigy. Like Michelangelo, he lived into his eighties. Like Sir John Vanbrugh his versatility extended to the theatre, for he wrote plays and operas; in fact, the typical background for an architect to have at this period, other than the plastic arts, was either the theatre or military engineering. The English essayist and traveller, John Evelyn, describes how, when in Rome in 1644, he attended the opera for which Bernini had 'painted the scenes, cut the statues, invented the engines, composed the music, wrote the comedy and built the theatre.'

The bronze baldachino, a tall canopy standing over the tomb of St Peter, has four twisted pillars, modelled on the pillars of the old St Peter's which were reputed to have come from the Temple in Jerusalem. The illusory scalloped awnings round the top, also in bronze and reminiscent of a mediaeval general's tent, are regarded by experts as the most superb feats of bronze casting. It certainly took so much bronze that they ran out of the material, and by order of Pope Urban VIII removed the bronze coffering from inside the vestibule of the Pantheon. In the wall above the baldachino, Bernini built the ancient chair, reputed to be St Peter's throne, into another illusion, known as the Cathedra Petri.

The mixture of architecture, sculpture, painting and trickery in these two pieces is excelled and exceeded in a more purely architectural work of Bernini's, or at least a work of architecture and planning, for half the magic of the colonnade he built round the piazza at St Peter's comes from its relationship with the environment. The colonnades, kept low to relate to Carlo Maderna's front, and providing welcome shade in the midday sun, have a profound symbolic significance. They suggest the embracing, protective arms of Mother Church, wrapped round the faithful in the piazza. Also, according to Bernini's brief, they draw the eye to the steps or to the window and balcony in the Vatican palace from which the pope gives his blessing.

Francesco Borromini (1599–1667), sculptor and mason, was very different from Bernini. He went to Rome in 1614 to train under Carlo Maderna, and Bernini. At the age of sixty-eight he died by his own hand. The complex, tortuous forms he evolved in his churches, particularly in S. Carlo alle Quattro Fontane, begun in 1633, are difficult for either layman or expert to understand without hard study and probably mirror the intricate obsessive labyrinths within his mind. For two centuries after his death he was considered deranged, and the choice by nineteenth-century art historians of the word 'Baroque', which meant misshapen, particularly of pearls, may have had something to do with the feeling in the eighteenth and nineteenth centuries that Borromini and his shifting architecture were uneasy and abnormal.

It is Borromini's juggling with shapes that is so fascinating. The fact that he had to work on tiny or awkwardly shaped sites does not seem to have curbed his swelling imagination, and this no doubt gave confidence to those who followed him, like Cosmas Damian Asam in Munich. The latter decided to build a little church, St John Nepomuk, on a site only thirty feet wide that adjoined his own house. He managed to pack the interior with swirling balconies and twisted pillars, throbbing passionately in gold, dark browns and reds. Borromini's San Ivo della Sapienza, the university church in Rome, was started in 1642 to fill in the end of an arcaded courtyard patterned with a star on its floor. But his plan for the church of wisdom looks back to the temple of wise Solomon and makes no concession to site difficulties. Its plan is formed by two triangles that interlock to form a star of David, whose points end, alternately, in semi-circles and half-octagons. The front giving onto the court is concave, and over all rises a rippling dome, very steep, in the form of a six-lobed cupola which is surmounted by a spiral lantern holding up the flame of truth. This form was to influence Guarini in his Chapel of the Holy Shroud in Turin.

However the oval is the classic shape of the Baroque. Ovals had been used before, of course. Serlio established the principle of using them in the fifth book of his seven books on architecture in 1547, and Vignola used a longitudinal oval in S. Anna. Now ovals may lie in the long direction of the church—from east to west—or transversely; several may be used, or they may be split in half and set back to back

San Ivo della Sapienza, Rome, by Francesco Borromini

to give concave curves on the exterior. Bernini used an oval across the width of the church in Sant' Andrea al Quirinale, which is known as the oval Pantheon. Carlo Rainaldi (1611–91) in the church of Sant' Agnese in Piazza Navona, on which Borromini put the façade, added two apse-like chapels at choir and entrance ends to make the plan of an octagon within a square into an east/west oval. Secular buildings were also oval, as, for example, the little Rococo Amalienburg Pavilion in the park of Nymphenburg Palace, Munich, by François Cuvilliés and François Mansart's Maisons Laffittes near Paris has oval rooms in its side wings. Le Vau's mansion Vaux-le-Vicomte (1657) has a central oval salon covered by a dome.

In San Carlo, Borromini twisted the four quadrants of a basically oval plan inwards to give undulating walls, and then used semicircular arches above the cornice to bring the walls back to the oval, from whence springs the coffered dome. The plan of the Abbey Church at Banz, Bavaria, is a spiral of interlacing ovals. Sant' Andrea and San Carlo both have oval domes, and the form even appears in oval staircases built into the fabric of a building. The magnificent staircase that Balthasar Neumann (1687–1753) built into the Episcopal Palace at Bruchsal, south Germany, in 1732, the end of the Baroque period,

S. Carlo alle Quattro Fontane, Rome, by Francesco Borromini

View into the dome of San Lorenzo, Turin

gives the impression that one is spiralling through space, from one podium to another.

Vierzehnheiligen is perhaps the most complex of all Baroque churches. From the outside it looks regular—a Greek-cross church with extended nave and aisles, polygonal side-chapels for transepts, altar in the east and twin towers on the façade. Inside, the visitor is stunned by the light and shadows that swell and ebb around the swooping vaults, by the Baroque architectural and decorative shapes in galleries or stucco; by much gold on white, and deep colours on the painted ceiling. There are no aisles; the church is open to shifting interpenetrating spaces. There is no dome; the altar is situated in the large longitudinal central oval which forms the nave, an anchored island floating in a sea of liquid light. When we examine the plan we see that this nave is strung between two smaller ovals, one forming the choir, the other the entry to the church, and bulging outwards a little on the façade to give the undulating wall line. The chapels in the arms of the cross are semicircular. Pillars and convex curves in the side walls indicate the position of two further ovals placed transversely between the altar and the entry area.

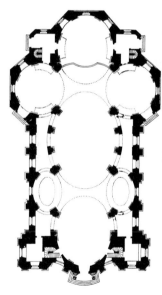

Vierzehnheiligen

Its complexity applies to the structure. Baroque structures were very advanced. If, after examining the Vierzehnheiligen, we look back to the early Renaissance buildings, we are struck by their structural simplicity—almost naïvety. The Palazzo Rucellai, for instance, consists of four solid walls holding up a shallow pent roof—about as primitive a structure as one could have. Rusticated stonework, pilasters, cornices, window frames are practically engraved on the side. In contrast, the Baroque architects' structural confidence seems unbounded. These men were in fact well capable of calculation. Many were engineers, Neumann and Guarini were mathematicians of note;

Great Cascade, Palazzo Caserta, Naples, by Luigi Vanvitelli

Sir Christopher Wren (1632–1723), architect of St Paul's, London, was reckoned a scientific genius, Professor of Astronomy at both London and Oxford Universities and a founder member of the Royal Society. They were ready to exploit the structural knowledge and expertise of the past without aesthetic or moral prejudice. So, in Sant' Andrea we have Bernini carving up his solid walls into niches, as did the ancient Romans; we have Guarini weaving ribs like webbing in catenary curves to support spires and domes in San Lorenzo and Il Sindone, relying on his knowledge of Gothic vaulting, spiced with piquancy of detail from Moorish vaults in Spain. And we find James Gibbs and Nicholas Hawksmoor, who with Vanbrugh worked in Wren's office, setting Gothic spires atop of classical churches. Curving wings and blocks, swirling vaults: the truth is that the Baroque had gone as far as it was possible with masonry structure. Further structural development had to await the discovery of new materials and the demand for new forms in the nineteenth century.

The Baroque architects matched their free-ranging experiments in structure by demolishing boundaries between one medium and another. Architecture and painting have their moment of intercommunion in the painted ceilings which opened up the roof to heaven by means of what the Italians called 'sotto in sù' (from below upwards). These were typical Baroque 'effects', common in both churches and palaces. Among the most famous is that of Il Gesù, and the Zimmermann brothers' pilgrim church at Steinhausen, Swabia, where colourful figures come and go above the false arches, painted in perspective, that frame the roof supposedly open to the heavens. In Bernini's Sant' Andrea, the theme of the saint's martyrdom, painted behind the altar, is carried upwards in a sculpture of his soul being carried to heaven, which is presumably located in the dome, where nude figures dangle

their legs over the cornice and gossiping cherubs perch all around like roosting doves. Sculpture is called in to support the fiction of a roof opening to heaven in the palace built for the Prince-Bishops of Würzburg by Neumann, Hildebrandt and others. Here, the staircase with its flowing patterns of balustrades sweeps up towards a ceiling on which Tiepolo depicted the four continents—a riot of violin bows, whirling cloaks, feathered head-dresses, girls riding crocodiles, ostrichs and camels. The gilt frame cannot contain the activity, and figures overspill the stage-like theatre-in-the-round. A gallant's legs hang over the edge, and a wolfhound and a little fat soldier appear to have toppled out onto the ledge below. Just as invention and reality mix, in the same way sculpture and architecture become interchangeable. In a similar conceit, shown at the garden room of the Belvedere, pillars assume the shapes of muscular giants carrying the weight on their shoulders.

Materials are also transmuted in these illusions: wood is carved and painted to look like cloth, rays lit by yellow light from a concealed source are fashioned from gilt and stream down on St Theresa, and on the Cathedra Petri, while in the Trevi Fountain in Rome stone is carved to resemble spray and spouting water. It is a transfixing experience to chance on the Fountain after wending through narrow back streets. Bernini conceived it, and two architects and two sculptors carried out this monument—to the indomitable spirit of man— that laps at the buildings on one side of a small enclosed square. It is impossible to separate the real from the sham in this powerful combination of classical figures and seething scatter of rocks, out of which wild sea horses and real waters froth and foam. There is a similar set piece in the grounds of the palace that Luigi Vanvitelli (1700–73) built for the Spanish King of Naples, Charles III, the Palazzo Caserta. In

Giant pillar supporting garden-room roof, Belvedere Palace, Vienna

one of two pieces depicting the legend of Diana and Actaeon, the sculptor has placed Actaeon, caught at the moment of being turned into a stag, at the base of the Great Cascade, cornered by slavering hounds, which leap up the rocks at him from the pool's edge.

This kind of effect was sought in two major planning schemes in Rome by the Popes. One was the Piazza Navona, now considered a museum of the Baroque, since it contains Rainaldi's Sant' Agnese with a front by Borromini, two fountains by Bernini and, in the Pamphili family palace, a gallery painted by Cortona. The most famous fountain, that of the four rivers, depicts the Danube, the Plate, the Nile and the Ganges, testifying, as does the ceiling at Würzburg, to the enormous interest in the countries being opened up to East and West by explorers and colonists. The other major town-planning scheme is the Piazza del Populo. It is a highly self-conscious piece of town planning and contains an obelisk between two churches, which appear to have twin elevations and domes. In fact, they stand on sites of different widths, and Carlo Rainaldi had to deploy some ingenious internal planning to create the matching effect on the outside.

We have seen how in Würzburg and Bruchsal, Baroque architects delighted in getting effects with flights of stairs. Bernini's Scala Regia, an early example, is perhaps the most famous. As in much of the best Baroque architecture, he was presented with a challenge—to make a 'royal' staircase leading into the Vatican Palace alongside the frontage and colonnade of St Peter's without detracting one from the other.

Piazza del Populo, Rome. Engraving by Giovanni Battista Piranesi

Composite of Christopher Wren's churches

Moreover, there was not much space. His solution was to have a passageway leading from the colonnade to the exit of the Cathedral's Galilee Porch. Here, a dramatic statue of the Emperor Constantine on a white horse distracts us cleverly from an inappropriate turn before the staircase is reached. Lined with arcades the grand staircase itself then ascends steeply, narrowing into a dignified tunnel-shaft, in the Mannerist manner.

Possibilities of using staircases outdoors for scenic effect were early appreciated in a hilly city like Rome. Francesco de Sanctis produced a masterpiece, the Spanish Steps, Rome. Unexpected curves, lines of steps and balustrades, where today flowers and souvenirs are sold, wind past the house where Keats died to where the sixteenth-century church with a frontage by Maderna, SS Trinità de' Monti, stands at the head of the steps like a grande dame receiving visitors.

The use of steps in conjunction with a church is also to be found in Portugal. The approach to the Bom Jesus do Monte, a twin-towered church near Braga, was laid out in 1723–44 according to the Stations of the Cross, the stages of Christ's journey from Pilate's Hall to his

Benedictine monastery, Melk

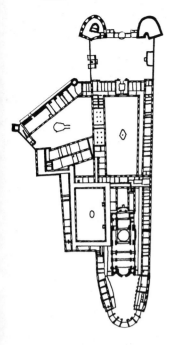

death on the cross. Zig-zag flights with fountains and obelisks at the angles link the chapels commemorating the fourteen Stations until the church at the top is reached.

Sometimes it is the siting that gives a building presence and drama. Juvarra assured the dominance of his Basilica at Superga by not only giving it a dome like St Peters, but also by setting it on a hill high above Turin. Baldassare Longhena's church, S. Maria della Salute, with crested pediments lapping halfway up its walls seems a creation of the sea because of its position, white as creamed surf among the red-tiled roofs, at the entrance to the Grand Canal in Venice.

But probably the most superlative siting is that of Jacob Prandtauer's Benedictine Monastery at Melk, Lower Austria, 1702–14, on a bluff above the Danube. Above the brown-green river and the grey-green outcrops of rock, the twin towers on the façade, the dome and the grey-green roofs of the detached church rise imperiously up from within a surround of monastic ranges with red-tiled roofs.

The British variations on this Continental style have been left to the end of the chapter, since their individuality sets them out of step with their European contemporaries, if for no other reason than that, unlike the other countries in which the Baroque flourished, England was Protestant. Anglican churches were therefore open halls and Protestant churches of the period present a harder outline in contrast to the curvaceous Baroque. A first glance at Sir Christopher Wren's greatest work, St Pauls' Cathedral, London, with its high, serene dome set around with cool, contained, closely-spaced slim columns— more like Bramante's Tempietto than like St Peter's—suggests that he belongs to the Renaissance rather than to the Baroque, but further study does not support this. On the secular palace-type side elevations, a swirling façade replaces transepts; and the front bulges between two towers reminiscent of Borromini's work. When one ventures inside and examines the black-and-white chequered tiling, the bold structure

Monastery at Melk by Jacob Prandtauer

Interior of St John
Nepomuk, Munich, by
Cosmas Damian Asam

Interior of Vierzehnheiligen
by Balthasar Neumann

Castle Howard, Yorkshire,
by Sir John Vanbrugh

of the Whispering Gallery encircling the dome, and then moves on to consider the piers that are hollowed out into enormous niches and placed diagonally to support a dome as wide as nave and aisles together, one recognizes the intrepid effrontery of Baroque massing. In the rebuilding of fifty-one churches in the City of London, after the four terrible days and nights of September 1666, during which four-fifths of the city was burned down, Wren showed an adventurously versatile eclectic response to the mammoth task before him, combining Gothic and Renaissance details and structure.

If there is a temptation to assign Wren to an earlier age, there is no question of this with Sir John Vanbrugh (1664–1726). The classic 'mighty forces struggling against overwhelming weights' of Baroque massing and the stirring panache of his soaring, vertical pillars, windows and turrets above the lake on Blenheim Palace, Oxfordshire, and Castle Howard, Yorkshire, have the unquestioned theatrical hallmark of the Baroque. After a brief association with Hawksmoor in Wren's office, Vanbrugh gained his first commission, Castle Howard, for the Earl of Carlisle in 1699. Untrained but confident, he came swaggering onto the architectural scene from more swashbuckling arenas: he had previously been an army captain, had been arrested as a spy in France and imprisoned in the Bastille, and had later gained fame as a Restoration dramatist. Walpole considered 'sublime' that quality of powerful excitement with which he would invest classical forms. That quality is to be found at Castle Howard, in the dome rising majestically above the pedimented south front, in the famed Great Hall with its shifting spaces and quivering shadowy hollows and in the narrow vaulted Antique Passage. He boasted of his special feeling for 'the castle air', and this is probably justified at Blenheim Palace, called after the victory in the war of the Spanish succession and presented by a grateful nation to the conquering general, the Duke of Marlborough. Its presence and enormous scale recall Versailles.

The last phase of the Baroque in France was called Rococo, an elegant, light-hearted décor, invented to suit Parisian tastes. The style first appeared in the classicist Jules-Hardouin Mansart's designs, executed for Louis XIV, for the Château de la Ménagerie, which was to be built for the thirteen-year-old fiancée of his eldest grandson. In response to the King's objections that the projected decoration was too sombre for a child, Claude Andran, Watteau's master, evolved a light delicate decoration of arabesques and filigree depicting hunting dogs, maidens, birds, garlands, ribbons, plant fronds and tendrils. Then in 1699, Pierre Lepautre applied arabesques to the mirrors and doorframes of the King's own apartments at Marly. The style was launched. By 1701 it had appeared at Versailles.

It took its name from *rocaille*, meaning rocks and shells, to indicate the natural forms of its decorations: leaf- and branch-shapes, sea-shapes—shells, surf, coral, seaweed, spray and spume—scrolls, C-and S-shapes. In France it remained delicate and elegant, providing exquisite rooms for the fashionable and intimate pursuits of dancing, chamber-music, etiquette, letter writing, conversation and seduction.

The architecture supporting the decoration became simpler. Rooms were more likely to be rectangular, possibly with the corners rounded off, painted in ivory white or a pastel tone, lacking pillars or pilasters and all but the simplest mouldings, so as to not detract from the gold arabesques with which they were covered. It was at this period that the term 'French window' came in to describe the fashionable attenuated windows which often stretched from floor to ceiling. Mirrors had already been used for brilliance of effect in grand salons, such as Louis XIV's Galerie des Glaces at Versailles, a barrel-vaulted room with a rich painted ceiling, whose arcade of seventeen windows down one side was matched by an arcade of seventeen mirrors down the other. In 1695 Fischer von Erlach added a more delicate version that might almost be called flimsy to the 'Viennese Versailles'—the Schönbrunn Palace, Vienna, built in rivalry of Louis XIV. Now mirrors of the flattering contemporary dark glass became customary over the mantelpiece; and walls were patterned with mirrors of all shapes, regular and irregular, whose frames were made of twigs or leafy shoots in gilt—slim, wispy, often trailing away in a vague open-ended S- or C-shape that knew nothing of symmetry.

By 1732, when Germain Boffrand created the Salon de la Princesse for the young bride of an elderly Prince de Soubise in his hôtel, or town-house, in Paris, French Rococo was at its height. It had spread even to town-planning in the Place de la Carrière, Nancy. The château built there for the French Queen's father, the dethroned Polish King Stanislas Leczinsky, was destroyed. But the Polish king's taste for the Rococo is still testified to by the curving arcades of open arches, built after 1720. They define spaces that open intriguingly out of each other, and involve an oval court, a triumphal arch and beautiful wrought-iron gates. Some time before that, Elector Max Emmanuel of Bavaria had discovered that the court dwarf, François Cuvilliés had a talent for architecture and in 1720 sent him to Paris to study for four years. He worked in the Munich Residenz, and between 1734 and 1739 he created the Amalienburg, the best known of the four Rococo pavilions erected in the extensive grounds of Schloss Nymphenburg on the outskirts of Munich. This stylish little *Pavillon de plaisance*, with a deceptively smooth and simple exterior, is embellished with charming details, such as a flight of semispherical steps leading to the curving projecting porch under a prow-shaped pediment, the corners sculpted to make them concave, and the slim bow-shaped pediments elegantly raised. Inside, a central circular hall, about forty feet in diameter, curving with the curve of the front façade, is provided on either side with the necessary services, bedrooms and gunroom. The hall, washed pale blue like the first morning of creation, is a room of oval-headed mirrors. These alternate with the windows and doors and are set at slight angles to proliferate the summer frivolity of the decorations. Silver-stuccoed ornament covers the walls in airy screens of verdure, musical instruments, cornucopias and shells; butterflies rise from the sun-spattered leaves, and grasses quiver around the roof cornice, while birds wing their way up into the blue heaven.

Spanish Steps, Rome, by Allesandro Specchi and Francesco de Sanctis

Staircase of Residenz Würzburg

Hall of Mirrors, Amalienburg Pavilion, Schloss Nymphenburg, Munich, by François Cuvilliés. Stucco by J. B. Zimmermann

S. Maria della Salute, Venice, by Baldassare Longhena

16

The Prophets of Elegance

Baroque and Rococo came to an abrupt end in Germany in the middle of the eighteenth century. As a rule, an artistic phase that has outlived its usefulness or relevance dies out during a span of several decades. It is very odd that this one came to an end so suddenly. With more sober and ponderous empires now assuming political power, Europe returned to the more sober and ponderous classical architecture, this time based on the Greeks.

There were several reasons for this. One was the changed atmosphere in Europe, culminating in the French Revolution of 1789, which seems to have led architects and their clients to search for more permanence and authority in their buildings than the Baroque could provide. Another was that the Baroque had only been taken up by certain regions, and with the shift in the balance of power, the architecture preferred by countries like France and Protestant Germany now came into its own. But the deciding factor in the break with the Baroque was a new enthusiasm that found expression in the fashionable taste of the time.

This was the new pursuit (at this stage scarcely a science) of archaeology, and, in particular, the exploration of Greek ruins, which were for the first time opened up to the gentlemen of Europe, and were included in the Grand Tour which formed part of their education. A spate of books, treatises, sketches, paintings and engravings, similar to the flood that accompanied the experiments of the early Renaissance architects, poured through France, Germany, England and Italy in the 1750s and 1760s. It was these works, within the changing political, social and emotional atmosphere, that hastened the demise of the Baroque.

The first, in 1753, was by an amateur in both archaeology and architecture, the Abbé Laugier (1713-69). In his search for authority, he reconsidered the basic design of the primitive hut, when architecture consisted of upright posts, cross-beams and pitched roofs, the genesis of the ancient Greek temple. This, he contended in his *Essai sur l'architecture* (1753), was how architecture should be ideally, with plain walls unarticulated by pilasters, pediments, additional attic storeys, domes or decorations of any sort. The first person to translate Laugier's theories into fact was Jacques Germain Soufflot (1713-80), who built the Church of Ste-Geneviève, Paris, in 1755, secularized during the Revolution and renamed the Panthéon. He did however use a dome, which he based on St Paul's. But he supported it almost entirely on pillars, joined together by straight entablatures, except for the four corners, where he borrowed from Gothic structure and introduced four triangular piers, with columns standing up against them. His intention that light should pass freely through the building

(opposite) Le Petit Trianon, Versailles, by Ange-Jacques Gabriel

Interior of Panthéon, Paris,
by Jacques-Germain Soufflot

was foiled later on, when the windows all round were filled in.

Five years after the Abbé's treatise, Le Roy produced his *Ruines des plus beaux monuments de la Grèce*, but this work was outdated in 1762 by the first volume of James Stuart and Nicholas Revett's definitively comprehensive and scholarly work *The Antiquities of Athens*. It was written after the English philosopher Lord Shaftesbury persuaded the two men to visit Athens in the 1750s. In 1764 in Germany, J.J. Winckelmann brought out his history of ancient art. Winckelmann never went to Greece, but the first sentence of his *Reflections* tells us clearly where his allegiance lies: 'Good taste, which is spreading more and more throughout the world, was first formed under Greek skies.' Architects, he felt, should strive for the qualities shown by the Greeks—noble simplicity, calm grandeur and precision of contour.

The profound influence which writers and intellectuals had on the artistic movements of the time must be taken into account in order to understand this period. We know of the effect of philosophical writings on the outbreak of the French Revolution and on the decision of the American colonies to break away from Britain. When we look at the Romantic Movement in Britain, we shall see how the writers of the time were involved in the development of the romantic landscape movement—the essayist, Joseph Addison, and the poet Alexander Pope, who commissioned William Kent to design him a garden, and the writer Horace Walpole. Probably as influential were the popular painters and engravers of the day, who liked to combine architecture, usually of an antique or ruined character, with the 'sublime' prospects of nature. Paintings by Claude Lorraine and Salvator Rosa were eagerly bought up and brought home as souvenirs by young gentlemen on the Grand Tour. Most influential of all was the etcher, Giovanni Battista Piranesi, whose dramatic scenes of ancient Roman remains and prison squalor conveyed an image of Rome which did much to shape European conceptions of the city. Piranesi's work was given an added boost in England through his friendship with the Scotsman, Robert Adam (1728-92). Adam, who went in for sketching rugged landscapes and had made a detailed study of Diocletian's Palace at Spalato, which he published in 1764, lived for a time, possibly intimately, with Piranesi in Rome. He returned to England and designed mostly in classical Greek and 'Etruscan' style the interiors in a series of country houses, and produced some of the finest eighteenth-century planned terraces in London and the New Town of Edinburgh.

The very architects whose work exemplified the classical revival were often equally effective when working in the Romantic idiom. In France, Ange-Jacques Gabriel (1698-1782) built in the grounds of the palace of Versailles one of the first perfect Neo-classical buildings, Le Petit Trianon. A little cube house in pale limestone and rose-pink marble with a long arcade effect across the front, it was built for Louis XV. It was later altered for Marie Antoinette. Gabriel's working life was long enough for him to complete two planned streets twenty years apart, Place de la Bourse, Bourdeaux, and Place de la Concorde,

La Superga, Turin, by Filippo Juvarra

Paris, both based on the Louvre Colonnade. The Place de la Bourse (formerly the Place Royale), which he built between 1731 and 1755, has Ionic columns and high French roofs, while the Place de la Concorde (1753–65) shows in contrast the two most typical features of the classical revival: giant Corinthian columns and long balustrades. In La Superga, Juvarra expressed his intention of moving away from Baroque and back to the purer classicism of Bernini. But the siting and the back-to-front plan of La Superga, with its jutting classical entrance portico tacked on to a front apse beneath a dome rising proudly above the city, suggests that he was merely juxtaposing these two styles; yet, such is the splendour and magnificence of this church that one should not regret the stylistic shortcoming.

It was in England that the two styles most patently overlapped. The English made an early return to classicism, not at first to the ancient forms of the Greeks, or even of the Romans (that was to come later), but to the gentler interpretation by Palladio. Between 1715 and 1717, a young Scot, Colen Campbell (1676–1729), produced a book of over one hundred engravings of houses in England, which he called *Vitruvius Britannicus*. In it, he praised both Palladio and Inigo Jones. Campbell put his theories into practice by building Houghton House, Norfolk, an Inigo Jones-type house, with a magnificent forty-foot double-cube room for the Prime Minister, Sir Robert Walpole. He also built a holiday villa at Mereworth, Kent, which closely followed Palladio's Villa Rotonda, with a round central hall, but dispensed with Palladio's symmetrical exterior staircases on two sides. A similar variation on the Rotonda theme was created by Lord Burlington when he built for himself, with the help of William Kent, a villa in London, Chiswick House, in 1725.

Tsarskoe Selo, Pushkin, by Bartolomeo Rastrelli and Charles Cameron

Richard Boyle, third Earl of Burlington (1694–1753), one of the
Whig politicians who had come to power with the accession of George
I, was an amateur architect. Inspired by *Vitruvius Britannicus* he
established a group of architects who took the work of Palladio as a
model. It consisted of people such as Colen Campbell, the young
painter William Kent, whom he had collected while studying in Rome,
and the poet Alexander Pope, and established himself as the virtual
dictator of taste in England until his death in 1753. The style was
carried as far as Russia, where a Scot, Charles Cameron, added a
wing to the imperial palace built by an Italian, Bartolomeo Rastrelli
(1700–71), with an Ionic colonnade facing the park, at Tsarskoe Selo,
Pushkin. Another Scot, James Gibbs (1687–1754), Jacobite and Catholic who had at one time studied for the priesthood and had also
studied the international Baroque under Carlo Fontana in Rome, one
would expect to be in opposition to Burlington's Whig establishment.
But even Gibbs' work on London churches, for example, St Martin-
in-the-Fields, where he combined a classical portico with a spire, is
never outrageously Baroque, and in the long, cool, dignified symmetry
of the Senate House at Cambridge University, he showed himself an
incomparable successor to Wren. That Gibbs' style is in harmony

The Marble Hall, Holkham Hall, Norfolk, by Richard Boyle, third Earl of Burlington and William Kent

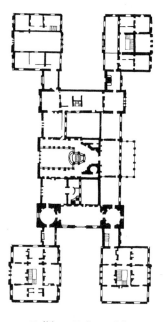

Holkham Hall, Norfolk

with Palladian elegance is shown by its popularity abroad—in America, where Palladianism was much emulated, and in the work of Australia's convict-forger architect (whom today she honours on her banknotes) Francis Greenway in St James Church, Sydney, of 1824.

England at this period was going through an agricultural revolution which was to transform the appearance of the rural landscape. A foremost figure in this transformation was Thomas Coke, Earl of Leicester, for whom, in 1734, Burlington and Kent built Holkham Hall in Norfolk. The surface of the house was in yellow brick, made locally, but, at Coke's request, fashioned after antique Roman brick. The house was planned with a central rectangular block, which presented a Palladian portico entrance to the deer park. On either side of the main block to front and back, connected by short low and recessed links, stand four smaller rectangular blocks. As a plan, it represents a valid extension of Palladio's service wings, simply repeated so as to face the back as well as the front. Yet the entrance hall is almost Baroque. The house had been commissioned to show off Coke's collection of antiquities, and the hall is on two levels, with an apse-like gallery round the inner end. This is reached by a staircase, gashed with a strip of red carpet, shaped like the train of a velvet cloak or an unopened peacock's tail. Pillars of brown-on-white Derby-

*Royal Crescent, Bath, by
John Wood the younger*

*Gardens at Stourhead,
Wiltshire*

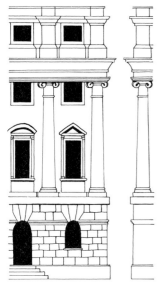

Palladian pillar and frontage juxtaposed

shire alabaster, based on the Temple of Fortuna Virilis in Rome, rise from this gallery level to support an extraordinary coved ceiling which, because it runs into the apse in a half-cup shape, reflects to some extent the curious form of the staircase.

The new elegance was not confined to country houses. John Wood the elder (1704–54) and John Wood the younger (1728–81), both architects of Palladian country houses, discovered a method of translating the simple sophistication of the Palladian way of building into the street. No later version, not even Robert Adam's planning of Charlotte Square, Edinburgh, a unified palace frontage, is quite as dramatic as the streets the Woods created in Bath, Avon. In golden-white Bath stone, the elevations are conceived as one continuous Palladian frontage. A pediment gives emphasis to the centre of Queen Square. An untrammelled lawn sweeps steeply down to the tree fringes from the elliptical curve of Royal Crescent. The masterly way in which they evolved this new and elegant face for quality planning can be seen by juxtaposing a Palladian pilaster against the frontage of a Bath terrace and noting how the proportions and the horizontal emphases are translated from one to the other. What has happened is that the pilaster has been extended sideways to form a street so that the base becomes the ground floor, sometimes rusticated, and the shaft of the pilaster is repeated as a colonnade or in the tall narrow verticality of the first floor windows. Details of architrave and frieze are matched in the cornice mouldings, and above that there may occur pediment or attic storey.

The Burlington school were important pioneers of the association of architecture and its environment which was part of the Romantic movement. It is to William Kent that we owe the start of the English landscape movement of the eighteenth century—the landscape of 'controlled nature'. Kent, in the phrase of the Prime Minister's son, Horace Walpole, 'leapt the fence and found all nature was a garden'.

This new awareness led to a total reversal of the Baroque relation between inside and outside. If we look at the most famous Baroque gardens, Le Nôtre's designs for Vaux-le-Vicomte and for Versailles, we see just how carefully and geometrically they were controlled— clipped hedges defining parterres, long avenues of trees leading to geometrically organized sheets of water, diagonal paths to fountains or shrubberies. Yet the inside of Versailles and of Vaux-le-Vicomte have the lavish warmth and excitement of painted vaults and carved cornices. In complete contrast, the eighteenth-century English country houses have serene interiors, while outside, nature is allowed to heave into mounds or fall away, paths, streams and lakes are given licence to twist or run straight, trees to grow very much as they want to do. Kent was followed by Lancelot Brown (1716–83), nicknamed 'Capability' Brown because he always enthused about the 'capabilities' of a site. Tree-planting was an art in which he excelled. His particular art of bunching and scattering of groups of trees is now taken for granted as a characteristic feature of the English landscape. So extensive was Brown's work that one landowner said he hoped to die before him since he wanted to see what heaven looked like before

Capability 'improved' it. Another gardener, Charles Bridgeman, is credited with the method whereby the entire landscape, as far as the eye could see, became part of the estate: he replaced fences dividing gardens from the surrounding pasture land by sunken fences called ha-has, which kept cattle out, but were imperceptible from terrace or drawing-room window.

Interaction between house and garden went one step further in the Picturesque Movement when the garden was embellished with delightful architectural features—bridges, temples and grottoes. Bridgeman's garden for the house that Robert Adam remodelled at Stowe, Buckinghamshire, now a public school, is an architectural treasure-trove of classical temples and bridges by the most renowned—Vanbrugh, Gibbs, Kent, 'Capability' Brown. There is even a copy of Roger Morris's Palladian bridge from Wilton House, set on a series of graceful arches. Colen Campbell made the designs for a Palladian house at Stourhead, Wiltshire, for the banker Henry Hoare in the 1720s. When Henry and his son Michael decided to make the complementary garden, they dammed the valley to the west of the village, and, inspired by the Aeneid, laid it out as an allegory of man's passage through life. The idyllic route suggests, rather, a passage through Elysium to the visitor who wanders round the triangular lake by verdant copse and dreaming waterlily, by dank green grottoes and exquisite temples, between pink, blue and mauve hydrangeas and over bridges whose curves are reflected in the water.

Kent's contemporary in France was Ange-Jacques Gabriel, who succeeded his father as chief royal architect in the 1750s. A consistent man, he retained his classical symmetry and composure, unadulterated, until the end. The same cannot be said of his successor, Richard Mique (1728–94), whose structures in the gardens of Le Petit Trianon, Versailles, represent the infection of English romanticism to produce what the French call *folies*. Here he built a delightful little temple, called the Temple of Love, embowered in weeping greenery, which owes something to Greece, to Rome and to England. He constructed an artificial peasant village called le Hameau, where the capricious Marie-Antoinette played at being a country girl and came to milk the goats from time to time. Mique was only one of a prolific generation

Château of Vaux-le-Vicomte by Louis Le Vau. Gardens by André Le Nôtre

Interior of Syon House, London, by Robert Adam

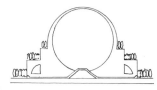

Section and elevation of Boullée's design for a cenotaph to Isaac Newton

of architects born between 1725 and 1750. Better known are Claude-Nicolas Ledoux and Etienne-Louis Boullée, both of whose work has an almost fantastic grandeur. In Boullée's case, little ever went further than the drawing-board. He is best remembered for a design for a monument to Isaac Newton, an enormous sphere, set into a double ring base, which demonstrates the desire to exploit the use of massive geometric figures.

Examples of Ledoux's work have survived. He built a ring of forty-five toll-houses around Paris, all with different plans and elevations, and basically classical in style; only four remain, of which the best is probably La Barrière de la Villette. As architect to the king, he was nearly guillotined, and many of his toll-houses were destroyed in the Revolution. In the late 1770s, he built a Greek revival theatre at Besançon. But one of his most interesting essays was an early example of industrial architecture, a city for chemical workers at a salt mine, La Saline de Chaux at Arc-et-Senan, on the river Loue near Besançon. Little is left today; the entrance is through a rough, strong row of Doric columns, stumpy and sitting on the ground without any base, while behind is a romantic grotto with round niches, in which are carved stone urns pouring out stone water.

Ledoux's columns reflect a controversy raging at the time as to what early Greek columns had really been like. The two distinguishing features of Neo-classical at this period were long colonnades and giant classical columns, whose proportions were supposed to be those of ancient Greece. It was a great shock to the classicists and antiquarians to discover that the true Doric order had been relatively short and squat, and had, most shocking of all, no base. What had always been pictured as Greek—the taller, slimmer version—was in fact Roman Doric if fluted and Tuscan Doric if unfluted. It is no doubt a good thing that these purists were spared the knowledge we now possess, that the early Greek temples were probably decorated in vivid colours.

The first example of the Doric revival appeared in England in 1758, in a temple built in the grounds of Hagley Hall, near Birmingham, by 'Athenian' Stuart, the author of *The Antiquities of Athens*. The most eminent classical buildings in this style, showing clearly the use of colonnades and antique columns, are to be found in Germany. Friedrich Gilly, who died in 1800 of consumption at the age of twenty-eight, left only drawings. But the dignity and quality of his designs for a memorial to Frederick the Great and the more original, less formally classic design for a national theatre in Berlin make us regret that he wasted some of his short life in studying knights' medieval castles in Prussia. His pupil Karl Schinkel (1781-1841) had more to offer the world, for he straddled several styles and several eras. He too had his romantic side: as painter and scenic designer, he produced a particularly memorable Neo-Egyptian palace for the Queen of the Night in a production of the Magic Flute in 1815. He extended his classical debt to Gilly by learning from Ledoux and Boullée, when, in 1803, he took himself to Paris and to Italy. But his eyes were not turned backwards only; he looked with keen interest towards the new productions of the Industrial Revolution—the factories and the machines they housed—and to the new materials coming into use—cast iron, papier mâché and zinc. Schinkel's two best-known buildings, the

Altes Museum, Berlin, by Karl Schinkel

Royal High School, Edinburgh, by Thomas Hamilton

Schauspielhaus, 1819–21, Berlin, and the Altes Museum, 1823–30, Berlin, are both in faultless Greek idiom. But there is something more than cold correctness in his building, and something almost spellbinding about the long low colonnade of the Altes Museum.

Similar architecture for a house of learning can be seen in the British Museum by Sir Robert Smirke (1780–1867), begun in 1823. James Gandon's Dublin Custom-House, William Wilkins' National Gallery in Trafalgar Square, London, the Greek Revival triple Ionic archway at Hyde Park Corner by Decimus Burton, and many other formal public buildings, were part of the Greek Revival movement initiated by Robert Adam and Sir William Chambers, who from 1760 were joint Architects of the Works to George III. Chambers was the most celebrated academician of his day. In Somerset House in the Strand, London, with its restrained though imposing Neo-Palladian façades around four sides of the courtyard, he established the Neo-classical style for government buildings in England. But he was as carried away by the romantic obsession with ruins and follies as were less establishment figures. When he designed a mausoleum for Frederick, Prince of Wales, in Rome, he made two meticulous drawings, one of the finished building, the other showing the building as a ruin, its beauty enhanced by the ravages of time. He published a book on Chinese architecture, and his pagoda in Kew Gardens is the only survivor of a Rococo fantasy of classical temples, Roman theatres, mosques, Moorish Alhambras and Gothic cathedrals built in the gardens during the 'Picturesque' vogue of the period.

Adam was less academic and more fashionable. His great enthusiasm, other than Diocletian's Palace at Spalato, was Etruscan architecture, particularly its decoration. Working with his brother James, he established a whole vocabulary of interior decoration that became enormously influential. After the 1770s there was scarcely an Adam house that did not have an Etruscan room. The white figures, urns and garlands in low relief against a pastel background such as Josiah Wedgwood adopted for the pottery he produced in the factory village he named Etruria in Staffordshire are a microcosm of Adam's prolific work in furniture, wall mouldings, mantelpieces, fanlights over doorways and, most beautiful of all, ceilings in delicate relief, often with a daisy shape in the centre and fan-like webs of garlands across each corner.

His Roman rooms show deeper colours—gilt and marbles on pillars and flooring in black, dark green and terracottas, as well as strongly masculine original detailing, such as his trick of screening off an apse or a shallow alcove with massive pillars. The marble pillars around the walls of the ante-room in Syon House, London, a Jacobean building remodelled, were dredged out of the Tiber to support only a decorated cornice carrying golden Greek figures.

Scotland was a hive of architectural industry and took to the Greek Revival style in its most exact form. Edinburgh was given the sobriquet of the Athens of the North when part of the Parthenon was built on Calton Hill as a national monument. Thomas Hamilton (1784–1858) reinforced this reputation when he built his faultless Greek

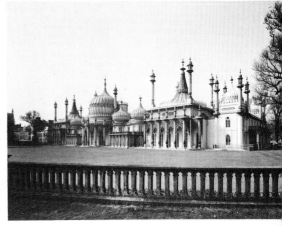

Royal High School in 1825-9. In Glasgow, the churches of Alexander Thomson (1817-75) were so literally Greek Revival in style that he was known as Greek Thomson.

In England, John Nash (1752-1835) was prepared to direct his fertile wits and sense of humour to any style of the past. He translated the picturesque of the country estate to the city in his Neo-classical terraces round Regent's Park, London, producing continuous frontages which were as impressive as those the Woods had made in Bath and as Adam, Playfair and others had done in the New Town of Edinburgh. He anticipated garden cities with his plans for self-contained villas around Regent's Park, each private in its own foliage but all possessing the park. He built Gothic in Devon, Italianate in Shropshire, and Old English thatched-cottage style at Blaize Hamlet near Bristol. During 1815 and 1821, he remodelled in Hindu style a Palladian pavilion built at Brighton for the Prince Regent by Henry Holland (1745-1806) in the 1780s. He decked out the classical symmetry of the main façade in Moorish arcades, and created a skyline that is a funfair of green copper domes and minarets. Inside, vulgarity of extravagance vies with exquisite craftsmanship in a series of individual rooms, the novelty extending even to the huge kitchen with pillars in the shape of palm trees—made in the new material, cast iron.

The period is best described as Romantic Classicism, because it was both classical and romantic. But it ends on a distinctly romantic note. The vogue for the antique and the picturesque, which we traced back to Piranesi's etchings, had placed such a cachet on melodramatic ruins—the 'ivy-mantled towers'—that men with more money than sense were actually building them. A striking example of this genre was Fonthill Abbey, Wiltshire, designed for William Beckford by James Wyatt (1747-1813), a rival of the Adam brothers, in 1796. It was a country house in the disguise of a mediaeval monastery on an attenuated cross-plan, its long wings housing, apparently, the church and various monastic ranges, partly in ruins. Its high polygonal Gothic tower collapsed in 1807, and the rest has since joined the tower as a ruin in earnest.

Somerset House, London, by Sir William Chambers

Royal Pavilion, Brighton, by John Nash

Mercederian Monastery, Quito

Sagrario Metropolitano, Mexico City

São Francisco de Assis, Ouro Preto, by Aleijadinho

17

How the Pioneers became Self-reliant

In the centuries we have just discussed, Europe had been preoccupied by what was going on within its own brilliant, vital confines. But archaeological excavations, travel, exploration and missionary work were all serving to open up territories hitherto unknown. The wider world now demands to make its contribution to our theme.

We are talking here not simply of European travellers dabbling in bits of foreign detail that they had come across in their travels, as today an artist may take a holiday in Africa, Mexico or the Andes to draw on the folk-art of an alien culture to enrich his own work with new themes and colour-schemes. That kind of interaction did, of course, exist. The early association between South America and Spain and Portugal led to the importation after 1500 of American Indian details into European architecture, with notable effect on the Plateresque type of decoration and the Churrigueresque in Spain and Portugal. And, as we have just seen, during the eighteenth and nineteenth centuries there was a vogue among the Romantics of Europe for all things Chinese. In architecture, it was apparent in the building of follies within great gardens, pagodas and bridges, nothing very serious. And the fashion for *chinoiserie*, a delicate decoration of wall surface, and furniture and porcelain whose motifs were drawn from Chinese artefacts (of any period) was apparent inside the house. Its applications are clearly as Rococo as Adam's 'Etruscan' Greek nymphs. Any country house with a pretension to being fashionable had to have a Chinese room.

That kind of interaction was little more than petty pilfering. It was another matter where the Europeans established colonies, or where missionary activity brought areas within the sphere and responsibility of a European country. For the English in America, it was the settlements of the eastern seaboard that were their progeny; while Canada, parts of Florida and Louisiana owed their existence to France. There were Spanish settlements in Florida, too, and South America was being opened up by both Spain and Portugal. Spanish missions, originally largely Franciscan, later Dominican and Jesuit, worked their way across South America, up the western seaboard of California, and eventually across to New Mexico, leaving behind charming whitewashed adobe churches with bell-towers in the gable, and mission buildings around courtyards which enclosed a garden, a graveyard for the brothers, and a fountain or well for the village water-supply. The Mercederian Monastery at Quito of 1630, with its two-storey loggia around the garden courtyard shows a more sophisticated form. But not all colonizers went West. India and Indonesia were settled, con-

Governor's Palace, Santa Fé

verted and exploited by the English, the Dutch and the Portuguese; Australia had yet to enter the picture.

The architectural style adopted in the colonies was at first a primitive version of that of the parent country at the time of colonization. Bit by bit, pragmatic adaptations due to climatic conditions, to the availability of local materials and the skills of local craftsmen, combined to produce a version that bore the hallmark of that particular country in its own right. In Brazil, where art was primitive and there was no tradition of building in stone, the architectural style tended to be a straight import from Portugal. In other areas, such as New Mexico, it was the native Indian adobe tradition that won.

In Santa Fé, outpost of the Spanish empire at the end of the Trail, building-heights are still strictly controlled. There is nothing today to distinguish the age and eminence of the Governor's Palace, just off the main plaza, from the surrounding buildings. Houses, government buildings and churches all tend to be built of Indian adobe brick, with the windows and doors moulded into curves that are typical of the medium, their wooden-raftered roofs often packed with a slim local tree, the palo verde. The Palace is a long, low one-storey building with a wooden loggia running along its length in whose shelter Indians from nearby reservations spread out rugs, basketwork and jewellery to sell to tourists. In contrast to that, a distinctive French flavour is apparent in the grid plan of New Orleans and in the colonnaded galleries of the humid towns of Louisiana, for example Parlange, Pointe Coupée Parish of 1750.

But it was in the churches of Mexico and Peru, some of the earliest colonial buildings still in existence, that there first appeared a combination of the traditions and talents of settlers with natives. Along with their motto 'For Christ and Gold' (an echo of the 'For God and profit' that a Renaissance merchant in Florence wrote on the fly-sheet of his ledger), the conquistadores brought with them their richly decorated form of Baroque. Once churches were built with local labour, further embellishments appeared, whose origins went back to the crafts and motifs of the Aztecs and the Incas, for both these Indian peoples commanded a mastery of masonry, carving and metalwork far exceeding that of their Spanish conquerors.

The Chapel of the Three Kings and the attached Sagrario (Sacrament Chapel) of the Cathedral at Mexico City are even more exuberantly encrusted with Churrigueresque than any Spanish model, all the more astounding because so much gilt paint was used. The mouldings are further serrated by the proliferation of a typical New World detail—the *estípite*, or broken pilaster. The cathedral, built in 1563, replaced a primitive structure which the conquistadores had built in order to obliterate the memory of the Aztec temple that had once stood on the same site. The Neo-classical west front with its twin towers in fawn limestone and the dome and lantern were all added much later. The cathedral at Zacatecas has similar Churrigueresque detail resembling lichens and plant forms swarming all over the façade and towers.

The church of São Francisco at Bahia (now Salvador) on the Brazilian coast, is later than the two Mexican cathedrals since it was started in 1701, but still bears the Aztec/Baroque forms in gilt wood and plaster. The cathedral in the ancient Inca city of Cuzco, in Peru, in contrast, chooses as its Spanish element the severe classicism of Philip II's Escorial, but with a different fluidity in slim pillars rising up the west front to a semicircular pediment. In similar vein, the original conception of the Jesuits' church in the same city, the Compañía, may have been Il Gesú in Rome, but it developed twin bell-towers, topped (in a very un-European manner) with little cupolas, each bound in with four tiny corner turrets.

The earliest church on the continent, said to have been founded by Cortez and built about 1521, is San Francisco at Tlaxcala, near Mexico City, where local cedar wood was used for beams. There is an example of late Spanish Gothic, with a Plateresque west front of 1521–41, at Santo Domingo (now Ciudad Trujillo) in the Dominican Republic. At about the time the Santo Domingo cathedral was being finished another church was being built in Mexico, San Agustin Acolman, which revealed Gothic and Moorish details grafted onto a basically Spanish Plateresque style. In the brilliant sunshine the ornament, carved by Indian craftsmen, shows up as incredibly incisive. The difficulties of responding to topographical conditions is well illustrated in the Cathedral at Lima. The first vaults, built in the mid-sixteenth century, were of stone—the material they would have chosen at home. Then after the first devastating earthquake, they tried brick. Finally in the eighteenth century they capitulated to nature and used wooden vaults with reed and plaster in-fill—a replaceable construction for future emergencies.

By the eighteenth century, when the Baroque was already out of fashion in Europe, South-American Baroque had found its own self-confident individuality—a combination of naivety with dazzling beauty, exemplified in two very different churches, the Sanctuary at Ocotlan, Mexico, and São Francisco de Assis, at Ouro Preto, Brazil. Their common ancestor was the front put on the Cathedral of Santiago de Compostella in 1667. But they were very different towers, with a change of gable and decoration, giving quite another proportion and outline to the church.

Ocotlan, a pilgrimage church of 1745, built where an Indian had seen a vision of the Virgin, rears up against the vivid Mexican sky across a wide empty plaza, with ranges of very Moorish buildings on either side—a double-storey arcade of wide round-headed arches on very slim pillars to one side, an archway into a pishtaq-like rectangular façade on the other. A round-headed panel of carved stucco in deep relief goes all the way up the west front between the two towers. The towers are in unglazed red brick on their lower reaches, quietly patterned all over in fish-scales, but at the top they suddenly burst into two-tiered, top-heavy white turrets, fretted and spiky. The interior was richly carved by a local sculptor, Francisco Miguel.

São Francisco at Ouro Preto was designed by a mulatto António Francisco Lisboa, better known by his nickname Aleijadinho, or Little Cripple. In 1766, in the gold-mining district of Minas Gerais, he started building this unique white church with contrasting lintels and cornices. Its proportions, the slim pillars on either side of the entrance section and the undulating cornice may suggest Borromini, but the two round towers and the extraordinary gable with spread wings is totally original. He also carved a dramatic series of life-size statues of prophets up the entrance stairway to the Conghas do Campo church, built in 1800, which has a presence reminiscent of Bom Jesus, Braga.

After that floridity—exuberant Baroque tempered with peasant innocence—it is almost a shock to find a style of severe simplicity in the dwellings of the early settlers on the eastern seaboard of North America. The Europeans who first landed in South America were conquerors; the first settlers in the New England states were pilgrims seeking freedom to worship and escape from want and fear. Their barns scattered round the States and Canada are beautiful primitive structures in oak and thatch or aspen shingle that bespeak different European origins. Their early buildings were simple frame houses, and settlers who became established and prosperous built in the classical Georgian style that they had left behind in England—but in wood, for in the New World they found little stone or lime. Swedish settlers of the sixteenth century brought with them the log-cabin technique, and by 1649 the first saw-mill was working. The very earliest houses, like Parson Capen House, Topsfield, Massachusetts, had timber frames and shingle roofs and were clad in clapboard. The upper floor jutted out over the lower in the jetty, typical of English frame Elizabethan and Jacobean houses. The windows, on the other hand, were not recessed as in English Georgian brick or stone, but flush with the wall, as suited timber. Quite a few examples still remain in Massachusetts and Connecticut: Longfellow House, Cambridge, of 1759, represents the type in a later, more elegant, form. By that time the house had grown a loggia, or a porch or balconies for sitting out in hot weather. The early houses with weather-boarding, small leaded window panes and a central chimney serving both downstairs rooms from fireplaces in a dividing brick wall, had coped excellently with the winter weather. Now that establishment gave more ease, consideration was given to the leisured summer hours.

Shirley Plantation, Virginia

Monticello, near Charlottesville, Virginia, by Thomas Jefferson

Early towns like Salem, Nantucket and Charleston retain charming tree-shaded streets lined with balconied houses. The typical low-pitched roof was often flattened at the top and edged with a wooden balustrade to form a terrace known as *captain's walk*. Handsome two-storey Palladian colonnades, with the tall slim pillars made possible by wood, and avenues of great trees were often features of the grand houses, which, like the tobacco planter's house, Shirley Plantation, on the James River in Virginia of 1723-70, often looked out across ample parkland, in a land where there was plenty of space. George Washington's timber Georgian house at Mount Vernon, Virginia, shows a similar shady gallery. Brick was commonly used in Virginia, and sometimes, as at Mount Pleasant in Philadelphia, 1761, rubbled walls were stuccoed over and scored to look like stonework, while brick was used for the quoins.

In the second capital of Virginia, Williamsburg, are the earliest Renaissance buildings in North America, William and Mary College (1695-1702), now entirely preserved and restored. They form a U-shaped college, consisting of classrooms flanked by the chapel and refectory wings, for which Wren may have drawn up the sketch-plans. By that time the thrifty homespun houses of the early settlers had passed. William Byrd, for example, imported English fittings for his gracious and ample brick house, Westover, in Charles City County,

The Lawns, University of Virginia, Charlottesville, by Thomas Jefferson

Virginia. Ballrooms and extensive gardens evoke a sophisticated society life in the Governor's Palace at Williamsburg.

Then classicism came to America through Thomas Jefferson (1743–1826), who was to write the Declaration of Independence and become President. He had served as ambassador at Versailles, at the time France was going through a Palladian phase, caught from the English enthusiasm. Jefferson returned to America inspired by Palladio and by the ancient Roman remains, particularly those at Nîmes, which he saw in the 1780s. He built himself a Palladian villa at Monticello near Charlottesville, Virginia, in 1770, which owed much to the Villa Rotonda. It had projecting bays and odd-shaped rooms such as he had seen in Parisian *hôtels*. It stands on a small hill looking towards the Blue Ridge Mountains and to the site where he later built the University of Virginia, and is full of light. It is larger than it looks at first, with extensive domestic quarters, including wine-cellars and stables built into a basement. It is a treasure-trove of quirky inventions—dumb waiters which swing out of sight, gadgets for opening shutters, beds that can be entered from two rooms—that testify to the genius of the man.

He planned his 'academical village' at Charlottesville (the University of Virginia) as a living museum of different sizes and types of classical buildings. Across the top is a library, modelled on the Pantheon and recently rebuilt; and then down either side of a series of leisurely sloping lawns are the buildings used as both classrooms and staff houses. This pattern became established as typical of the campus of an American university. Around the lawns are gardens of scented shrubs that separate the main quadrangle from the houses originally built to accommodate the slave servants of the early students. It is only slightly less grand than the plan created by L'Enfant for Washington, the gracious capital city on the banks of the Potomac river. Its great Mall is studded with monuments to American origins, and it is laid out in a grid crossed diagonally by avenues which bear the names of the states to which they point. The Palladian White House, designed by an Irishman, James Hoban, with porticoes added by Benjamin Latrobe, stands aloof just off the Mall with a suitable air of reticence and good breeding. It does not dominate Washington; but it does reflect its elegance.

The Roman grid around the central square, where the church and the town meeting-hall stood, became typical, a planning exercise derived from France and Ireland rather than from England. The characteristic American church of the period, such as Christchurch, Boston, or St Michael's, Charleston, was strongly in debt to Wren's city churches and to James Gibbs, particularly in the common combination of classical temple porticoes with a more Gothic spire. Then Latrobe, in the Catholic Cathedral at Baltimore of 1805–18, created a spacious, vaulted interior with America's first coffered dome by adapting the French and English classical influences of his training.

For classicism had come to America with Jefferson and was to mark the point at which the new country entered the architectural lists with an originality that prefigured the major role she was to play in the next two centuries. That originality was to be seen first in the grand buildings for government, commerce and finance in which classicism had already shown its power. Latrobe's Bank of Philadelphia was one such example. Then William Strickland (1788–1854), the William Wilkins of America, undeterred by a difficult corner site, achieved his stunning piece of Greek Revival in the Philadelphia Merchants' Exchange of 1823–4, giving his approach an elevational dignity with a colonnaded apse and, with spectacular economy, surmounting his building not with a dome but with a simple tempietto lantern. An English architect, and an amateur at that, Dr William Thornton, started the Capitol at Washington with a basic Parthenon shape; but the feature that gives it its world-famous silhouette, Thomas Walter's

Philadelphia Merchants' Exchange by William Strickland

Parkville, Melbourne

Town Hall, Calcutta. From a drawing by R. Harvell and F. C. Lewis in Views of Calcutta *by J. B. Fraser, published in 1824*

St James Church, Sydney, by Francis Greenway

triple-tiara dome, places this building firmly in the nineteenth century: he made it of cast iron.

Across the globe cast iron figured in the intricate lacework balconies and railings that were to become characteristic of suburban Melbourne and Sydney. This was a more sophisticated use of iron than the homely cast-iron roofs that are a feature of the Australian house-type, largely because they respond so well to the summer climate. Because of the way the states sold off narrow-fronted blocks of land to settlers, the characteristic Australian development was a row of narrow one-storey boxes, often with extensions 'tacked-on' at the back and with balconies, also roofed in cast iron, wrapped around as many sides of the house as the owner could afford. The less vernacular and more pretentious Georgian or classical-style buildings are generally of a lower quality than those of North America.

Not so the public buildings for New South Wales commissioned by Governor Lachlan Macquarie from his aide-de-camp, Lieutenant John Watts and the York convict-architect Francis Greenway, which date from 1815 onwards. They include St James Church, Sydney, with typical careful Greenway brickwork and copper-sheathed spire. It started construction as Law Courts and had to be redesigned by the long-suffering architect when the Commissioner from the English Home Office cancelled plans for a cathedral on another site.

Tasmania has some of the continent's oldest buildings, with some charming Georgian houses in Hobart, kin to the terraces of Brighton, Sussex, with views out to sea. Perth's Mediterranean climate encouraged a Victorian interpretation of Italian Renaissance. In the Titles Office Building, Cathedral Avenue (1897), smooth rich red brick combines with ranks of white colonnaded balconies under wide shadowy coffered eaves.

The eighteenth- and nineteenth-century upsurge of buildings of commerce and authority, erected in Neo-Palladian or Neo-classical style, was not limited to the Australian state capitals. Throughout the British Empire, from the West Indies to Malaysia, rose ponderously, in Palladian or Roman Doric, buildings with the 'Government look', typified in the Town Hall of Calcutta, as well as in churches built after Gibbs, such as those of Calcutta and Madras, often designed by soldier-architects.

18

The Rise of the Iron Masters

By the opening of the nineteenth century any certainty apparent in the architecture of the age of elegance in the preceding century had evaporated. The agitation brought in by the French Revolution of 1789 had never fully subsided; a different kind of society began to take shape, not immediately but by the end of the Napoleonic wars, effectively from the 1820s.

It was an age of uncertainty. But it was also an age that witnessed the emergence of a powerful new force in society—the bourgeoisie. The bourgeoisie were the real victors of the French Revolution and its aftermath. Work and leisure were shaped by them, no longer by the great aristocratic patrons of the eighteenth century and not yet, if indeed ever, by the working classes in whose name the revolution was said to have been made. The architecture of the nineteenth century was designed to meet middle-class aspirations.

There was another revolution every bit as influential as the French, the Industrial Revolution. It was cradled in Britain, from roughly 1750 to 1850. It began with the exploitation of natural phenomena, especially water and coal, found its first achievements in Britain and then spread with a relentless force throughout the world. The urban population dramatically increased, towns and cities multiplied in number and size, a new urban society emerged. The demand for new buildings was greater than ever before. Many of them, as we shall see, were unprecedented, designed to satisfy the needs and demands of a changing society.

To the fashionable architects the central—and often stated—problem was to discover a style appropriate to this time of change. They had inherited from the previous century the understanding and experience of classicism, with all the clarity of its formal language. Above all, classical and Neo-classical architecture expressed authority. They needed authority. The rival to the classical system was Gothic. The Romantic movement in art and literature found in the soaring attenuated forms of the Gothic style a suitable background for imagination and mystery. There were plenty of other styles, Renaissance and Baroque, Chinese, Saracenic, about which more was being discovered every year. But Classical and Gothic were the main contenders in the Battle of the Styles. Revived Gothic in particular went through the usual phases of growth and maturity—from superficial whimsy to a more basic understanding and thence to the freedom of personal expression. No one had a greater or more lasting influence than the prolific writer and critic, John Ruskin.

Appropriately, the finest illustration of the stylistic predicament was the very seat of law-making in Britain, the Houses of Parliament. In 1834 a fire destroyed the Palace of Westminster, except for the

Great Hall. The competition for a new palace to house Lords and Commons was won by Charles Barry (1795–1860) in 1836. Barry was a skilled exponent of the classical style. He had created the very symbol of the rise of middle-class political power in the Travellers' Club (1827) and the Reform Club (1837) in Pall Mall. Both were in his Italianate manner. Their elevations were immensely influential and, with various adaptations, spread through the country's public and commercial buildings and housing developments of the mid century. Inside the Reform Club had a large glazed court, a prototype of the central hall common to later nineteenth-century monumental planning. With his usual concern for technical modernity, Barry installed a very advanced steam kitchen for the famous chef, Alexis Soyer.

His problem with the Houses of Parliament was that the government had decided that the new building should be in the style thought to represent England at its best—Elizabethan or Jacobean. That required greater knowledge of late Gothic than Barry possessed. He had produced a logical classical plan, which could easily have been given classical elevations. To make them Gothic he recruited the greatest living authority on Gothic, Augustus Welby Northmore Pugin (1812–52). Pugin designed the elevations, the details, and the interiors, using stone, brass, plaster, paper and glass with a tremendous vital intensity. The House of Commons was bombed during the Second World War and has been restored; the House of Lords remains in its full glory and testifies to the adaptability and richness of the Gothic style.

In addition to the Houses of Parliament Pugin designed several hundred churches, five cathedrals, a number of great houses and wrote and published major works on Gothic architecture and furniture; he exhausted three wives, countless contractors, finally himself, and died insane at the age of 40. His influence was profound, for he supplied the vocabulary of Gothic. More important, he announced the two principles upon which he believed architecture should depend—that there should be no features about a building which are not necessary for convenience, construction or propriety, and that ornament should be limited to the essential structure of the building. He found these characteristics in Gothic. And since Christianity, in particular Catholicism, was the way to salvation, Gothic or Pointed architecture had ultimate authority. Of his many churches the one least changed, with its elaborate colour and furnishings, is St Giles, Cheadle, in Staffordshire, built from 1841 to 1846.

The strange thing is that although Pugin, and many architects who

Houses of Parliament, London, by Sir Charles Berry and A. W. N. Pugin

Interior of House of Lords by A. W. N. Pugin

followed him, detested the world of industry and reacted against it strongly, which ultimately led to the Arts and Crafts movement of the end of the century, his principles, in all their seriousness and simplicity, and their emphasis on function, were those you might associate with the Industrial Revolution. It is to the effects of that revolution that we must now turn.

Leading up to it was the work of the great engineers and surveyors—Telford, who at the turn of the century and in its early decades built bridges, roads, canals and churches; the Stephensons, who built bridges and railways; Brunel, who built bridges, roads, railways and ships. The buildings and artefacts of industry provided knowledge and experience that could be adapted to architecture, which now grew at an unprecedented rate. The Albert Dock in Liverpool, for example, designed by Jesse Hartley and opened by Prince Albert in 1845, was a vast warehouse scheme covering seven acres, with iron-framed buildings clad in brick and resting on massive cast-iron Doric columns, one of the masterpieces of industrial architecture. On the other side of the Pennines a young architect, Cuthbert Brodrick, won the competition for Leeds Town Hall in 1853, and created the very symbol of civic pride in one of the new wealthy industrial cities. It radiated confidence with its great rectangular plan and gigantic Corinthian order; dominating everything was its tall French-looking Baroque tower. A few years later, Brodrick made another symbolic gesture. The Grand Hotel at Scarborough, 1863–7, was, as its name implies, the grandest hotel of its time, spectacularly located on the edge of a hill above the sea. It was a middle-class dream. It used brick and terracotta and had an original roof line with bulging towers. It was brilliantly planned and used the latest service technology available.

I have selected these buildings because of their merit, but also because they represent the demand for buildings which had either not existed before or, if they had, had played only a minor role in the history of architecture. With increased wealth and increased population, the task of creating country houses for the new rich and city churches for the new urban poor provided plenty of work for domestic and ecclesiastical architects. But the buildings that dominate the nineteenth century are not so much those as clubs, government buildings, town halls, hotels and a vast array of others—banks, offices, libraries, museums, galleries, exhibition buildings, shops, arcades, law courts, prisons, hospitals, schools, colleges, and the more obvious products of the industrial age—railway stations, docks,

Reform Club, London, by Sir Charles Barry

Albert Dock, Liverpool, by Jesse Hartley

bridges, viaducts, factories and warehouses. We shall see some of these taking over the architectural scene in other countries.

That was one major change. The other major change was brought about by the Industrial Revolution, mainly by the transformation of building technology. This transformation came in the form of new, man-made building materials, new structural techniques and new technical services. Together they produced a universal structural system that could be applied to the new building types.

The structural possibilities of iron were first demonstrated on a dramatic scale in England in 1777 at Coalbrookdale by the iron bridge that crossed the river Severn. Within a few years iron was being extensively used for columns and frames, together with hollow clay tile floors, to provide a fireproof construction for the mills. By the beginning of the nineteenth century that system developed into a complete internal skeleton of stanchions and beams. The skeleton, which had from the beginning been one of the basic methods of building, had come into its own again.

The advantages of iron over masonry in terms of strength without bulk and of economy led to its adoption for more fashionable buildings—churches, large houses with roofed courtyards, clubs, public buildings. In 1839 the roof of Chartres Cathedral was replaced with a new cast-iron roof above the stone vaults; and iron was used for the roofs of the New Palace of Westminster a few years later. After the 1850s its use declined for a time, mainly because of architects' preferences for other materials and the influence of Ruskin. But for the bulk of ordinary buildings in what has recently come to be known as the Functional Tradition—in bridges, railway stations, conservatories, market halls, shops and offices—iron was an obvious choice.

Iron—at first, cast iron and wrought iron (made more flexible and strong in tension as a result of an invention patented in 1785), and then steel, following the invention of the Bessemer process in 1856— lent itself to the most dramatic and large-scale enterprises. Other materials familiar in preceding centuries took on a new life or new

Town Hall and Victoria Square, Leeds, by Cuthbert Brodrick. From an old photograph

characteristics. Advances in plate-glass manufacture in the 1840s, coupled with the lifting of duty and tax, ensured its widespread use from the 1850s onwards. Bricks, hitherto handmade, were mechanized and there were new types and a huge variety of shapes, patterns and colours. And traditional craftsmanship began to change, sometimes to the dismay of architects and critics such as Ruskin.

Interior and exterior views of the Crystal Palace, London, by Joseph Paxton

Craftsmanship changed through the production of manufactured building elements and prefabrication. It followed that the operations on the site were also mechanized. That in itself required larger organizations than the old craft firms could cope with; hence the rise of the large building contractors. The needs of industry led to the development of new technical services in heating, ventilation and sanitation, which began to be applied to domestic architecture as well. Central heating, not used since the time of the Romans, reappeared in the form of steam-heating systems in the early nineteenth century; cold- and hot-water systems and sanitary plumbing developed rapidly in the second half of the century. Gas lighting came to London in 1809 and that brought a new dimension to living—urban night-life. In 1801, Volta demonstrated to Napoleon the production of electricity from a pile battery; by the 1880s electric light was available to those who could afford it and were prepared to take the risk of using it. Lifts, telephones and mechanical ventilation were introduced in the last decades of the century. However much people may have regretted or been frightened by the scale and rapidity of the changes, what had been produced in a hundred years was a whole new range of possi-/ bilities, and therefore a new aesthetic and a new challenge to the designer. How was he to cope with change and express architectural qualities in such a revolutionary milieu?

One building more than any other in Britain brought these discoveries together and became the most influential innovation of its time, influencing, because thousands of people came to see it, the architecture of the world. That was the Crystal Palace in London, housing the Great Exhibition of 1851. Everything about it was symptomatic of and a portent of the future. It was the brain-child not of an architect, but of a gardener, Joseph Paxton (1801–65). He brought to the problem of a vast space the lessons he had learned in building greenhouses at Chatsworth. The Crystal Palace was prefabricated, it was light and transparent, supported and enclosed by iron and glass. Its form was

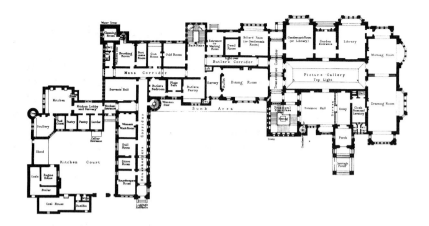

Bear Wood, Berkshire.
Ground-floor plan

revolutionary in that it was indeterminate; there was no reason why it should not be made bigger or smaller, longer or wider. It had no conventional style. Its erection depended upon railway transport and sophisticated organization of the site. It was constructed in nine months. And it could be taken down and put up again, as it was at Sydenham in 1852, where it survived until it was destroyed by fire in 1936.

Because of the vast output of construction in Britain—it must for many years have seemed like a vast building site, especially in the towns and cities—it is impossible to do more than note a few typical buildings. Of those that consciously followed some sort of style by choosing to use Romanesque or Gothic in one of its many forms or derivations are the Natural History Museum, London, by Alfred Waterhouse (1830-1905), in yellow and blue terracotta with lively animal detail, the Law Courts, London, by G.E. Street (1824-81), the swan-song of the Gothic revival in England and of the architect, who died of overwork, and the Royal Infirmary, Edinburgh, by David Bryce, a very successful Scottish architect with many dramatic buildings in Edinburgh to his credit. The most original architect within that tradition was William Butterfield (1814-1900), whose All Saints, Margaret Street, London, 1847-59, was seen at the time as the complete demonstration of the principles of Pugin applied to the high-church practice of the Church of England. The church, vicarage and hall are closely grouped around a small court; the spire is tall and the nave high. And it is full of ingenuity in, for example, the roof trusses, the highly decorated flat surfaces and the frank expression of materials with inherent colour. It is Victorian architecture at its most uncompromising. Gothic was no longer a revival; it was a vehicle for personal expression.

Oriel Chambers, Liverpool, built by Peter Ellis in 1864 was more original in its construction as well as in its function as offices. It used a light iron frame and masonry piers and provided a neat solution to the problem of creating an interesting rhythm with plate-glass fenestration by using shallow oriels the height of the building. There is one other essential feature of nineteenth-century architecture which can only be appreciated by looking at a plan.

Bear Wood in Berkshire was designed for the owner of *The Times* by Robert Kerr, the author of *The Gentleman's House*, a standard book on nineteenth-century domestic design. In the event it was a failure as a house and in its appearance, which is not worth illustrating. But its planning illustrates Victorian architecture at its most ingenious. Advanced technology is exploited for plumbing, gas lighting, central heating and fireproof construction; the plan is a *tour de force* of planning, with intricate lines of communication between the multiplicity of rooms, the separation and definition of every function and different spaces for each, including stairs for bachelors.

That brilliance in planning was even more dramatically demonstrated in France, with the design of the Opéra, Paris, by Charles Garnier in 1861–75. Stylistically, it is a triumph of sumptuous historicism, with wonderful colour inside and out and plastic Baroque forms and sculpture. But the plan is exquisite. Most people find it difficult to read a plan, but this one is worth studying; it shows the architect's mind working on every function and space, every corner and detail. In the nineteenth centuy the French became the leaders of monumental planning and have remained so until today.

Apart from planning, there are two other aspects of nineteenth-century French architecture to be emphasized, which show the range of problems that architects and engineers set out to solve. The first, which affected other European countries, was, as the Opéra itself demonstrated, the theory of 'architectural polychromy'. The spokesman for the theory was a not very good architect, J.-I. Hittorff, who based his beliefs on discoveries made about ancient Greek buildings. In 1823 he found evidence at Selinus and Agrigentum that classical Greek buildings had been highly and even vulgarly coloured. In the 1820s and 1830s there was heated discussion; such a belief after all threatened the purity of Neo-classical conventions. But Hittorff was not only interested in colour as an archaeological curiosity, he needed the authority of antiquity to back up his proposals for a new architecture. In England, Owen Jones (1806–89) took up the theory enthusiastically and brought brilliant colour into the Crystal Palace interior.

Interior of All Saints, Margaret Street, London, by William Butterfield

Plan of the Opéra, Paris

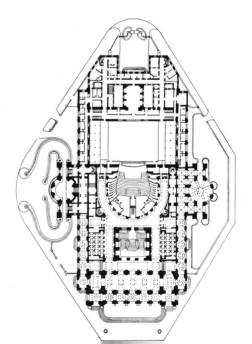

Staircase, the Opéra, Paris

*Interior of Bibliothèque
Sainte-Geneviève, Paris,
by Henri Labrouste*

In Copenhagen, Gotlieb Bindesbøll (1800–56) designed a museum in 1839 with classical shapes and rich primary colours. If the Parthenon had been covered with vivid colour and gilt on its columns, the new architecture could afford similar splendour.

The second aspect of French nineteenth-century architecture was the exploitation of structure. The writer and architect Viollet-le-Duc (1814–79) demonstrated in his massive and influential publications on architecture (*Entretiens sur l'architecture*, 1872) how the principles of Gothic architecture could be interpreted and developed through structural technology. The architect who made the most effective use of a structure integral with plan and appearance was Henri Labrouste. In the Bibliothèque Sainte-Geneviève in Paris of 1843–50 and in the reading-room for the Bibliothèque Nationale of 1862–8, he produced light and lively interiors, however uninteresting the exteriors might be. Slender iron columns support shallow arches and delicate domes, and the spaces created inside are one of the great achievements of metal architecture. By applying the new technology to his analysis of the needs of a modern library to be used by many people, he produced a space which combines ingenuity with elegance.

If Labrouste created some of the finest rooms, it was the engineer Gustave Eiffel (1832–1932) who gave Paris its most conspicuous and most visited monument, the Eiffel Tower of 1887–9. Eiffel had designed many bridges (as well as the frame of the Statue of Liberty) and was an engineer of exceptional distinction. The Tower was the signpost of the Paris Exhibition of 1889, and for many years the world's tallest structure. Its elegance and economy, with the main structural elements strongly emphasized and knitted together with a metal web of great complexity, was a presage of the future. However much disliked and criticized at the time, it was a work of engineering that demonstrated spatial possibilities for later structures and also for the decorative arts.

In Germany and Austria, the same preoccupation with style and the same adventure with structure and space can be seen. In Austria at the height, and not long before the dissolution, of the Austro-Hungarian Empire, classical styles seemed most appropriate. There were some outstanding Gothic churches, like Heinrich von Ferstel's Votivkirche in Vienna of 1856–79. More serene is the Parliament building (1873–83) by Theophil Hansen (1813–91), a long symmetrical building in beautifully correct Greek style. The Burgtheater is bolder, with its curved front facing the Ringstrasse, the road encircling the central area of Vienna and one of the first exercises in the planning of ring roads. It was a masterly feat in imaginative classicism, designed by Gottfried Semper (1803–79) and built from 1874 to 1888.

German architects, flourishing in a nation forming itself into a greater power under Bismarck, seem to have swung between a tough classicism and the most reckless fantasy. In the Altes Pinakothek in Munich, one of the great picture galleries of the century, Leo von Klenze produced a plan (1826–36) that was to influence the design of such buildings throughout Europe. It is High Renaissance in style, but, as in the French examples, it is the plan that makes it historically important. The immense length of twenty-five bays is divided into three parallel rows, the central one containing top-lit galleries, the loggia on the entrance front giving full longitudinal access to them.

The rich and mad Ludwig II of Bavaria inspired or drove his architects into realms of fantasy, an escape from the industrial world. He built three famous palaces, whose cost eventually impoverished him. Linderhof of 1870–4 is a Rococo fantasy, Herrenchiemsee of 1878–86 recalls the glories of Versailles, but Neuschwanstein of 1868–86 was the last word in Romanticism, a fairy castle on a mountain, complete with decorations of Wagnerian legends.

The rest of Europe reveals the same diversity, with national and regional overtones. Brussels' Palais de Justice was in Neo-Baroque; Amsterdam's Rijksmuseum in a free Renaissance style which hid vast internal courts of iron and glass; Milan produced one of the best examples of the new roofed pedestrian streets in the Galleria Vittorio Emanuele II of 1865–7. It has a vast cruciform plan, its arms meeting

Neuschwanstein Castle, Bavaria, by Edward Riedel

Galleria Vittorio Emanuele II, Milan, by Giuseppe Mengoni

The Capitol, Washington, completed by T. U. Walter

in a 128 feet diameter octagon at the centre that rises to a height of 96 feet. It was a grand, expensive shelter for shopping and social intercourse, built with English money and technical advice. The most successful extravaganza of the whole period was in Italy in the monument to Victor Emanuele II, Rome, built from 1885 to 1911. It towers over the Piazza Venezia and glares down the Corso, a stunning if vulgar tribute to the founder of a nation.

The main themes of nineteenth-century architecture are to be found in Europe. But by the end of the century, Europe seemed to have exhausted itself and to be waiting for disaster, and the story of architecture shifted to America, by then the centre of economic power with its vast natural resources. For most of the nineteenth century, America, Australia and New Zealand reflected the concern with style and new functions that preoccupied Europe.

Among the outstanding buildings in the United States at this time are the Pennsylvanian Academy of the Fine Arts (1876) in Philadelphia by Frank Furness in fanciful, colourful and original Gothic, and the Public Library (1882–92) in Boston, by McKim, Mead and White, a Cinquecento essay of compelling elegance and exquisite craftsmanship. As in Britain, the greatest demonstration of national pride and confidence was in government building—the Capitol in Washington. The central portion with its portico had been built at the end of the previous century and the beginning of the nineteenth. Now, from 1851 to 1867, Thomas U. Walter extended it hugely and, in effect, created a new unified complex on a dramatic scale. Its most distinguished architectural feature is the great central dome, 207 feet high and 94 feet in diameter, which has a cast-iron shell.

The nineteenth century had changed the whole architectural landscape with a wealth of new buildings demonstrating a massive variety of taste. The climax of nearly a century of experiment came at the turn of the century. To that climax in the United States we must now turn.

19

Expectancy: the Turn of the Century

The period with which this chapter deals is relatively short, between 1880 and 1920. But it is a most distinctive and stimulating moment in architectural history. It saw the formulation of theories and slogans and the creation of some extraordinary masterpieces and new types of building which were to change the shape of towns and cities.

It was an exciting, almost hysterical time. In both Europe and America cities grew, and sophisticated technology developed at amazing speed. Music and the visual arts were as lively as at any time in history. In Europe it was almost as if everyone was waiting for a storm, a cataclysm, which indeed broke with the Great War of 1914–18. It was the age of apprehension. But if there was a nervous excitement in Europe, there was a growing self-confidence in America. The mounting confidence of a rich nation aware that its resources could buy almost anything was irrepressible.

In the 1880s and 1890s an architectural revolution was under way in America, in particular in Chicago. The major influence on the growth of what came to be known as the Chicago School was Henry Hobson Richardson (1838–1886), who had worked for Labrouste in Paris and returned to America at the end of the Civil War. He started his practice by winning a competition in 1866. He developed a very personal heavy style, of which the Marshall Field Warehouse in Chicago of 1885–7 is a well-known example. It became the model for the new generation of Chicago architects. The building which best gives some idea of his power as a designer is the Crane Library at Quincy, Massachusetts, of 1880–3. His training in Romanesque is apparent in the elevations, but the design is informal, a skilful combination of mass and line and heavy detail interpreted in a personal way.

Crane Library, Quincy, Mass., by Henry Hobson Richardson

Richardson had a national reputation. What brought the Chicago School into prominence was the disastrous fire of 1871. It swept across the river and destroyed much of the city centre, including a number of cast-iron buildings which were not built of fireproof construction. The opportunity and the challenge provided Chicago architects with a programme of building which had in its very nature to dispense with historical styles. In doing so it set the scene for the modern movement.

The crucial event in that movement was the skyscraper. It is generally accepted that the first definitive skyscraper was the Home Insurance Building, Chicago, built in 1883–5 by William le Baron Jenney (1832–1907). Of fireproof construction, it has a metal frame clad in brick and masonry. But Jenney could not quite abandon traditional detailing on the exterior and had not really mastered the challenge of giving a new shape to such a new kind of building. In the 1890s, a few years after the the fire, skyscrapers were built by Burnham and Root, Holabird and Roche, Adler and Sullivan. They effectively established the Chicago School and the essential outlines of twentieth-century commercial architecture.

What made multi-storey buildings possible was the lift, invented in 1852 and made widely available by the invention of Siemen's electric lift in 1880. There was now no reason why buildings should not become higher and higher. A new style of building and a new cityscape had arrived. Outstanding among the early skyscrapers in Chicago are Burnham and Root's Monadnock Building of 1889–1901 (constructed of solid masonry) and Reliance Building of 1890–4 (using a metal frame). In Buffalo, in 1890, Louis Sullivan (1856–1924), one of the most cultivated of all American architects, designed the Guaranty Building. Then, in the Carson, Pirie and Scott Department Store, Chicago, of 1899–1904, he demonstrated his mastery of the new form.

Reliance Building, Chicago, by Daniel Hudson Burnham and John Wellborn Root

Sullivan was the most intense and logical architect of his generation. A brief explanation of the Store is enough to demonstrate the essential elements that made it a prototype for countless twentieth-century offices and department stores. There are ten floors of offices, covered with white terracotta tiles hung on the steel frame, punctuated by even rows of large windows. These floors sit on a two-storey base (which is what a shop needs) framed as part of the metal structure. Panels above and around the main doorways are filled with luxurious Art Nouveau decoration in cast iron. Logic and fantasy went hand in hand, as they had in the nineteenth century; a repetitive mass building needs its own distinctive decoration. Sullivan's principle, inherited from nineteenth-century theorists, that 'Form Follows Function' was to provide a slogan for many years to come.

The two principal materials for the new high and massive buildings were steel, which as we have seen had been pioneered in Britain and brought into general use in America, and reinforced concrete, which was developed in France. By 1892 François Hennebique had perfected a system for the best location of steel reinforcement in concrete; the combination of the compressive strength of concrete with the tensile strength of steel in a homogeneous grid was one of the turning-points of architectural history. It provided a new structural material for the

new forms and big spaces of modern architecture.

Carson, Pirie, Scott Department Store, Chicago, by Louis Sullivan

One of the first examples of reinforced concrete was Anatole de Baudot's church of St-Jean de Montmartre in Paris of 1897–1904. De Baudot (1836–1915) had been a pupil of Viollet-le-Duc and followed his master's ideal of using modern technology to develop further traditional structural principles: starting with neo-Gothic, he re-examined its forms and reduced them so that only the essentials remained. Elimination of unnecessary detail and expression of structure are basic to any understanding of modern architecture.

The architect who brought that approach in France to its first satisfying climax was Auguste Perret. In 1903 in his apartments at 25 bis Rue Franklin, Paris, he went further than the Chicago architects had done. He realized that the eight-storey frame made load-bearing walls unnecessary; since the walls held nothing up, the building could have open space inside. He clad the frame on the outside with tiles decorated with a flower motif. But the structural elements are freely

25 bis Rue Franklin, Paris, by Auguste Perret

Expiatory Temple of the Sagrada Familia, Barcelona, by Antoni Gaudí

expressed, razor-sharp and deeply modelled to give clear vertical movement to the building. Perret made the new concrete architecture respectable with that block of apartments. Twenty years later, in 1922–3, he was to reveal in a church on the outskirts of Paris, Notre-Dame du Raincy, how a traditional plan could lead to a spatial concept equal to the vision of the great Gothic designers. Segmental vaults of *in situ* reinforced concrete were elegantly supported on a few slender shafts, so that a new light and airy space was encircled by non-load-bearing screen walls of pre-cast concrete units filled with coloured glass.

The French delight in decorative detail led, surprisingly, to the creation of a new kind of expressive space. Hector Guimard (1867–1942), who designed the entrances to the Paris Métro in 1900, was an exponent of the fashionable Art Nouveau. Its characteristics were the whiplash line, abstracted biological and botanical decoration, asymmetry and a wide repertoire of materials, all of which allowed for personal expression and novel decorative themes.

In Brussels the initiator of Art Nouveau was Victor Horta (1861–1947), whose Hôtel Tassel of 1892–3 had a novel plan and made use of many levels. But his masterpiece was the later Hôtel Solvay of 1895–1900. The staircase hall has all the characteristics of Art Nouveau—flowing curves and a frankly decorative display of wrought iron. It was a theme that gave the whole interior of the house a stylistic unity. Hector Guimard gave an even fuller demonstration of Art Nouveau architecture in his Castel-Béranger, Paris. He used many different materials on the façade and made the forms flow so that they suggested living organisms. For a short time it looked as if a wildly imaginative and flexible system had been invented, which would spread every-

where; its sudden death was caused by the inappropriateness of Art Nouveau for ordinary building functions.

But it did play a part in one of the most extraordinary manifestations of originality ever seen in the history of architecture. It happened in northern Spain, in the work of Antoni Gaudí. Art Nouveau in Spain was known as *Modernismo*, and Barcelona was the centre of a wave of organic design. Gaudí, born in 1852, was the most inventive and the most idiosyncratic. He died after being run over by a tram in 1926. His funeral procession was one of the longest ever seen in the city; his death was mourned as a national calamity.

The masterpiece for which Gaudí is best known, unfinished at his death, was the Expiatory Temple of the Sagrada Familia in Barcelona. He took over a neo-Gothic design by another architect and transformed it into a huge cathedral. The four tapering towers of the east transept, the Nativity façade, were one of the few parts that were completed. They are over 350 feet high, punctuated with louvres (designed to release the sound of long tubular bells) and finished at the top with fantastic finials of glass, ceramic and tile. The carvings of human figures, animals, plants and clouds are naturalistic. Every bit was supervised and some were even put together by Gaudí himself, who gave up all other work and moved into the crypt, where he lived in squalor until his death.

His secular buildings and landscapes have an originality even more dramatic than his cathedral. The Casa Battló in the centre of Barcelona is known as the House of the Bones; for its structural members at the front have warped surfaces which are bone-like in shape. In the Casa Milá, a large block of apartment flats, also in Barcelona, the exterior seems like waves, and the interior has no right angles. He used

Stairwell of Hôtel Tassel, Brussels, by Victor Horta

Crypt of Santa Coloma de Cervelló, Colonia Güell, by Antoni Gaudí

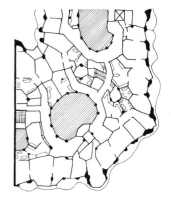

Casa Milá, Barcelona

parabolic arches and allowed an amazing roofscape to be shaped by the differing heights caused by the differing spans. In the Güell Park, he made a landscape of unusual diversity, with waving forms, strange stone arcades and evocative sculptures. He made an architecture out of his exceptional understanding of the structure of natural forms— of shells, mouths, bones, gristle, lava, vegetation, wings and petals. He created a fantasy of colour and light.

Most fascinating of all his creations is the crypt of the church of Santa Coloma de Cervelló, where in addition to elaborating upon natural forms he worked out his own system of structural determination. He used a web of strings in tension with weights attached. The shape created thus in tension would, if you imagined it upside down, give the natural shape for a structure made of stones in compression. The strange twisted shapes of the columns and the vaults are the outcome of this experiment. No buttresses are necessary, as in Gothic buildings, he said, because the members are at the correct angle and slope to resist the forces laid upon them.

Gaudí's favourite geometric shapes were the paraboloid, the hyperboloid and the helicoid, which can be found in nature. However crazy the shapes look, they are in fact carefully thought out, structurally sound and geometrically precise. He went further than anyone in creating an architecture based on the apparently irregular, but in reality functional, shapes and colours of nature.

If France, Belgium and Spain were the cradles of Art Nouveau, its sprightly forms were introduced to Britain in the illustrations of Aubrey Beardsley. In architecture, it expressed itself not only in original forms, but also in the more solid and functional approach of the Arts and Crafts Movement.

Pugin, as we have seen, had proclaimed the main principles of a functionalist architecture. Ruskin had extended Pugin's ideas enormously and emphasized the importance of the craftsman in providing quality in decorative form. What was now added was the belief that architecture was an expression of society. William Morris was the major figure in the second half of the nineteenth century in the promotion of the Arts and Crafts movement, which he saw as not just an artistic but also a social programme. For his own house in Bexley

Red House, Bexley Heath, Kent, by Philip Webb

GROUND FLOOR PLAN

Heath (1859-60), he commissioned Philip Webb to design a dwelling which would be mediaeval in style, but contemporary in its frank expression of materials. It is of brick and tile, sparse in detail, substantial in construction and homely in appearance. Webb and Morris set out to create an honest architecture and succeeded; it is a landmark in architectural history.

Ground-floor plan, Deanery Garden, Sonning-on-Thames

Deanery Garden, Sonning-on-Thames, by Sir Edwin Lutyens

Having eschewed conventional classical or Gothic detail, architects were able to point to the moral virtue of using materials honestly and at the same time enjoy the rich textures and varied forms of traditional native architecture and of craftwork made from natural materials. Hence the revival of interest in native vernacular.

The architects who dominated this period, including Webb, were Charles Annesley Voysey (1857-1941), the finest exponent of the vernacular, Richard Norman Shaw (1831-1912), the most successful architect of his generation, and Sir Edwin Lutyens (1869-1944). Lutyens designed more than a hundred houses, as well as major public buildings, of which the greatest is the Viceroy's House for the new capital of India, New Delhi. Among his houses, the one which best exemplifies his work is the Deanery Garden at Sonning on the Thames of 1901. It is a middle-sized house set in a delightful English garden created by Gertrude Jekyll. The materials are used in a natural way and frankly expressed. But what is original about this and all of Lutyens' work is the plan. We saw in the last chapter how the planning of buildings became a preoccupation with architects in the nineteenth century. Lutyens brought even more originality into that planning. He made access and entry to his houses an adventure full of surprises. In an apparently axial house, one might have to change direction several times before finding the main rooms. At the Deanery, the way through from the road to the garden is sometimes semi-enclosed, sometimes open, with spaces and rooms opening off it. The garden elevation at the end is one of the finest asymmetrical compositions in English architecture.

Charles Rennie Mackintosh (1868-1928) is seen today as one of the most original and historically important architects. He designed houses and some very original tea-rooms in Glasgow which took their character from his own version of Art Nouveau. His major work was

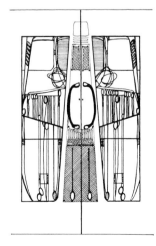

Art Nouveau symbol by Charles Rennie Mackintosh

Library of the Glasgow School of Art by Charles Rennie Mackintosh

Town Hall, Stockholm, by Ragnar Ostberg

the Glasgow School of Art, won in a competition and built in two phases, from 1896 to 1899 and 1907 to 1909. The directness of the main elevations, apart from some delightful play with curved and twisted forms in wrought iron, is the simple outcome of putting rooms and studios together in the most functional way. Inside, it is another experience. The main studios, main exhibition spaces and staircases demonstrate his mastery of the nature of different materials. The library is remarkable. Mackintosh used verticals, horizontals and gentle curves in timber to work out a richly decorative space, defined and shaped by columns, beams, cover plates and hanging frets. All the details are his—the light fittings, the door furniture, the windows, the periodicals table. He was considered a failure in his time, and he left Glasgow. He spent his later years in London and then in France, making the most entrancing watercolours of landscapes and flowers.

The Arts and Crafts movement in England and Scotland had an influence on the Continent through *Das Englische Haus*, written by Hermann Muthesius, an attaché at the German embassy in London, and published in Berlin in 1904–5. It described the work of most of the architects we have discussed in this chapter. In the work of the older generation, the themes reflect those of Britain and that balance between a passion for the expression of structure and the exploitation of decorative detail. The exhibition hall at Darmstadt, 1907, by Joseph Maria Olbrich (1867–1908) is a major example. More expressive was the work of Otto Wagner (1841–1918) in Vienna, who set out to distill classicism to a point where all that remained was a logical statement of material, structure and function. His Majolica House of 1898 is plain, dignified and finely proportioned; the decorative majolica spreads right across the upper four floors in coloured tiles. In the Post

Office Savings Bank (1904–6) he suppressed his liking for ornament and decoration and left a beautifully constructed building that relies for its effect simply on the forthright statement of construction and function. The most extreme exponent of this kind of Functionalism was Adolf Loos, who in 1908 proclaimed that 'Ornament is crime' and converted people to a belief that was to take half a century to eradicate.

In the Netherlands, the major buildings of the period were more personal and expressive. Outstanding is the Exchange, Amsterdam (1898–1903), by H.P. Berlage. It had a modern function that Berlage wished to express without stylistic mannerisms. But he also wanted his building to enjoy the attention and admiration of the many people who would use its halls and corridors. He therefore brought together many painters, sculptors and craftsmen to work on its fine spaces. The interior has a fine massive dignity and a most attractive character.

The mood spread widely. In Silesia, Max Berg was responsible in 1911–13 for the Jahrhunderthalle at Breslau, erected to mark the centenary of the nation's rise against Napoleon. It is a stupendous structure in reinforced concrete, with the largest span of its type, great internal arches and stepped concentric rings. Even more emotional in its effect was Ragnar Ostberg's Town Hall at Stockholm. It took twenty years to build, from 1904 to 1923, but has always been recognized as a triumph of what is best described as the Modern Traditional school. It is beautifully sited by the water, and has a romantic style that combines lightness with firmness and gives it a dignified presence as a unique national symbol.

To see the full expression of the period we must return to America. The Chicago School survived into the early years of the twentieth century, but was never again as influential as it had been in the last decade of the nineteenth. But by that time, it had produced a definitive genius, whose individuality and long career took him from that movement through at least two others and well into the middle of the twentieth century. That was Frank Lloyd Wright, who was born in 1867 or 1869 (no one knows which) and died in 1959. After working for Louis Sullivan, whom he always referred to as 'Lieber Meister', he started his own practice in the 1890s. His work spanned seventy years of extraordinary versatility in the handling of steel, stone, red wood and reinforced concrete, extending geometrical plans and silhouettes to create a new and exhilarating relationship with the natural environment.

Wright had no doubt that he was a genius and the greatest architect of his time. His life was full of drama, including the burning of his house twice and the murder of his wife and her children, and divorces. He wrote copiously and was a well-known public figure. His autobiography is one of the most compelling accounts ever told of an architect's life. His book *Testament* (1957) brings together the theories and personal beliefs that inspired his work. He was regarded as possibly the greatest American of his generation.

In 1889 he built his own house in Oak Park, Chicago, and in the next few years he built many other houses in that rich suburb. They

Martin House, Buffalo, by Frank Lloyd Wright

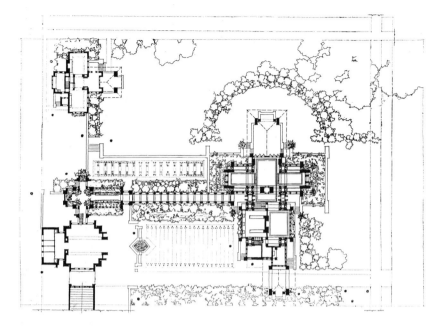

were complemented by the Unity Church, an influential design that took the basic elements of the scheme—church, entrance and parish hall—and composed them into simple cubic shapes. To understand his houses, it is best to look at one of his typical plans, that of the Martin House at Buffalo. The basic form results from the crossing of axes. The extension of these axes into the garden forms other contained shapes which, characteristic of Wright's style, provide a single spatial experience through the interpenetration of internal and external shapes. He had an exceptional understanding of three-dimensional geometry, possibly instilled in him by his early education at a Froebel kindergarten. Especially interesting is his ability to make the internal

Robie House, Chicago, by Frank Lloyd Wright

Majolica House, Vienna, by Otto Wagner

Falling Water, Bear Run, Penn., by Frank Lloyd Wright

spaces flow into one another. Corners of the rooms are virtually dissolved, walls become screens, the horizontal emphasis is maintained by low sweeping ceilings and roofs and by long clerestory windows, often leaded, and the levels change so as to define rooms without barriers or doors. He created, he claimed, the open plan.

Of his many 'prairie houses' one of the best known and most accessible is Robie House, Chicago, 1908-09. In it, he combined the traditional virtues of craftsmanship and good detail with modern technical installations. Behind the exquisitely laid brickwork, stone copings and leaded windows were electric lighting and heating systems of the most advanced type of their time. But his work demonstrated not so much the technology as the dramatic composition of roofs and the flow of the interior spaces into one another, which changed for ever the concept of a house as a collection of boxes.

Wright's career was several times given new directions by his constantly questing and inquisitive mind. By the time he had finished the Imperial Hotel in Tokyo (1916-22), whose brilliantly original structure enabled it to survive the earthquake of 1926, and returned to America he was already regarded as an old master. He then proceeded to startle the world with an even more dramatic series of houses, of which Falling Water at Bear Run, Pennsylvania (1935-7), is probably the most frequently illustrated house of the twentieth century. Like his earlier houses, it is brilliantly organized. The stepped sections of reinforced concrete thrust outwards from a core of masonry to hover in overlapping planes above the rocks, trees and falling water. He mastered an apparently impossible site and created the most vivid example of man-made form complementing nature.

At almost the same time, he built Taliesin West at Phoenix, Arizona. It was to be a winter home, which would also be a house and an atelier for his many pupils; it is still the spiritual home of the Wright admirers. Ordered by 45° diagonals, the structure is of what he called desert concrete—with big boulders of local stone as aggregate, timber framing and canvas awnings—a succinct statement of his concept of organic architecture, adaptable forms and natural materials in unity with the site, in this case, a response to the harmonies and rhythms of the Arizona desert.

The turn of the centry produced an architecture that was international in its conception, but highly personal and idiosyncratic in its national manifestations. It was the last time that architects would have the opportunity of expressing such individuality in their work. After the calamity of World War I, Europe, the Americas and the East were entering a new phase of internationalism, which suggested not so much variation as much as uniformity. That was represented by the International Style.

20

Function and Anonymity

The term International Style was coined in 1932 by the organizers of the first International Exhibition of Modern Architecture at the Museum of Modern Art in New York. Since that time, despite many criticisms and complaints that it does not accurately reflect the actual situation, it has come to represent the mainstream of modern architecture from about the 1920s to the end of the 1950s. The book produced for the exhibition declared that 'there is now a single body of discipline, fixed enough to integrate contemporary style as a reality and yet elastic enough to permit individual interpretation and to encourage natural growth. ... There is, first, a new conception of architecture as volume rather than mass. Secondly, regularity rather than axial symmetry serves as the chief means of ordering design.'

The need for order was in a sense true of the whole of the period. The cataclysmic events of the First World War and the Russian Revolution of 1917 changed Europe's internal order. The years that followed saw the rise of authoritarian socialist and fascist states in Europe, a succession of economic crises and finally another world war (1939–1945). What emerged from all that was a mass culture—of production, consumption and communication.

Architects and planners, as the designers of a new society, went to great trouble to identify themselves with international themes. The Congrès Internationaux d'Architecture Moderne (CIAM) was founded in 1928. They lasted in one form or another until 1959, but their earliest declarations were the most lasting in their impact. 'It is only from the present', they declared, 'that our architectural work should be derived.' They hoped to 'put architecture back on its real plane, the economic and social plane' and specifically stated that 'The most efficacious production is derived from rationalization and standardization.'

In order to see the movement taking shape and understand why it became an obsession with several generations, we must look at the work and ideas of some leading exponents, always recognizing that they, the mainstream architects, saw themselves as part of a social revolution; architecture was to become, not just a witness to, but a definitive agency in, the creation of a new society. It was in every way logical and in keeping with that ideology that for the first, and possibly the only, time in the history of architecture, the housing of the ordinary man and woman became the vehicle for great architecture, the material out of which, like the cathedrals and palaces of an earlier epoch, great architectural statements were to be made.

The towering genius of the movement was one of the founders of CIAM, Charles-Edouard Jeanneret (1887–1966), better known as Le Corbusier. Writer, painter, architect and town-planner, he was re-

Villa Savoye, Poissy, by Le Corbusier

Villa Savoye, Poissy

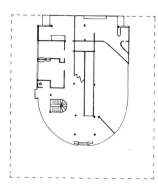

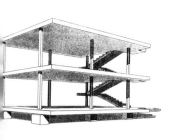

Dom-ino skeleton (as drawn in Oeuvre complète, *vol 1, 1910–29)*

sponsible for a stream of ideas about architecture and town-planning long before he began to put up buildings. Every few years he published his designs and projects, along with his own precise aphorisms and uncompromising statements. His was the most pervasive influence on modern architecture, for good or ill. An understanding of the work of Le Corbusier is indispensable for an understanding of modern architecture.

In his seminal first book *Vers une architecture*, 1923, translated into English under the title *Towards a New Architecture*, Le Corbusier announced the five points of a new architecture—free-standing supports (pilotis), the roof garden, the free plan, the ribbon window and the freely composed façade. We can see all of them in his Villa Savoye at Poissy (1928–31), which is an elevated white concrete box cut open horizontally and vertically. As with the paintings of the period, it is a crucial part of the concept that the observer is not standing in one fixed place, but is moving around. As he does so, the forms of the building overlap and become sometimes solid, sometimes transparent. The pilotis free the ground; at the same time the roof garden re-creates in the air the land that is lost below.

We can best understand that concept by looking at a plan. We saw how the Victorians changed the planning of buildings by analysing needs and finding a space and a shape for each function. We then saw how Lutyens created new plans by making the way through a house an unusual adventure, and how Frank Lloyd Wright freed the plan altogether by opening corners, making spaces flow into each other and eventually to the outside. Le Corbusier had a quite different concept in his mind. He saw the internal space or volume as a big cube and then divided it up both horizontally and vertically, so that one part of the cube might contain taller rooms and other parts smaller and lower ones. He saw the building in the way the Cubist painter interpreted objects; he was, after all, a painter, and he saw the shapes as if *he* was in movement.

The freedom of the plan and of the façade are explained by another simple, but profoundly influential diagram. The project for the

Dom-ino House was published in 1914. It is simply a frame (the basis for low-cost housing) consisting of two concrete slabs kept apart by columns and linked only by an open stair. The plan is quite independent of the structure; the walls and windows can be put where the designer wants them, or glazed throughout. Whereas for virtually the whole of architectural history, walls were used to hold the floors and roof, now they could go anywhere and could be moved. It is a deceptively simple diagram that affected the whole future of architecture.

The other crucial element in Le Corbusier's theories was the creation of the *Modulor*, a scale of architectural proportions based on the human body and the golden section. We saw that Renaissance architects, such as Alberti, worked out systems of proportion that gave their buildings authority and their followers a working set of dimensions that lasted for several centuries. Corbusier went further and produced a flexible system that he used in all his later buildings.

In the Pavillon Suisse at the Cité Universitaire, Paris (1930–2), he

Le Corbusier's modular man

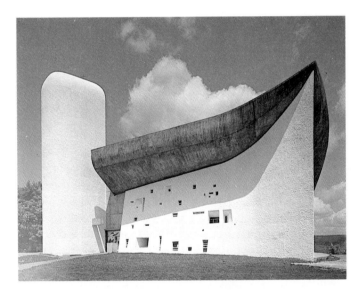

Notre-Dame-du-Haut, Ronchamp, by Le Corbusier

Interior of Notre-Dame-du-Haut by Le Corbusier

Pavillon Suisse, Cité Universitaire, Paris, by Le Corbusier

Unité d'Habitation, Marseilles, by Le Corbusier

used pilotis and ribbon windows. He introduced the idea of a hierarchy of functions—the repetitive function of the forty-five bedrooms for the students is expressed in a slab raised above the ground on massive supports. The communal areas at ground level flow freely, enclosed by a wall of random rubble stonework. Nearly twenty years later he applied those discoveries on a colossal scale in the revolutionary building which was the greatest single influence on mass housing in the post-war years, the Unité d'Habitation, Marseilles (1946–52).

With all its dimensions carefully taken from the Modulor, the great block of 337 split-level apartments in 23 different types rides on top of massive pilotis of concrete marked with the lines of the timber shuttering in which it was poured. The apartments have internal stairs; they are entered from wide internal corridors or streets. There are seventeen floors. About a third of the way up, the internal corridor is a two-storey shopping mall. And on top, there is not just a roof garden but a fantastic landscape, unlike anything Le Corbusier had done before. With concrete and planting, it incorporates a gymnasium and running track, a nursery school, tunnels and caves for children to play in, a swimming pool, seats, a cantilevered balcony and a restaurant, all grouped like a huge continuous sculpture, in which the most dramatic features are the huge tapering funnels for sucking air out of the building. Far from being the cold-hearted rationalist that one of his sayings suggested, that 'the House is a machine for living in', he saw and ultimately expressed in his buildings the great ideal which he announced from the start, that 'L'architecture est le jeu savant, correct et magnifique des volumes assemblés sous la lumière'; in a free translation this statement reads 'Architecture is the masterly, correct and magnificent play of masses brought together in light.'

As if to confound his critics, Le Corbusier produced in 1950–5 a small church which is considered by many to be the greatest single architectural work of the century. The Pilgrimage Chapel of Notre-Dame-du-Haut at Ronchamp (1950–4) on a hilltop in the Vosges mountains contains a (reputedly) miraculous statue which attracts thousands of people on special occasions. The chapel is designed so

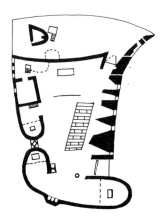

Plan for Chapel of Notre-Dame-du-Haut, Ronchamp

that major services can be held outside. Inside it is small, with three smaller chapels rising up and shaped at the top to let light in. The whole chapel is a study in light. On one side the walls are immensely thick, with deep irregular windows filled with coloured glass; on other walls, tiny windows are tunnels punctured through at different angles. As the sun moves around, the whole interior changes and seems to live. The roof is a huge concrete shell sagging down in the middle and reaching up at the corners to the sky, so that the whole building is seen as pointing out as well as inviting in. For all its apparent irregularity, it is in fact planned around a series of right angles and parallel lines, all dimensioned according to the Modulor. Le Corbusier had said 'Our eyes are made to see forms in light: cubes, cones, spheres, cylinders or pyramids are the great primary forms.'

Le Corbusier's output was considerable and so was his influence. His monastery at La Tourette, near Lyons (1957), became the model for many community buildings in other countries, none more successful than St Peter's College at Cardross in Scotland by Gillespie, Kidd and Coia (1964-6). In the period of his most massive output he designed the central government buildings in the new capital of the Punjab at Chandigarh, with the Himalayas as a backdrop. The Legislative Assembly (1956) is a truncated cooling tower; the Courts of Justice (1951-6), in raw concrete, have a gargantuan umbrella of shallow vaults, which span the High Court, the courtrooms and the portico which lies between them. The Secretariat (1951–8) is a monolith of reinforced concrete cut open by a 'brise-soleil' to allow the passage of breezes while giving shelter from the sun.

We have looked at some of Le Cobusier's buildings in detail because they provided much of the vocabulary of the modern architect and became effectively symbols of the time. But he was by no means alone in developing modern architecture. To see the International Style in many of its other manifestations, we must move around Europe and then cross to the Americas.

The sharp divisions within the movement were especially marked in Germany after the First World War. On the one hand, there was the faction represented by Erich Mendelsohn (1887–1953) in his Einstein Tower at Potsdam (1919-21). Designed as an astronomical laboratory for great scientists, it in fact enabled the architect to make an expressive statement about science in flowing forms of plastic concrete (actually clay tiles covered with stucco). On the other hand, the dominant side of the movement was more anonymous and formal.

In 1911, Walter Gropius and Adolf Meyer designed the Fagus Factory at Alfeld-an-der-Leine. They interpreted its walls as a smooth glass and steel membrane barely interrupted by structural piers. Gropius went on to found a school of design, the Bauhaus, that was to have the most far-reaching effects upon architectural education, especially in the United States. The Bauhaus was founded in 1919 at Weimar, transferred in 1925 to Dessau and closed in 1933 when its leading teachers left for the United States to escape the Nazi regime. It taught design, building and craftsmanship. Under Gropius' direction and with outstanding artists such as Paul Klee, Wassily Kandin-

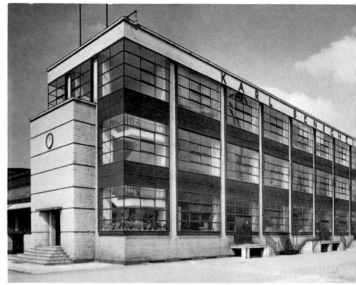

Einstein Tower, Potsdam, by Erich Mendelsohn

Fagus Factory, Alfed-an-der-Leine, by Walter Gropius and Adolf Meyer

Bauhaus, Dessau, by Walter Gropius

sky and Laszló Moholy-Nagy on the staff, it insisted, as William Morris had done, on the fundamental unity underlying all branches of design and emphasized the necessity for a rational and systematic analysis as the start of any programme for serious building.

The buildings for the Bauhaus itself, designed by Gropius in 1925–6, were a precise demonstration of these principles. They were composed of simple elemental shapes, articulated according to their function, arranged on a pin-wheel plan with glass corners, presenting an ever-changing sequence of solid and transparent. The teaching of the Bauhaus spread world-wide. So did the form of the building. So did the influence of its teachers, above all Mies van der Rohe, whose housing for the Weissenhofsiedlung at Stuttgart of 1927 was one of

Schroeder House, Utrecht, by Gerrit Rietveld

Town Hall, Hilversum, by Marinus Dudok

the pioneer terraces of flat-roofed housing, which, for good or ill, was to have a crucial effect on the development of domestic architecture.

In the Netherlands, a group of artists and architects who called themselves De Stijl was formed in Leiden in 1917. They published an influential magazine under that name, inspired by the work of the artist Piet Mondrian, who used interlocking geometric forms, smooth bare surfaces and primary colours in his paintings and constructions. The Schroeder House in Utrecht of 1923–4 by Gerrit Rietveld (1888–1964) is the outstanding exponent of De Stijl aesthetics. It is a cubist construction of smooth planes at right angles, set in space and articulated by primary colours. Inside, the walls slide away to make a large uninterrupted space. Outside, it is an abstract sculpture, as is

Penguin Pool, London Zoo, by Berthold Lubetkin

Stairway of Royal Festival Hall, London, by Robert H. Matthew

Rietveld's well-known chair of straight lines and primary colours for those who would sacrifice comfort rather than their deeply felt aesthetic convictions. More authoritative was Dudok's Town Hall at Hilversum (1930), which has a deceptively simple appearance, using the fine Dutch tradition of brick-building to create a dignified civic building without pomposity. Inside, the spaces and colours are finely chosen and immensely restful. With its blend of the conservative and the radical British architects in particular found it much to their liking.

The International Style was given a sharp injection of radicalism in Britain by a number of refugees from totalitarian regimes on the Continent. The first example of the style in Britain was the house *High and Over* at Amersham (1929–30) by Amyas Connell, who had returned from a sojourn at the British School in Rome (where he had learned about the work of Le Corbusier) and designed this house for the Director of the School, to the great disgust of the local residents. Before going to America, Gropius spent some time in Britain, where he was employed on some influential school buildings and worked with the young architect Maxwell Fry, whose Sunhouse in Hampstead (1936) was one of the outstanding examples of International Modern before the war. But it was Berthold Lubetkin, an émigré from Russia, who made the most dramatic impact. His Penguin Pool at London Zoo (1934), its astonishingly simple spirals of concrete descending to the water, was the most sophisticated of all the animal houses in that lively zoo. With Highpoint I and II at Highgate, London, his firm Tecton (which recruited some of the outstanding designers of the next generation) created the most accomplished examples of the International Style in Britain—tall, clean-lined and very expensively finished in reinforced concrete.

But the International Style did not really get under way in Britain until after the Second World War. Then the lead was taken by public architects' offices, notably that of the London County Council under the leadership of Robert Matthew. The Royal Festival Hall, the centre piece of the Festival of Britain of 1951, was a key building on three counts. First, it was the first public building to use the style; second, it had a magnificent sequence of flowing interior spaces that are wholly characteristic of the Modern Movement; and third, it was the first building comprehensively to demonstrate the application of the new acoustics. It became the major international influence on concert-hall design.

In an undulating parkland among mature trees, the same office established at Roehampton, London, an outstanding estate of what came to be known as mixed development—a mixture of slab and point blocks of eleven storeys along with single-storey, two-storey and four-storey blocks. It became internationally famous and was a characteristically British modification of Le Corbusier's theories fused with lessons learned from Scandinavia. Now that the inadequacies of high-rise living have been disclosed, the estate looks less attractive; in its day it seemed a heroic image of a post-war society housed on a massive scale.

In Scandinavia the International Style had been accepted without anxiety and struggle before the war, in domestic and in public buildings such as museums, universities, churches and hospitals. Of the best-known projects, the Forest Crematorium, Stockholm (1935–40) by Gunnar Asplund (1885–1940) gives an indelible image of dignity and repose with the simplest of geometric forms by the sensitive composition of the chapels, crematorium, columbarium and cross. The work of Alvar Aalto (1897–1976) in Finland is in a class of its own. Aalto was a public figure and almost a national hero—a very independent master who combined romance with technology in a number of buildings that are both practical and intensely personal. One such building is the Civic Centre at Säynätsalo of 1950–2. It is a small collection of pitched roof buildings in red brick, wood and copper, containing a council chamber, municipal offices, library, shops, bank and post office, grouped around a raised green courtyard in a picturesque composition. Aalto succeeded in making a vernacular, humane architecture inspired by the landscape of his country, a free expression that totally avoids doctrinaire severity and is in the great tradition of national romanticism.

London County Council housing at Roehampton, London

Crematorium, Stockholm, by Gunnar Asplund

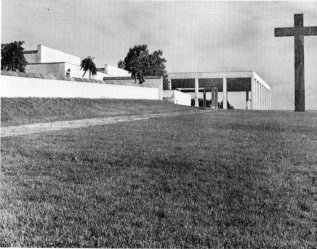

Civic Centre, Säynätsalo, by Alvar Aalto

Glass House, New Canaan, Conn., by Philip Johnson

But, the United States, with its remarkable lack of public control and available money, provided the opportunity for some of the most spectacular achievements of the Modern Movement.

One of the first essays in the International Style was R.M. Schindler's Lovell Beach House at Newport Beach, California (1925–6). Schindler had been born in Vienna, where he was influenced by Otto Wagner. He emigrated to the USA in 1913. But it was through commercial building that the movement was most quickly spread. The Wall Street crash of 1929 brought to an end the boom in office building which had followed the First World War. By that time the Empire State Building (1930–2) was already planned. It was for a long time the tallest building in the world. The Rockefeller Center, New York (1930–40), by Reinhard and Hofmeister and others applied the theme on an even more extensive scale. A group of office and leisure buildings on a twelve-acre site, it is a stylish composition that exploits the lines and planes of vertical movement.

The refugees from the Bauhaus had their effect. Gropius and Marcel Breuer, the most brilliant student the Bauhaus ever had, brought its tenets to the USA in a modest little house for Gropius at Lincoln, Massachusetts (1937–8), applying American timber building techniques to the massing of European Modern. Supremely influential was Mies van der Rohe, Gropius' colleague and successor at the Bauhaus, not only in his own buildings, but also in the work of the Americans who worked with him.

Philip Johnson (b. 1906) took up Mies's themes of steel and glass, shown in his project for a glass house, and created for himself at New Canaan, Connecticut, an exquisite group of buildings (1949) which are a rigorous exercise in transparency, using the outside view as the walls. From Mies's projects for glass skyscrapers of 1923, the influential firm of Skidmore, Owings and Merrill found inspiration for the first actual realization of his visionary ideas. Lever House in New York (1951–2), became the model for tall buildings all over the world—the curtain wall of blue-green glass in light steel sections wrapped round the outside of the main structure of the building, the technology of the services, which set an international standard, and the basic arrangement of a tall, thin slab above a low podium containing the entrances and larger social areas.

Mies himself went on to design, among other projects, the Lake Shore Drive Apartments, Chicago, of 1951. The sixteen-storey blocks have an exacting discipline, which is extended even to the tenants, who are expected to keep their standard-coloured blinds in the right position so that the elevations look properly ordered. He worked with Philip Johnson on what seems almost the final building of this school. The Seagram Building in New York of 1958 was set back so as to give a full view of the thirty-eight-storey block, whatever the cost of leaving land vacant. The headquarters of a whisky firm who spared no expense, it was an advance upon the Lever building, brown in the colour of its glass and its bronze surface beams, monumental in some of its detail and rich in its finishing materials. After that, it was difficult to see what more could be done in the way of refinement: the next generation began to look for something more personal.

In South America a more spectacular architecture was rising. The main influence was Le Corbusier, who had gone to Rio de Janeiro in 1936 as consultant on the design of the new Ministry of Education building, one of his typically influential designs using a brise-soleil screen shading the glass wall. After the Second World War, Brazil exploded in a stunning architecture of its own. Lúcio Costa was the planner of the new capital of Brasilia, won in a competition in 1957. The architect for most of the central buildings was Oscar Niemeyer. The President's Palace, a rather pretentious version of a house on pilotis expresses Niemeyer's flamboyant personality and probably something of Brazil's pride in its new capital. The complex at the centre, dominating the Piaza of the Three Powers, defines its separate functions in different elementary geometric shapes. The three smooth

Rockefeller Center, New York, by Reinhard, Hofmeister; Corbet, Harrison, Macmurray; Fouilhoux and Hood

Lever House, New York, by Skidmore, Owings and Merrill

Government Buildings, Brasilia, by Oscar Niemeyer

Church of the Miraculous Virgin, Mexico City, by Félix Candela

basic solids have almost as great a power as Boullée's visionary geometric schemes (see Chapter 16). The twin towers house the administrative offices, the dome holds the Senate Chamber and the saucer the Assembly Hall. There is something almost unreal about the pure geometry of Brasilia, which may have something to do with its general unpopularity nowadays—an architect's dream, it is said, that paid little attention to the needs of people.

In Mexico, the new architecture was given a spectacular turning by Félix Candela (b. 1910), who came to Mexico after the Spanish Civil War and set up as an architect and builder. He is especially noted for his development of the hyperbolic paraboloid, a warped surface which is generated by straight lines and can be economical to construct. An unusual man with a rare understanding of three-dimensional geometry and of the properties of materials, he was influenced by Gaudí, as can be seen in his first major work, the Church of the Miraculous Virgin, Mexico City (1954). Its structure consists of a dramatic series of twisted columns and double-curved vaults which are in fact hyperbolic paraboloids. A conventional church plan is transformed into an original and distinctive magical interior.

Here the possibilities inherent in the International Style and the technical developments that came with it may be said to come to an end. By the end of the 1950s architects appeared to be yearning for something which would combine originality and individuality, without sacrificing to the imperative of functionalism. Indeed, as the shape of the world was changing, so were the conceptions that people held about space. The search for a new style was to start again.

21

Many Directions

To the men and women responsible for the genesis of the International Style, it was the culmination of everything—an architecture for everyman in every country in every way, in a brave new world that was smaller than ever before. But the story of architecture has no ending. The human mind is endlessly ingenious and inventive. While some architects may have thought that they had reached a final answer, others were thinking out buildings that would upset the *status quo* just as the modern movement upset it early in the century.

It has been said by an informed critic of the contemporary scene that the Modern Movement came to an end in July 1972, when the Pruitt Igoe flats in St Louis were blown up. They had been completed in 1955; they had received an award from the American Institute of Architects. They had been vandalized, defaced, mutilated and had witnessed a higher crime rate than any other development of their type. The incident was not the last. In 1979, two multistorey blocks of flats in Liverpool, built in 1958, were similarly demolished. There are more on the way down as I write this. The irony is that those buildings were intended to be the architecture of everyman, housing for people.

What had happened during those last twenty years? What happened was that both parties—architects and observers—lost confidence in what they had seen as the Modern movement. For the observers it happened mainly in the sixties, not just in England and America, but all over the world. The buildings that dropped most in public esteem were the two kinds which made up the bulk of the Modern Movement and characterized the modern cities—mass housing and office development. The arms of the movement reaching out to social democracy in housing areas and to commercial success in city centres suddenly seemed to be enfolding a monster. Critics who had in the sixties talked of architects as the heroes of the new society now believed that actually they had been wrecking cities and treating people with the utmost contempt.

As for the designers, they were no longer so certain where they were going. As in many aspects of life, it is when people are least sure of themselves that they become most dogmatic; there is no need for dogma in a world of moral certainty. So architecture, whatever the public may have thought, started to go in many directions. Instead of recognizing one mainstream, architects started out along different paths, some of them quite irreconcilable with each other. Not only that. They fell for what designers have often fallen for, but not so dramatically until this century—the 'isms' of art and architecture. Apart from the revival of traditionalism, there were Brutalism, Historicism, Constructivism, Futurism, Neo-plasticism, Expressionism, Utilitarian Functionalism, the new Empiricism, Organicism, Meta-

Byker Wall, Newcastle, by Ralph Erskine

Philharmonic Concert Hall, Berlin, by Hans Scharoun

Willis, Faber and Dumas offices, Ipswich, by Foster Associates

bolism, Neo-Metabolism, and Post-Modernism. And, though not actually an -ism, the most popular of all—the vernacular. Perhaps this means only that, like most things in our society, architecture is characterized by pluralism.

The one aspect of architecture that proceeded steadily on its way, sometimes despite architects, sometimes in answer to challenges presented by them, was the development of technology. Technology advanced dramatically, not so much through new discoveries as through the refinement of the innovatory ideas of the early twentieth century.

There have been significant developments in the use of most materials in structural design. Reinforced-concrete shells, used at the TWA terminal at the J.F. Kennedy International Airport, New York, have been developed. In steel, the space frame, a three-dimensional system for evenly distributing the load in all directions, has achieved remarkable spans; if bent into a sphere, it becomes a geodesic dome. The warped surfaces introduced by Candela have spawned a large family of spatial structures, requiring different kinds of analysis from structures that could be reduced to two dimensions. Dramatic experiments have been made with cable net roofs and with pneumatic structures, in which the air inside the building, with only a little more pressure than that exerted by the air outside, holds up a plastic envelope without supports but with anchorage—a reversal of traditional structure. Such developments are only in their infancy.

Traditional structures have been much refined. In order to resist wind loading at great heights, the traditional high-rise frame has developed hybrid forms such as the stiff core, the cross-wall and the braced outer skin, so that the building in effect acts as a vertical cantilever. Some materials have been industrialized so that more components are prefabricated. This trend has had a very uneven history, but it may be assumed that more components are likely to be made in a factory and bought, so to speak, off the peg, as a considerable proportion of a modern building is already.

It is, however, the development of the technical services in a building, together with new ones such as air conditioning and acoustics, that has made the most fundamental alterations to the way buildings are conceived, constructed and used. High buildings in particular are differently conceived if all their services, from lifts to water and air, are conditioned. On the other hand such services are intensive consumers of energy. A turning-point for some countries—and it may be for the future of their architecture—was the oil crisis of 1973, as a result of which more consideration is being given to alternative sources of energy, such as sun, wind and water. There have also been many attempts to improve the efficiency of the conventional use of energy in buildings.

Ultimately the architect of today or tomorrow has to master the technology available to him on an unprecedented scale. The generation of a new building, therefore, depends greatly upon the decisions taken at the earliest moment about what portion of the cost will be spent on the technical services and what portion on the accommoda-

Velasca Tower, Milan, by BBPR

Interior of TWA Terminal, John F. Kennedy Airport, by Eero Saarinen

tion. And that will affect the whole style and appearance of the building as well as its convenience. Firmness, commodity and delight have a meaning extended by modern technology.

To see what is happening we can look at what has come to be known, since the mid-seventies, as Post-Modernism. It seems a self-contradictory term, like talking about post-now; what is means is that much of the architecture is a reaction against the kind of architecture represented by the International Style. Some early Post-Modern manifestations happened in Italy, where the Velasca Tower in Milan (1956-7) by Belgiojoso, Peresutti and Rogers was a deliberate protest against the blandness and smoothness of Modern. The top eight floors of the twenty-six storey tower are spread out on enormous chunky concrete brackets three floors deep. The windows are scattered across the façade as if someone had thrown a handful of windows at it. It was a rude comment upon the formality and smoothness of the usual modern office block.

At much the same time, Eero Saarinen startled America with his supple, soaring and birdlike TWA Terminal at the J.F. Kennedy International Airport, New York, 1956-62. Suddenly, in place of anonymous Modern, here was something dynamic, but also symbolic of the flights which are the *raison d'être* of the building. An even more intense and dramatic designer was Louis Kahn (1901-74), whose Richards Medical Research Building in the University of Pennsylvania (1958-60), with its 'served' and 'servant' spaces composed so that the outside looks like huge ducts, became a model for students. His National Assembly Hall for Dacca of 1962 revived the use of *beaux-arts* principles. The Modern movement wss taking on new and more emotional overtones.

If those buildings signalled one part of the opening campaign, the architect who expressed the mood most clearly and concisely, both in words and in actions, was Robert Venturi (b. 1925). His book *Complexity and Contradiction in Architecture*, 1966, makes the case for something more than the simple unitary forms of the Modern movement; he wanted an architecture of meaning and popular interest in place of its abstractions. The house he built for his mother at Chestnut Hill, Philadelphia, in 1962–4 is recognized as a key example of the complex, unexpected and metaphorical language of this school of design. The ambiguity is even more unexpected in buildings like Franklin Court, Philadelphia, where you look at the new buildings through a stainless steel skeleton that suggests the outline of the former house.

Venturi and his partner Rauch were expressing a mood that was to result in some unusual and exciting changes. In Spain and then in France, the Catalan architect Ricardo Bofill has constructed some richly colourful bright red and yellow complex buildings. His Palacio d'Arbraxas on the outskirts of Paris is a housing mass of ten storeys containing four hundred flats, given rhythm by huge Ionic columns in concrete. The complex of Les Arcades du Lac at Marseilles is punctuated by five huge arches. The 386 low-cost flats have been described as monumental classicism or technological classicism; he has, not for the first time in modern history and probably disastrously, made housing into a public monument.

That search for a new classicism, for what has come to be known as Post-Modern Classicism, is nowhere more skilfully represented than by the work of Charles Moore in the USA, an erudite professor of architecture at the University of Los Angeles and a brilliant designer of classical pastiche. His house at Santa Barbara in California expresses the spatial concept of classical buildings. His Piazza d'Italia in New Orleans is a delightful public space, with fountains, coloured façades, screen walls and classical details like Ionic capitals carried out in stainless steel. At the University of Santa Cruz in California he has created a stage setting called Kresge College, an irregular walk through groups of residences and a landscape arranged in a form that would have delighted a picturesque architect of the early nineteenth century.

If the International Style was looking towards unity, anonymity and simplicity, the Post-Modern period looks towards complexity and fun. It calls upon historical memories (but not historical accuracy)

House at Chestnut Hill, Philadelphia, by Robert Venturi

Piazza d'Italia, New Orleans, by Charles Moore

Hyatt Regency Hotel, San Francisco, by John Portman

US Pavilion, Expo '67, Montreal, by Buckminster Fuller

and the local context. It exploits the vernacular, likes buildings to be metaphorical, to have ambiguous kinds of space, uses a plurality of styles, even in one building, and goes in for images and symbols. No longer does the Post-Modern architect look for a single way to a true modern style or for utopian solutions; he looks for individuality and lots of different ways; he says goodbye to Mies van der Rohe and comes back again to Gaudí and the Le Corbusier of Ronchamp.

So Roche and Dinkerloo set up the Ford Foundation Headquarters, New York, in 1967. It has a vast greenhouse-like foyer, soaring up twelve storeys, with offices and communal areas wrapped round two of its sides. John Portman has designed, and as a developer built, some astonishing Hyatt Regency Hotels, like the spectacular one in San Francisco, which have vast landscaped interior volumes dripping with plants and expressing a luxury that transforms a stay in a hotel into an exotic experience. In Canada, at the Expo '67 Exhibition in Montreal, the USA employed its most brilliant as well as most verbose engineer Buckminster Fuller to make its pavilion, a huge dome 254 feet in diameter, a geodesic structure of triangles and hexagonal elements covered with a plastic skin. Fuller believes that whole communities could live in such a 'benign physical microcosm', and it is possible that that will happen one day. At the same exhibition the most memorable permanent exhibit was the Habitat housing by Safdie and colleagues, a piling up of 158 prefabricated dwellings in a calculated appearance of disorder, an attempt to provide an informal urban life combining privacy, social contact and modern amenities.

In Germany, Hans Scharoun (1893–1972) produced in his old age the Philharmonic Concert Hall, Berlin (1963), which may at first sight seem a wilful personal expression, but is in fact a rational solution to the acoustical problems and the desire to create a rapport between audience and orchestra. The fantastic spatial elaboration is the result of a creative acoustical arrangement of seats in 'vineyards' stepping up and around the players, a successful response to the exacting demands of the great orchestra it houses. When the Olympic Games were held in Munich in 1972, the great stadium was a vast tent roof, using the principle of tension in opposite curvatures, by the engineer Frei Otto with the architects Behmisch and Partners. A web of steel cables covered by transparent plexiglass sheets was suspended from

Habitat Housing, Expo '67, Montreal, by Moshe Safdie

Olympic Stadium, Munich, by Frei Otto, Behmisch and Partners

poles by steel ropes to provide an undulating translucent weather-shield that is virtually shadowless.

Britain was less adventurous in structure, more experimental in style and environment. After a strange interlude known as the New Brutalism, in which buildings were made of steel or concrete so as to look as unattractive as possible, some notable advances have been made in the environments of buildings both inside and out. The *Economist* Buildings, London (1962–4), by Peter and Alison Smithson are three towers of varying heights in an eighteenth-century setting; they were an exercise in Renaissance planning. With the Engineering Building for Leicester University (1963), James Stirling and James Gowan created an original complex of teaching workshops, research laboratories, lecture halls, staff rooms and offices, using a ruthlessly logical interpretation of the building's functions and economics to create some distinctive imagery. In the National Theatre, London, Sir Denys Lasdun (b. 1914), one of the descendants of Tecton, created another unattractive exterior in concrete, but some wonderful interior spaces surrounding and leading into the three contrasted theatres.

But perhaps the outstanding success of the diverse movement was the offices for Willis, Faber and Dumas, Ipswich, by Foster Associates in 1974. The three-storey deep-plan block covers the whole of the irregular site and is wrapped within an undulating window wall of solar-resistant glass panels, behind which some highly mechanized environmental control systems provide unusually fine working conditions. The reflections in the glass wall are the dominant feature of the building, an ever-changing pattern of colour and light. At the Hillingdon Civic Centre, 1977, Andrew Derbyshire of Robert Matthew, Johnson Marshall and Partners gave the most extensive demonstration of the 'vernacular' yet seen, with roofs cutting across at various angles and brick patterns making the most of the native tradition. But considered by many the outstanding example of Post-Modernism in Britain is the Byker Wall in Newcastle, 1977, a long waving line of housing in patterned brick with thick landscape by Ralph Erskine, who made it an exercise in community architecture, involving the tenants at every stage of the design.

Paris received the most spectacular example of modern architecture reconsidered. The Centre Pompidou (1972–7) was designed by an Italian, Piano, and an Englishman, Rogers. What was required was a stack of uninterrupted internal spaces and the technical infrastructure for the display of objects and for other functions, such as library and information service. The demand was met in the most drastic modern way, by leaving the inside clear and putting all the workings on the outside—pipes, tubes, escalators and structure. Compared with a traditional building, a modern building is upside down, inside out and back to front. In Belgium at the University of Louvain, Eugène Kroll showed, in the student residences and plaza, that it could also seem to be falling down.

Japan, and other regions of the Far East, has seen some of the most dramatic examples of advanced experimental architecture. In structure, for example, Kenzo Tange, the brilliant disciple of Le Corbusier, created a fine exercise in imaginative structural gymnastics for the two sports halls for the Tokyo Olympics in 1964. They are covered with enormous tent-like roofs, whose sheets are slung from steel

Economist *Buildings, London, by Alison and Peter Smithson*

cables, seeming to reflect the spirit and vigour of sporting activities. Tange had already designed some huge projects such as that for a city projecting into Tokyo Bay. The Japanese architectural scene is full of such adventures—housing reaching into or even under the sea, huge stepped housing blocks, complicated office environments, buildings capable of expansion and contraction and change—the theme of the Metabolists, who try to create architecture from an understanding of what happens in biological processes.

The most memorable is the Nakagin Capsule Tower in Tokyo by Kisho Kurokawa of 1972. Japan's developments in industrialized systems of prefabricated housing are among the most advanced in the world. Kurokawa provided a framework for a plug-in system of small living units comprising a bath, double bed, kitchen, storage and sitting area, all in a space measuring eight by twelve feet. Each unit has its own controls for heating, ventilating and air conditioning. To the observer, it is rather like an ancient Japanese wood puzzle and the interlocking geometry of their temple timber structures. Kurokawa is said to have remarked about the capsules that 'They're bird cages. You see in Japan we build concrete-box birds' nests with round holes and place them in the trees. I've built these bird nests for itinerant businessmen who visit Tokyo, for bachelors who fly in with their birds.'

The most spectacular—and in some ways the most unsatisfactory—of all the contemporary public buildings is the Opera House in Sydney. It was started by a young Danish architect Jørn Utzon in 1959, after he won the competition for it, and completed by the team of Hall, Littlemore and Todd in 1973. Utzon sketched out the most imaginative and expressive set of reinforced concrete shells on a spectacular mole jutting out into Sydney harbour. Beneath them—or within the granite-clad podium on which they sit—are a concert-hall, an opera-house, a theatre, a cinema and restaurants.

In fact they are not shells, which would have been impossible to construct on such a scale, but pre-cast concrete sections finished with ceramic tiles on the surface. Utzon resigned before the work was finished, and the final interior bears no relation to the exterior. Yet it

Centre Pompidou, Paris, by Richard Rogers and Renzo Piano

National Gymnasium,
Tokyo, by Kenzo Tange

Nakagin Capsule Tower,
Tokyo, by Kisho Kurokawa

remains one of the most dramatic and inspiring architectural images of the twentieth century. Architecture is again capable of making a great statement and filling people with wonder.

My final example is also in the East, and it is under way as I write these words. The new Hong Kong and Shanghai Bank in Hong Kong promises to enshrine, at considerable expense, the most advanced use of technology—not only in its computerized heating and ventilating systems, communications, controls, lighting and acoustics, but also in its materials, which draw upon the developments of astronautics. In that, it may bring architecture full circle. For at many times in history, architecture has embodied the most advanced technology of its time. Now it promises to use the advanced technology of space.

And yet, in a sense the story of architecture can never come to an end. As every new departure changes the immediate scene, it also changes the shape of history. With every new discovery we find ourselves looking back for traces of its origin—for the influences that consciously or unconsciously have played upon the designer in his search for form.

But as we pause, we must ask whether there is a pattern to the story. Do certain themes emerge from this review of the whole of architecture, over something like 6000 years, which help us to answer the question that I asked at the beginning—why is it like that? There is of course no simple answer; for the story we have been following shows that there have been many different answers and no doubt there will be many more.

All architecture reveals the application of human ingenuity to the satisfaction of human needs. And among those needs are not only shelter, warmth and accommodation but also the needs, felt at every moment in every part of the world in endless different ways, for something more profound, evocative and universal, for beauty, for permanence, for immortality.

Opera House, Sydney, by Jørn Utson

Hong Kong and Shanghai Banking Corporation Headquarters by Foster Associates

Further Reading

The primary sources of architecture are not books, but the buildings themselves. In writing my version of the story, I have made use of buildings, places visited, books, articles and plans too numerous to mention, and have talked to architects and critics. I would particularly like to record my debt to Alan Luty of the School of Architecture, Leeds Polytechnic, and to the staff of the Polytechnic library.

The following list is not exhaustive, but is intended as a guide to the periods and places dealt with in the book. The books listed will serve as a guide to the buildings and to the available literature about them.

Basic texts (such as Vitruvius, Abbé Suger's treatise on the rebuilding of St-Denis, and the classic texts of Renaissance theorists such as Alberti, Serlio or Palladio) are not included. Fundamental to any serious study of architecture, they can be found in specialist libraries.

Although the European tradition of architecture is extensively dealt with in all its aspects, only a few books give world coverage. These include my own *Pocket Guide to Architecture*, published by Mitchell Beazley in 1980, and *The World's Great Architecture* published by Optimum Books, 1980, which I edited. The most accessible authority is *A History of Architecture* by Banister Fletcher, published by the Royal Institute of British Architects and London University (Athlone Press), now in its 18th edition (1975). In early editions, architecture outside the European tradition was dealt with under the heading 'The non-historical styles'; today, all the world's major buildings are covered, with background information, descriptions, dimensions, illustrated with photographs, plans and detailed drawings.

A vast body of background material, profusely illustrated, has been produced in the last twenty years, and will repay exploration. These include the series entitled a 'living record of history', published by Thames and Hudson (produced from 1960 onwards), especially:

> *The Birth of Western Civilisation* (ed. Michael Grant)
> *The Dark Ages* (ed. David Talbot Rice)
> *The Flowering of the Middle Ages* (ed. Joan Evans)
> *The Age of the Renaissance* (ed. Denys Hay)
> *The Age of Expansion* (ed. Hugh Trevor-Roper)

The following books, not related to a particular period, may be helpful:

> CLIFTON-TAYLOR, ALEC, *The Pattern of English Building*, London 1972 (on use of materials)
> COWAN, HENRY J., *The Master Builders*, Sydney and London 1977 (on structural evolution)
> PEVSNER, NIKOLAUS, *An Outline of European Architecture*, Penguin, Harmondsworth, 1943
> JELLICOE, GEOFFREY and SUSAN, *The Landscape of Man*, Thames and Hudson, 1975 (on landscape and architectural environment)

The list that follows is arranged according to chapter.

1 GUIDONI, ENRICO, *Primitive Architecture*, Abrams, New York, 1978
   RUDOFSKY, BERNARD, *Architecture without Architects*, Academy Editions, London, 1973

2 GIEDION, SIGFRIED, *The Beginnings of Architecture*, vol. 2 of *The Eternal Present* (2 vols), Oxford University Press, Oxford, 1964
   PIGGOTT, STUART (ed.), *The Dawn of Civilization*, Thames and Hudson, London, 1961
   JAMES, E. O., *From Cave to Cathedral*, Thames and Hudson, London, 1965

3 DE CENIVAL, JEAN-LOUIS, *Living Architecture: Egyptian*, Oldbourne, London, 1964
   SMITH, W. STEVENSON, *The Art and Architecture of Ancient Egypt* (rev. ed.), Penguin, Harmondsworth, 1971

4 VOLWAHSEN, ANDREAS, *Living Architecture: Indian*, Macdonald, London, 1969
   ROWLAND, BENJAMIN, *The Art and Architecture of India* (rev. ed.), Penguin, Harmondsworth, 1971

5 SICKMAN, LAURENCE and SOPER, ALEXANDER, *The Art and Architecture of China* (3rd ed.), Penguin, Harmondsworth, 1968
PAINE, ROBERT TREAT and SOPER, ALEXANDER, *The Art and Architecture of Japan* (rev. ed.) Penguin, Harmondsworth, 1975.

6 ROBERTSON, DONALD, *Pre-Columbian Architecture*, Prentice-Hall, Englewood Cliffs and London, 1963
HEYDEN, DORIS and GENDROP, PAUL, *Pre-Columbian Architecture of Mesoamerica*, Abrams, New York, 1975

7 MARTIN, ROLAND, *Living Architecture: Greece*, Oldbourne, London, 1967
LAWRENCE, A. W., *Greek Architecture*, Penguin, Harmondsworth, 1968
SCULLY, VINCENT, *The Earth, the Temple and the Gods*, Yale University Press, 1962

8 PICARD, GILBERT, *Living Architecture: Roman*, Oldbourne, London, 1965
WARD-PERKINS, JOHN B., *Roman Architecture*, Abrams, New York, 1977

9 MACDONALD, WILLIAM L., *Early Christian and Byzantine Architecture*, Prentice-Hall, Englewood Cliffs and London, 1962
KRAUTHEIMER, RICHARD, *Early Christian and Byzantine Architecture*, Penguin, Harmondsworth, 1975

10 KUBACH, HANS ERICH, *Romanesque Architecture*, Abrams, New York, 1977
OURSEL, RAYMOND and ROUILLER, JACQUES, *Living Architecture: Romanesque*, Oldbourne, London, 1967

11 HOAG, JOHN D., *Islamic Architecture*, Abrams, New York, 1977
MICHELL, GEORGE, *Architecture of the Islamic World*, Thames and Hudson, London, 1978

12 GRODECHI, LOUIS, *Gothic Architecture*, Abrams, New York, 1977
ACLAND, JAMES H., *Mediaeval Structure: the Gothic Vault*, University of Toronto Press, Toronto and Buffalo, 1972
HOFSTATTER, HANS H., *Living Architecture: Gothic*, Macdonald, London, 1970
FRANKL, PAUL, *Gothic Architecture*, Penguin, Harmondsworth, 1962

13 MURRAY, PETER, *Renaissance Architecture*, Abrams, New York, 1971
HEYDENREICH, LUDWIG H. and LOTZ, WOLFGANG, *Architecture in Italy, 1400–1600*, Penguin, Harmondsworth, 1974
WITTKOWER, RUDOLF, *Architectural Principles in the Age of Humanism*, Alec Tiranti, London, 1962

14 BENEVOLO, LEONARDO, *The Architecture of the Renaissance*, 2 vols, Routledge and Kegan Paul, London, 1978
ALLSOPP, BRUCE, *A history of Renaissance Architecture*, Pitman, London, 1959
HUGHES, J. QUENTIN and LYNTON, NORBERT, *Renaissance Architecture*, Longmans, London, 1962
SUMMERSON, JOHN, *The Classical Language of Architecture*, BBC/Methuen University Paperbacks, London, 1963/4
Architecture in Britain, 1530–1830, Penguin, Harmondsworth, 1970

15 MILLON, HENRY A., *Baroque and Rococo Architecture*, Prentice-Hall, Englewood Cliffs and London, 1961
BAZIN, GERMAIN, *Baroque and Rococo*, Thames and Hudson, London, 1964
BLUNT, ANTHONY (ed.), *Baroque and Rococo: Architecture and Decoration*, Elek, London, 1978

16 WITTKOWER, RUDOLF, *Palladio and English Palladianism*, Thames and Hudson, London, 1974
CROOK, J. MORDAUNT, *The Greek Revival*, Murray, London, 1972
GERMANN, GEORGE, *Gothic Revival in Europe and Britain*, Lund Humphries, London, 1972
WATKIN, DAVID, *The English Vision: the Picturesque in Architecture*, Murray, London, 1982

17 PIERSON, WILLIAM H., *American Buildings and their Architects: the Colonial and Neo-classical Styles*, Doubleday, New York, 1970

18   HITCHCOCK, HENRY RUSSELL, *Architecture: Nineteenth and Twentieth Centuries* (4th ed.), Penguin, Harmondsworth, 1977

DIXON, ROGER and MUTHESIUS, STEFAN, *Victorian Architecture*, Thames and Hudson, London, 1978

GIROUARD, MARK, *The Victorian Country House*, Oxford, 1971

19   RUSSELL, FRANK, *Art Nouveau Architecture*, Academy Editions, London, 1979

20   HATJE, GERD (ed.), *Encyclopaedia of Modern Architecture*, World of Art Library, Thames and Hudson, London, 1963

PEVSNER, NIKOLAUS, *The Sources of Modern Architecture and Design*, World of Art Library, Thames and Hudson, London, 1968

BENEVOLO, LEONARDO, *History of Modern Architecture*, 2 vols, Routledge and Kegan Paul, London, 1971

GIEDION, SIGFRIED, *Space, Time and Architecture*, Harvard University Press, Cambridge (Mass.), 1963

BANHAM, REYNER, *Theory and Design in the First Machine Age*, Architectural Press, London, 1960

LE CORBUSIER, *Towards a New Architecture*, Architectural Press, London, 1970

HITCHCOCK, HENRY RUSSELL and JOHNSON, PHILIP, *The International Style*, Norton, New York, 1966

21   JENCKS, CHARLES A., *The Language of Post-Modern Architecture* (3rd ed.), Academy Editions, London, 1981

Late Modern Architecture and Other Essays, Academy Editions, London, 1980

Acknowledgements

The publishers wish to thank all individuals, photographers' institutions, and photographic agencies who have kindly supplied photographs for publication in this book. Numerals indicate page numbers.
A.C.L., Brussels, 251 (left); Aerofilms, Boreham Wood, 130, 162, 163, 184, Aerofilms/Castle Howard Estate, 209 (btm); 223; Alinari, Florence, 91, 108, 112, 114, 135 (btm); 166 (right), 171, 173, 174, 175 (top and btm), 176, 177 (left and right), 180 (top right), 188, 199 (btm), 201, 203, 204, 205, 217, 246 (left); Anderson, Florence, 100 (btm); 102, 165, 170, 179, 180 (top left), 199 (top), 202; Architectural Association, London, 248, 270 (right); *Architectural Review*, London, 276 (right); Bauhaus Archiv, Berlin, 264 (btm); Bildarchiv Foto Marburg, 25, 101 (btm), 122 (top), 187 (left), 197, 208, 225 (left), 245; Osvaldo Böhm, Venice, 122 (btm); J. Bottin, Paris, 78, 83 (btm); Boudot-Lamotte, Paris, 116, 135 (top), 143, 214, 218; Caisse Nationale des Monuments Historiques et des Sites, Paris, 126 (btm), 150, 181, 244 (left and right), 261 (top); Camera Press, London, 10 (top); J. Alan Cash, London, 62, 65, 70 (btm); Ted Colman, Oxford, 279; The Conway Library, Courtauld Institute, University of London, 117, 148 (top), 155, 166 (left), 265 (btm); *Country Life*, London, 253 (top left and top right); Roy C. Craven, Gainsville, Florida, 76, 78 (btm), 79, 80, 81, 82 (top), 228 (btm right); Mrs B. J. Crichton, Anglesey, 207; F. H. Crossley, 128 (left); William Curtis, 250 (left), 256 (btm); Department of the Environment, London, 193 (top), 227 (left), 238 (right); Douglas Dickens, London, 54 (btm); C. M. Dixon, Dover, 107; Ediciones Poligrafa, S.A., 250 (right), 251 (right); Elsevier Archive, Amsterdam, 53; Embassy of Ecuador, London, 228 (top); Foster Associates, London, 272 (btm), 281 (btm); Foto Lauterwasser, Berlin, 272 (middle); Giraudon, Paris, 100 (top), 153 (right), 183, 261 (btm); Greater London Council, Department of Architecture and Civic Design, 266 (right), 267 (left); Richard and Sally Greenhill, London, 61; Sonia Halliday, Weston Turville, 123, 148 (btm); Hamlyn Picture Group Library, 47; Robert Harding, London, 64 (top); Held-Ziolo, Paris, 110 (top); Lucien Hervé, Paris, 260 (btm), 226 (left and right); A. A. van Heyden, Amsterdam, 37; Hirmer Fotoarchiv, Munich, 27, 30, 31, 35, 88; Michael Holford, Loughton, 213 (top); Holle Verlag, Baden-Baden, 36; Angelo Hornak, 235 (btm), 249; *Japan Architect*, 280; Japan Information Centre, London, 64 (btm); 67, 70 (top), 71, 73; A. F. Kersting, 42, 45, 46 (btm), 49 (btm), 51 (top), 52 (btm), 85, 95, 106, 136 (btm), 145 (btm), 147, 191, 209 (top left and right), 212 (btm), 213 (btm), 219, 220, 221 (btm), 224, 252; Library of Congress, Washington, 232, 233 (btm), 235 (top), 246 (right), 247; Mansell Collection, London, 89 (left), 103, 206, 236 (left); Mary Evans Picture Library, London, 241 (left and right); MAS, Barcelona, 160, 187 (right), 190; Mitchell Library, Sydney, 236 (right); Norman McGrath, New York, 275; Münchner Olympiapark, 277 (btm); Municipal Archives, Amsterdam, 192; Museum of Finnish Architecture, Helsinki, 268 (left); National Film Board of Canada, Ottawa, 277 (top); National Monuments Record of the Netherlands, The Hague, 193; Novosti Press Agency, London, 124; Paul Popper Ltd, London, 136 (top); Jeremy Preston, North Shields, 272 (top); Psychico, Athens/N. Tombazi (photographer), 89 (right); Royal Commission on the Ancient and Historical Monuments of Scotland, 225 (right); Royal Commission on Historic Monuments (England), London, 12, 14, 129, 159, 164 (btm), 189, 227 (right), 238 (left), 239 (right), 240, 243 (left); SCALA, Florence, 96 (top and btm), 115, 127, 178 (top and btm), 212 (top); Ronald Sheridan's Picture Library, Harrow, 10 (btm); Edwin Smith, 254 (left); Alison and Peter Smithson, London, 278; Sean Sprague, London, 81 (btm); Staatliche Museen zu Berlin, 19; Alex Starkey, London, 145 (top); Ezra Stoller, New York, 268 (right), 269 (right); Studio Morlet, Bourges, 153 (left); Sundahl, 267 (right); Thames and Hudson, London, 18; TOP Agence, Paris, 128 (right); TWA, New York, 274 (right); Victoria and Albert Museum, London, 239 (left); Roger Viollet, Paris, frontispiece, 39, 46, 119, 138, 146; Vision International/Paolo Koch, London, 66; Weidenfeld and Nicolson, London, 254 (right); Roger Wood, London, 141; Xinhua News Agency, Peking, 59 (right); ZEFA, London, 44; The Zoological Society of London, 266 (left).

Index